RETURNS OF WAR

NATION OF NATIONS: IMMIGRANT HISTORY AS AMERICAN HISTORY

General Editor: Matthew Jacobson
Founding Editors: Matthew Jacobson and Werner Sollors

Beyond the Shadow of Camptown: Korean Military Brides in America
Ji-Yeon Yuh

Feeling Italian: The Art of Ethnicity in America
Thomas J. Ferraro

Constructing Black Selves: Caribbean American Narratives and the Second Generation
Lisa D. McGill

Transnational Adoption: A Cultural Economy of Race, Gender, and Kinship
Sara K. Dorow

Immigration and American Popular Culture: An Introduction
Jeffrey Melnick and Rachel Rubin

From Arrival to Incorporation: Migrants to the U.S. in a Global Era
Edited by Elliott Barkan, Hasia Diner, and Alan M. Kraut

Migrant Imaginaries: Latino Cultural Politics in the U.S.-Mexico Borderlands
Alicia Schmidt Camacho

The Force of Domesticity: Filipina Migrants and Globalization
Rhacel Salazar Parreñas

Immigrant Rights in the Shadows of Citizenship
Edited by Rachel Ida Buff

Rough Writing: Ethnic Authorship in Theodore Roosevelt's America
Aviva F. Taubenfeld

The Third Asiatic Invasion: Migration and Empire in Filipino America, 1898–1946
Rick Baldoz

Race for Citizenship: Black Orientalism and Asian Uplift from Pre-Emancipation to Neoliberal America
Helen Heran Jun

Entitled to Nothing: The Struggle for Immigrant Health Care in the Age of Welfare Reform
Lisa Sun-Hee Park

The Slums of Aspen: Immigrants vs. the Environment in America's Eden
Lisa Sun-Hee Park and David Naguib Pellow

Arab America: Gender, Cultural Politics, and Activism
Nadine Naber

Social Death: Racialized Rightlessness and the Criminalization of the Unprotected
Lisa Marie Cacho

Love and Empire: Cybermarriage and Citizenship across the Americas
Felicity Amaya Schaeffer

Global Families: A History of Asian International Adoption in America
Catherine Ceniza Choy

Who's Your Paddy?: Racial Expectations and the Struggle for Irish American Identity
Jennifer Nugent Duffy

Islam Is a Foreign Country: American Muslims and the Global Crisis of Authority
Zareena Grewal

Soft Soil, Black Grapes: The Birth of Italian Winemaking in California
Simone Cinotto

African & American: West Africans in Post–Civil Rights America
Marilyn Halter and Violet Showers Johnson

Citizens of Asian America: Democracy and Race during the Cold War
Cindy I-Fen Cheng

From the Land of Shadows: War, Revolution, and the Making of the Cambodian Diaspora
Khatharya Um

The Cultural Politics of U.S. Immigration: Gender, Race, and Media
Leah Perry

Whiteness on the Border: Mapping the US Racial Imagination in Brown and White
Lee Bebout

Strange Fruit of the Black Pacific: Imperialism's Racial Justice and Its Fugitives
Vince Schleitwiler

The New Immigrant Whiteness: Neoliberalism, Race, and Post-Soviet Migration to the United States
Claudia Sadowski-Smith

Colonial Phantoms: Belonging and Refusal in the Dominican Americas, from the 19th Century to the Present
Dixa Ramírez

Girlhood in the Borderlands: Mexican Teens Caught in the Crossroads of Migration
Lilia Soto

Returns of War: South Vietnam and the Price of Refugee Memory
Long T. Bui

Returns of War

South Vietnam and the Price of Refugee Memory

Long T. Bui

NEW YORK UNIVERSITY PRESS
New York

NEW YORK UNIVERSITY PRESS
New York
www.nyupress.org

© 2018 by New York University
All rights reserved

References to Internet websites (URLs) were accurate at the time of writing. Neither the author nor New York University Press is responsible for URLs that may have expired or changed since the manuscript was prepared.

Library of Congress Cataloging-in-Publication Data
Names: Bui, Long T., author.
Title: Returns of war : South Vietnam and the price of refugee memory / Long T. Bui.
Description: New York : New York University Press, [2018] | Series: Nation of nations : immigrant history as American history | Includes bibliographical references and index.
Identifiers: LCCN 2018012206| ISBN 9781479817061 (cl : alk. paper) | ISBN 9781479871957 (pb : alk. paper)
Subjects: LCSH: Vietnamese Americans. | Vietnamese—United States—Historiography. | Refugees—Vietnam (Republic) | Vietnam War, 1961–1975—Refugees.
Classification: LCC E184.V53 B84 2018 | DDC 973/.0495922—dc23
LC record available at https://lccn.loc.gov/2018012206

New York University Press books are printed on acid-free paper, and their binding materials are chosen for strength and durability. We strive to use environmentally responsible suppliers and materials to the greatest extent possible in publishing our books.

Manufactured in the United States of America

10 9 8 7 6 5 4 3 2 1

Also available as an ebook

CONTENTS

Note on Language	ix
Introduction	1
1. Archival Others: The Vietnamese as Absent Presence in the Historical Record	25
2. Refugee Assets: The Political Reeducation of Personal Trauma and Family Bonds	57
3. Dismembered Lives: The Fractured Body Politics of the "Little Saigon" Community	87
4. Militarized Freedoms: Vietnamese American Soldiers Fighting "Future Vietnams"	122
5. Empire's Residuals: The Return Migration of Former Exiles to Globalizing Vietnam	169
Epilogue	201
Acknowledgments	205
Notes	209
References	219
Index	239
About the Author	251

NOTE ON LANGUAGE

Modern Vietnamese is a monosyllabic tonal language that uses diacritical marks in written form. However, many Vietnamese living overseas have adopted different linguistic and writing patterns. The compound word "Vietnam" has somewhat displaced the once common spelling, "Viet Nam," in English, though the latter has regained popularity. Working between multiple languages lends visibility to the ways language can change depending on context or historical periods, thus creating inevitable problems and a variety of confusions of which readers must be aware. In Vietnamese, a person's last name or family surname comes first, and this causes confusion when names appear with the surname last in Western sources but first in Vietnamese sources. I have chosen to faithfully present names as I am introduced to them by primary and secondary sources. I often refer to the "American War" when talking from a Vietnamese perspective, but then refer to the "Vietnam War" when speaking from the U.S. context. I employ the phrase "South Vietnam" to refer to the former Republic of Vietnam (RVN) (1955–1975), but this term may be confused with the general territory of Vietnam's southern region. Most of the time, I am referring to the RVN, except when I explicitly refer to the south as purely a geographic space. The creative language I employ throughout the book offers a mix of anecdotes, puns, colloquialisms, and academic jargon that speaks to the creative disorderly nature of writing about the structure of memory and identity. This decision to include both formal and informal elements encourages readers to make their own sense of things as they are presented in the text.

Introduction

I grew up in a refugee family with vivid, lingering memories of war. Throughout my childhood, members of my clan would speak about Vietnam, but not about the war. Yet, the Vietnam constantly being referenced was the former republic of South Vietnam, the fledgling nation-state created with great fanfare as an ally of the United States in 1955 that later hemorrhaged, leading to a communist takeover in 1975. Though this ghost nation was firmly fixed at the center of Vietnamese diasporic exile imaginary, it was a place I found difficult to contemplate or imagine. Born a few years after the end of the Vietnam War, and with little actual knowledge of the war, I grew up with no memories of my own about what was formerly and officially called the Republic of Vietnam (RVN) or South Vietnam. However, this political entity still has staying power for me, my family, and my community. It is the place that many of my relatives still call "home" after so many years living abroad. In "Little Saigon" refuge enclaves, you can still hear about how "we" refugees must remember our heritage as South Vietnamese and honor our protectors and saviors, the Americans. The potency of this country I never knew, combined with the constancy to this fervent devotion to the United States, have prompted questions this book tries to answer. How does the stunning loss of South Vietnam instill a need to stage a return to the war's history again and again? How did the tense, often negative relationship between the United States and South Vietnam create a lasting bond that persists, one that created new social and economic bonds? How do people remember South Vietnam, and what price do they pay for remembering a lost nation?

Most of the material presented here in some way touches upon aspects of my life, a testimony to the sensitive nature of doing research on one's community, not just as an intellectual journey but as a personal exploration. Various chapters represent aspects of this journey. As discussed in chapter 1, interest in Vietnamese refugee histories led me to visit the Vietnam Center and Archive (VNCA) in Lubbock, the largest holding of Vietnam War–related documents in the country outside the federal government archives and brought me back to my birthplace nestled deep in the heart of the Texas. My parents arrived there in the 1970s as refugees but left for Houston a year after my birth in search of better job opportunities and a larger co-ethnic population. While other members talked about the war, my parents never mentioned it or how they came to the United States to give wide berth to a traumatic generational history. There exist no letters or photographs. This void in my family history inspired my unexpected journey back to Lubbock three decades later, a local search that turned up transnational connections. At the VNCA, I searched for the stories of South Vietnamese refugees who, like my parents, came to the United States without any personal belongings. Thus, my return to the archive is a return to my own history, and the recognition of non-Vietnamese in crafting the place of Vietnamese in US history. The visit to the archive marked a homecoming of sorts, a visit to my "roots," a place to peel away the foggy layers of historical knowledge. Chapter 2 considers fictionalized memoir as a form of political reeducation insofar as the knowledge passed down from one generation to the next involves not only the transmission of trauma, but also a hardy economic asset offering hard lessons in survival from past prisoners of war in France, in the United States, and in other parts of the world. This chapter explores the challenges of remembering for Vietnamese refugee subjects in the face of postwar historical amnesia and trauma, and the economization of those things. It illustrates the ways the first and second generations must recuperate the political reeducation of South Vietnamese soldiers to understand the causes behind their own precarious lives "after" war as refugees. Chapter 3 considers two community protests that involved me and many friends, as we were accused by protesters of disrespecting the sanctity of our South Vietnamese heritage. The nation's original dismemberment by war, as a foundation for community dismemberment afterward, sparks constant fighting among different constituencies. Chapter 4, which discusses Vietnamese American soldiers and their stories of service in Iraq and Afghanistan, brings home the issue of multiple loyalties, a topic still resonant in many refugee families including my own, where all the men including me served in the military, either for the United States or South Vietnam. Chapter 5 follows a cohort of Vietnamese Americans, many of whom were former refugees, who have left the United States to return to South Vietnam in pursuit of better economic opportunities in a country that awkwardly seeks to embrace these national traitors. Inspired by the return migration of so many of my friends and colleagues, these now "glocal" informants helped me question my constant desire to come back to the very country my family had left long ago. The epilogue describes the problems of the South Vietnam refugee as a global model of success without accounting for the price they paid for losing the war.

This book examines new visions about South Vietnam as a reflection of the political views of its exiled refugees, the mangled historical policies of the American warfare state, and the neoliberal economies of present-day institutions like state archives, tourism, and the military. Focusing on the South Vietnamese side helps to truly "Vietnamize" the legacy of war, exposing a critical perspective that had been repressed within Vietnam's communist national imaginary and reprogrammed through the "Americanization" of the war's memory in popular Hollywood films (Ikul 2001). Drawn from the early twenty-first century, my case studies address the interplay of history and memory from different angles. What makes these examples compelling are the ways they catalog the efforts to rebrand the blotted image of South Vietnam and put it back on the map. As an intellectual exercise in political theory, *Returns of War* aims to revisit the term "Vietnamization"—the program that ran from 1969 to 1972, intending to extract U.S. soldiers from Vietnam and let the South Vietnamese fight their own battles—using it to explore problems of Vietnamese attempts to attain freedom and how they become legitimate as well as legible subjects of popular knowledge. It plays with the term Vietnamization, employing it far differently than Richard Nixon ever did, speaking to the unfulfilled wishes of the South Vietnamese to become a self-governing, self-sufficient people. I want to redeploy this controversial Cold War term to reveal the ways this supposedly discrete governmental decision is still with us, especially for refugees.

The Vietnamization of the Vietnam War was initially intended solely as a military maneuver, a bureaucratic and logistical transference of manpower, from the Americans to the South Vietnamese. Yet, Vietnamization was always far more than that. It has seeped into culture and memory, and I explore this cluttered arena through remembrances and consecrations of South Vietnam, raising the following key questions: Where is South Vietnam today and how do individuals, groups, and institutions map this supposedly disappeared geopolitical entity onto new "Vietnamized" spaces? How does the "premature death" of South Vietnam refract the derailed hopes for postcolonial freedom for the Vietnamese people? How and why do people even want to raise and hold onto the country's memory? How does memory connect with class, inequality, migration, labor, state power, and international political economy? To begin to tackle these pressing queries, it is essential to first discern how and why South Vietnam became America's sullied "ally." Ultimately, this book has two major purposes: One is to examine South Vietnam's domestic and diasporic populations to better understand Vietnamese political history. Another is to critique U.S. foreign policy, exploring the ongoing imposition of American imperialism and cultural paternalism on Vietnam and beyond.

The Vietnamization of the Vietnam War

On November 3, 1969, newly elected U.S. president Richard Nixon, in a much-anticipated televised speech, unveiled the Vietnamization of the Vietnam War, a strategy to excise all American troops and military presence from the region.[1] This was an about-face in U.S. foreign policy from defending at all costs America's ally, South Vietnam, against the onslaught of communist North Vietnam. Handing over total responsibility for winning the war to America's beleaguered friend, this executive decision established a multipronged, and concomitant task: "Defending South Vietnam, winning the war, achieving peace and preserving American 'honor'" (Kimball 2006: 59). Originally conceived by Secretary of Defense Melvin Laird and later officially adopted by Nixon, Vietnamization put a name to Cold War machinations and the hurdles of procuring both economic and political freedom for a foreign people whose future remained uncertain. While the military buildup of South Vietnam was the litmus to curb a communist takeover of Southeast Asia, Vietnamization was a global test case for U.S. contingency plans for de-escalation and ramping up local fighting forces and aid to repel "anti-democratic" forces. Nixon sought to prevent more deaths of American soldiers by supplying more combat training to South Vietnamese troops in modern military tactics and weaponry, shifting the burden of ground fighting to their battered partners while the United States would supply air protection. Vietnamization undersold the extent to which this could cause more problems later for South Vietnam and tipped the scales of war in favor of the northern Democratic Government of Vietnam (DRV) and the southern-based communist Viet Cong (PRG), pushing America's run-down friends to the brink of collapse.

By this time, the United States was facing strong public opposition to its involvement in this Vietnam War. According to Nixon, Vietnamization offered "a plan in which we will withdraw all our forces from Vietnam on a schedule in accordance with our program, as the South Vietnamese become strong enough to defend their own freedom."[2] Announced a few months earlier, in July 1969, at a press conference in the U.S. colony of Guam, Vietnamization was a cornerstone of the Nixon Doctrine, which essentially proclaimed that all U.S. allies were expected to take care of their own military defense from now on, and the leader of the free world would only support them from afar. While President Johnson had "Americanized" the war in Vietnam, Nixon sought to reverse this trend by "Vietnamizing the search for peace" (ibid.). As a declaration of independence for the country, Vietnamization mobilized whatever little popular support existed for the "political integrity of South Vietnam and, curiously, for the legitimacy of American soldiers fighting to preserve its integrity as a nation" (ibid.). Losing the war was not an option, but letting a friend go without support would spark violence, Nixon claimed, in the Middle East, the Western Hemisphere, and everywhere else.

With the Vietnamese fighting among themselves, Nixon initiated a salvo of aerial attacks and secret bombings of the country, making Vietnamization a smoke screen from behind which the United States could secretly and indiscriminately bomb the country as well as neighboring countries like Cambodia and Laos, a means of achieving "disengagement with escalation" with the appearance of "Asians killing Asians," a civil war with native people stuck in a "bloody test of arms and will" (Kimball 2011: 217). As subterfuge, it hid the fact that *most* of the carnage related to the war took place *after* the implementation of this policy. Things took a turn for the worst, where vows for the extraction of American military presence in the region led to more killing, mostly Vietnamese

(Asselin 2002: 22). It is generally agreed that Vietnamization fundamentally changed the nature of war since the United States no longer engaged in search and destroy operations, switching from an aggressor to an "advisory" role. The rhetorical message behind Vietnamization—South Vietnamese independence supported by the United States—was garbled by the political situation in the country and the question of who was in charge (Gartner 1998). While the South Vietnamese seemed to be taking charge of things, the policy allowed for a realignment of U.S. power in the Asian Pacific as it "internationalized" the Vietnam War, converting U.S. military bases in Okinawa, Japan, and the Philippines into the outposts for intensified aerial campaigns throughout Southeast Asia (Man 2014: 276).

Vietnamization epitomized more than Nixon's evolving foreign policy, but a hope for risk-adjusted returns on the war and economic investment in its global circle of "friends," an ongoing reminder of the debt the latter might owe to their colonial creditor and paymasters for helping them out. Lending U.S. "aid" to the South Vietnamese on borrowed time, Vietnamization was far more than a military directive or benchmark of political success; rather, it was a double-dealing sham and back-door decision pointedly matched to the "bottom-line" interests of a government engaged in far-off fighting with overstretched resources. In a secret exchange with Nixon three years later, Secretary of State Henry Kissinger made an ominous remark demonstrating Vietnamization in action:

> If a year from now or two years from now North Vietnam gobbles up South Vietnam, we can have a viable foreign policy—if it looks like as if a result of South Vietnamese incompetence . . . so we've got to find some formula that holds the thing together a year or two, after which—after a year, Mr. President, Vietnam will be a backwater. If we settle it, say, this October, by January '74 no one will give a damn. (Hughes 2010: 501)

With a time line in mind, Kissinger seems to give free rein to America's Asian partner in planning and sealing its own fate. The prevarication of national self-determination and the business of defending of freedom was the setup for Vietnamization, as evident in a passage from Nixon's Vietnamization speech:

> The defense of freedom is everybody's business not just America's business. And it is particularly the responsibility of the people whose freedom is threatened. When you are trying to assist another nation defend its freedom, U.S. policy should be to help them fight the war but not to fight the war for them. In the previous administration, we Americanized the war in Vietnam. In this administration, we are Vietnamizing the search for peace. (Nixon 1969)

Nixon's policy established the pretext for extending U.S. goodwill throughout Asian countries apparently imperiled by the shadow of the Iron Curtain by forcing them to take care of their own business. A compromising move to "buy" more time during a game-changing moment in the war, Nixon's announcement to Vietnamize the conflict in Vietnam served as an abnegation of U.S. responsibility for escalating and Americanizing the war in the first place. This proved to be a poorly advised plan of action because the "puppet troops" of the South Vietnamese military were supposedly ill-equipped in defending themselves against their more inspired and wily communist opponents (Jervis 2010). In the ensuing years of Vietnamization's implementation, thousands more RVN soldiers perished and the communists extended their territorial influence.

As later revealed in declassified government tapes, President Nixon postponed full discharge of U.S. troops from Vietnam until after his reelection in 1972, prolonging military evacuations long enough to "make Saigon's fall look like Saigon's fault" (Hughes 2010: 500); this, coupled with the reelection of South Vietnam's President Nguyễn Văn Thiệu, who torpedoed opponents using American backing as leverage, hobbled the country's democratic potential. Along with an autocratic decision to use any means to squash dissent, the U.S. policy of Vietnamization served as a continuation of war by other means, governed by the credo that "indigenization" of the conflict "could improve the military situation for South Vietnam" (Hughes 2010: 505). It sought to "de-Americanize" the conflict but served as a strategic cover-up for U.S. escalation of the war effort (Kimball 2011: 225). The policy attempted to bring "honorable withdrawal" and "honorable peace" to the United States by diverting attention away from American wrongdoings toward a fully domesticated theater of war, allowing final judgment for the conflict's outcome to be reserved for the Vietnamese people despite the terrible hand they had been dealt (Hanhimaki 2004: 43).[3] The popular lore in South Vietnam as a friend/ally of the United States was always held in dispute, but that friendly relationship needed to be emphasized to implement the plan of Vietnamization. The private government memos leaked by the Pentagon Papers outlined the U.S. Defense Department's raison d'être for U.S. military presence as helping the "people of South Vietnam to enjoy a better, freer way of life . . . to emerge from the crisis without unacceptable taint from methods used . . . NOT to 'help a friend'" (Gravel 1971: 643). The memos also expressed fears that South Vietnamese could attack Americans when the former realized that the United States was leaving them. Upon hearing about this, Henry Kissinger said, "If we pulled out and left them in the lurch, we may have to fight the South Vietnamese" (ibid.).

Exposing several U.S. presidents and their deep involvement in Vietnam, despite their promise not to get involved, *The Pentagon Papers* released in 1971 bluntly revealed that South Vietnam was "essentially the creation of the United States" (Zinn 2003: 350). For all the edification of the South Vietnamese as friends, these secret government documents confirm the Johnson administration's view of South Vietnamese *not* as friends of the United States deserving of support, but as a sad, bewildered people deserving of a better "Americanized" way of life. Like Lyndon B. Johnson, Nixon felt it necessary, after providing "enough" support, to let go of this friend, now deemed a political "liability" and moral hazard; at the same time, he wanted to maintain a hold over them. In this way, the master discourse of Vietnamization does not completely mesh with the U.S. government's secret relations with foreign nations. The lopsided relationship between South Vietnam and the American Goliath was filtered through jingoistic "visions of righteousness"—a lexicon of war to bamboozle the masses—and revisionist ideas of the United States as a patron of South Vietnam, rather than as a foreign power that "invaded South Vietnam, where it proceeded to compound the crime of aggression with numerous and quite appalling crimes against humanity throughout Indochina" (Chomsky 1991: 30). Clearly, in the historic and allegorical case of South Vietnam, freedom is tied to being "unfree" and "unfreedom" (both the actual lack of freedom and the sense of feeling imprisoned or held back despite being a technically "free" person). The theme of freedom appears in my case studies; and despite all the issues presented henceforth, like the globalization of Vietnam under communist controls, or protests among Vietnamese Americans, the question of social, economic, and political freedom relates back to the project of freeing South Vietnam not only from the communists but from the Americans as well.

Vietnamization, too, is not a military policy, but an ideology and discourse manifested from and informed by culture. It laid out an "imperial contract" between the United States and its foreign allies, one that ensured continued neocolonial relations of domination based on stereotypes. In her interpretation of Carl Schmidtt's distinction between friends and enemies as the basis for political society, Denise Ferreira da Silva (2005) finds that the expanding boundaries of U.S. empire requires the reconfiguration of those racial "others of Europe" within the shifting divide between "true friends" and "new friends." As opposed to its true friends in NATO (North Atlantic Treaty Organization), the new friends based in Third World places like Saigon, Vietnam, or Fallujah, Iraq need to be developed modern subjects-in-becoming within a Eurocentric idea of the government and "rights of man." Their poverty and lack of self-development render "the newcomers to the territory of freedom both unreliable friends and indistinguishable from the enemies of freedom" (2005: 125). As unreliable friends due to their economic and political underdevelopment, South Vietnam could never stand equal to its ally, the United States. Claiming to wean these Southeast Asian children off America's teat, U.S. military officials rated their Vietnamese counterparts poorly in combat preparedness, looking upon them as "little people," "animals," "squint eyes," and "gooks," and failing to distinguish between foe and friend. This added up to a lot of misunderstanding and a decisive breakdown of relations between the U.S. military and the army of South Vietnam (ARVN). Sour relations contributed to the ARVN's many problems: high defection, poor morale, ineffective training, and uncoordinated leadership. Per military historian Gregory Daddis, "Vietnamization could not undo racism or years of critical attitudes held toward Asians"; it instead revamped those same attitudes (2011: 170–171). The South Vietnamese were depicted as an inept and guileless by America's top statesman, undeserving of further assistance from the United States. President Nixon noted in a private conversation to advisors: "Well, if they're that collapsible, maybe they just have to be collapsed . . . We've got to remember, we cannot—we cannot keep this child sucking at the tit when the child is four years old" (Hughes 2010: 505).[4] Not only does this graphic metaphor hold forth the notion of South Vietnam as dependents of American beneficence, it pinpoints the careless, rather callous attitude of the Nixon administration toward the Vietnamese people.

An Imperial Contract between Friends

Returns of War reflects upon the contradictory process of societies both expunged and embraced by Western imperial powers, recognizing Vietnamization as what Denise Ferreira da Silva calls a "governing political signifier" for what South Vietnam means (2007: xxxii). That politics can have a cultural dimension is not surprising when one views Vietnamization as not just a political failing of the South Vietnamese government, but a cultural failing of the South Vietnamese people to win independence for themselves, unable to achieve freedom and be modern. Using culture to show the scripting of the South Vietnamese as lost "travelers on the road to transparency," the book marks their position as those "placed outside history . . . fixed in an earlier time or altogether outside time" (168, 166). This is more than a political issue, as the problem of economics bears weight on the exchange as a problem of the relationship between the West and "the rest." In this manner, the "new territories" of consumption and investment such as South Vietnam have been "mapped onto previous racial and colonial (imperial) discourses and practices" (Chakravartty and Silva 2012: 60). My use of economic metaphors like returns of war and others perhaps gets at this financialization of everyday life, which has both a geopolitical and historical basis.

In popular writings by the American news media, South Vietnam's crippled ability to become an independent nation on its own was time and again attributed to the economic and political deficiencies of the local people. This rhetorical sleight-of-hand in Vietnamization discourse suggested that the South Vietnamese then must be *made* free by a superior paternalistic power able to act as a guarantor of life, liberty, and happiness. Vietnamization is part of an older colonial strategy, one used earlier to justify U.S. colonization of Samoa, the Virgin Islands, Guam, Hawai'i, and Puerto Rico. Comparable to the U.S. strategy of "Filipinization" in the Philippines at the turn of the twentieth century, Vietnamization essentially proclaimed that the South Vietnamese republic and its "natives" were not strong enough to be on their own, and required the United States to help them find their way. As a different kind of colonial formation, "United States policy makers cast this alleged temporary relation as a tutelary project aimed at preparing otherwise incompetent, effectively infantile populations for self-government" (Goldstein 2014: 16). Going beyond the racial suggestion of disability, Vietnamization formed a new "imperial contract," offering another source (and possibly theory) of dependency that marks the unfair trade balance and exchange between imperial powers and their colonial subjects now labeled as "allies." South Vietnam, of course, was not a colony of the United States in the formal sense, but the comparison is relevant because the prickly history of U.S. involvement in other countries forms the larger colonial background for Vietnamization, and why this program—seemingly innocent in giving a nation the right to fight for its own freedom—was so controversial and remains so even now.

In the United States, the name "South Vietnam" describes dependency and tragic victimhood as shown by the perceived dishonesty of RVN government leaders needing U.S. foreign aid, Saigonese prostitutes needing American GIs and dollars, and finally, the neediness of the "boat people" escaping their country requiring adoption by American families. While in communist Vietnam there was silence or repression about South Vietnam, in the United States there is general ignorance about America's former and belittled friends, if not misinformed by cultural typologies that habitually sort South Vietnamese into ill-fated "freedom fighters," unfortunate "boat people," criminalized poor "welfare cheats," or assimilable "model minorities" (Nguyen 2006: 14). All this focus on individuals and group distinctions distracts from the structural processes of nation-building and empire-building, which created those social categories.

The U.S. discourse of South Vietnamese cultural impoverishment and deficit enabled the justification for Nixon's feigned support for the country's political sovereignty under Vietnamization, which worked in concert with the U.S. mainstream media's scapegoating of the fledgling Republic of Vietnam government (RVN) for the problems of the war. For the ARVN soldiers struggling to hold onto a dream of liberation that might not come true, the war became "no longer about the freedom and independence of South Vietnam but rather about the long-term stability of families" (Brigham 2006: 109). The press, politicians, and eventually even the president himself upbraided the RVN for its incompetence, maligned the South Vietnamese soldiers who were unable to properly handle "modern" military equipment, and looked down on the local civilians who were unwilling to protect their own homes (Willbanks 2004: 287). As a way of making imperial personhood, the idea was that if the South Vietnamese nation could not muster enough strength to stand on its own to carry out the anti-communist mission without the United States, rising to the occasion to stand on its own and stay the course, so the story went, the debacle that followed was the fault of *those* people for not loving freedom enough to fight or die for it. Vietnamization, in other words, updates the old Western "civilizing mission" of *helping others help themselves*, infusing this ever-problematic effort with a postcolonial maxim: *We can't help you if you can't help yourself*. As cultural historian Patrick Hagopian (2009) writes, the Vietnamese were considered childlike in their endeavors to develop as a nation in need of U.S. tutelage:

> The U.S. commander in Vietnam, General William Westmoreland, justified the American military effort in Southeast Asia by saying that Vietnam reminded him of a child—it had to crawl before it could walk and walk before it could run. Thus, pro-war propaganda overlaid two images: the South Vietnamese state as a child, a newly found "nation" in need of tutelage and support; and South Vietnamese children as representative inhabitants of the country. The two child images converged in their ideological meanings, because by protecting the children, the United States forces helped the young nation, and vice versa. (321)

If these adopted children were abandoned by their parents, they would become orphans, but, eventually, the childlike nation must learn to walk on its own. The drawing of curtains on the nation by the war's end led many South Vietnamese to become seen as infantilized refugees, again needing to be adopted, protected, and sponsored by Americans.

As a plan for decolonization steeped in imperialist thinking, Vietnamization deferred decolonization to the extent that the United States did not fully give independence to South Vietnam as the Americans retained custody of the country's freedom. Put differently, the program of Vietnamization signifies the on-the-surface liberation of a foreign people by the United States, the latter pretending that its "temporary" occupation of Vietnam was never a form of imperial imposition. As a racial project, too, it tailors the European mission of molding nonwhite populations into Westernized "modern people." In other words, Vietnamization is still going on and serves as a neocolonial discourse, referring at once to the condition of being dominated by an external force and being without self-determination (and thus needing that external push). As two historians put it, "Vietnamization involves more than just the asking of new questions. It also aims to provide new answers for some of the oldest and most persistent questions about the war" (Miller and Vu 2009: 2). As a framework, it helps uncover the histories of American war-making, things now being defoliated in the thick jungles of our historical memory.

Returns of War contends with the inescapable shadow of the Vietnam War, but more specifically the shadow of South Vietnam upon current events, written and completed during a time when a global "War on Terror" compels the United States to follow errant commitments abroad just as it did in Vietnam. As the country enters new quagmires without proper endings, such conflicts are routinely compared in the press to the controversial war waged decades earlier in Southeast Asia. Media comparisons of the U.S.-led conflicts in Iraq and Afghanistan—news reporters dubbed them Obama and Bush's Vietnam—with the epic war in Vietnam symbolically and synecdochically linked American aggression across world stages and historical periods. The analogizing of the U.S. wars in the Arab world as "another Vietnam" stamps out the specificity of the Vietnam War to help explain the sense of déjà vu experienced by the United States in its many geopolitical shell games. American politicians and pundits point to our recurring "Vietnam Syndrome," summoning the shame of U.S. military losses in the Vietnam War as the model—depending on whether one is a peace dove or war hawk—for later wars. In the overuse of the term "Vietnam Syndrome," South Vietnam's legacy is resuscitated in sporadic fashion to justify U.S. incursions in distant places that are supposedly going to collapse from terrorism—much like the Cold War truism that weak nations would fall like dominoes to the red menace (Carter 2008). The popular portrait of the South

Vietnamese government as a shoddy regime that fell effortlessly to communism—due in whole or in part to Vietnamization policy—makes it the prime example of what to do or what not to do to other countries. As a nation considered deceased, unable to return to its original form, after being deserted by the Americans and overtaken by communists, South Vietnam's memory inspires further thinking about the recursive power of war. Vietnamization even inspired the British pacification of North Ireland through a strategy of "Ulsterisation" (Kiernan 1974: 323). A better explanation of how the Vietnam War constitutes a flash point in larger anticolonial struggles and Cold War geopolitics in Vietnam is long overdue.

The Neocolonial History of South Vietnam

The Vietnamese people first engaged in anticolonial struggles against the French in the 1880s, fighting to gain independence as a sovereign nation. Attempts by the French to strip the power of Vietnam's young emperor, Hàm Nghi, drove the royal family to flee the capital city in Central Vietnam. High in the mountains, a guerilla anticolonial movement was forming that loathed any form of external control. European cultural influence and efforts to create a colony amenable to its interests spurred a growing sense of nationalism among sectors of Vietnam's educated elites (Chesneaux 1955). French military commanders recruited support in the south, where it had established a colony for two decades, enlisting pro-French collaborators and wealthy Vietnamese in its fight against nationalist forces in the north. The strongman tactics by which the French suppressed northern rebels and their supporters served to stimulate further hatred of the colonizers. With the outbreak of World War II, France found itself busy fighting a war on its own continent to deal with a colonial war in Asia. Anticolonial resistance took definitive shape as a mass populist movement in the 1940s with a coalition of forces led by leader Hồ Chí Minh and his Việt Minh nationalist party.

During the first Vietnam War or "First Indochina War" (1946–1954), the French were on the losing end of their own finagling in overseas territories, failing to crush the stirrings of Vietnamese nationalism. Undaunted, France sought to reclaim its wayward colonies again after World War II. This project of restoring French sovereignty in Indochina was bankrolled by the United States (which paid for 80 percent of this war effort) and approved by President Truman, backsliding on the promise of President Woodrow Wilson to respect the self-determination of all people. Inspired by the American colonial resistance to England, Hồ Chí Minh had earlier appealed to Wilson for assistance against the French, but his requests were repeatedly rebuffed. Such negligence was motivated by racism as Wilson and subsequent American presidents did not consider the Vietnamese "fit" for self-rule, especially given the weakness of the Saigon-based Bảo Đại imperial regime in southern Vietnam, the puppet regime of France. The Americans wanted to turn South Vietnam into a "protected" territory, but the pretenses of the United States as a democratizing force in the world meant the Americans would retain "temporary" control over the country, until they felt the Vietnamese were ready to stand on their own. The U.S. Cold War policy of containment, the domino theory, and fears of Soviet involvement (who supported the Việt Minh) could not hide the fact that American intervention mostly represented the neo-imperialist principles of "power acquisition in the international arena" (Soddu 2012: 7).

With the sound defeat of the French again by the Việt Minh at the Battle of Điện Biên Phủ, plans for a postcolonial Vietnam were articulated in the 1954 Geneva Peace Accords: A demilitarized zone along the seventeenth parallel would temporarily divide the country into two parts, with the northern region controlled by the Việt Minh and the southern region under the informal "administration" of the United States, until national elections were held in 1956 (Bradley 2000). Soon after, the Republic of Vietnam (or South Vietnam as it was and still is called colloquially) was decreed an independent state by Ngô Đình Diệm, a renegade politician and former French colonial bureaucrat. This illegal action, a violation of the Geneva treaty, was supported by the United States. Diệm's declaration stymied any progress toward national elections, which at the time many predicted the very popular Hồ Chí Minh and his party would win (Vlastos 1991: 55–57). In the ensuing years, John F. Kennedy sent military advisors and soldiers to the country, later supporting a coup to overthrow Diệm to produce a more manageable local administration. Through such actions, the Americans succeeded in "mapping their own imaginative geography, [where] American policymakers attempted to transmute a colonial war into a civil war through the creation of South Vietnam" (Tyner 2009: 49). Despite President Kennedy's inaugural speech in 1961 stating that the fight to create South Vietnam was a "limited war," the deracinated efforts to unify Vietnam ignited an even bigger war.

With France's imperial clout in Indochina waning, the United States adopted an aggressive policy of "containment" to stanch the tide of communism believed to be flowing into Southeast Asia, sparking the Second Indochina War, or what is called "the Vietnam War" in the United States and "the American War" in Vietnam. Redeploying similar colonial language used by the French to shortchange Vietnamese independence, the United States took over the imperial reins to assume power as the new regional hegemon, another colonizer trying to succor the South Vietnamese people to desire a "better" life (SarDesai 2005).[5] Countries like South Korea, benefiting from U.S. foreign aid and Western offerings of "a better life," furnished economic monies and military troops to the U.S. cause in Vietnam. President Kennedy dispatched military advisors and the Green Berets to help overthrow the insubordinate Diệm dictatorship regime. Successive administrations continued to display erratic behavior as these regimes existed semi-autonomously. With South Vietnam technically under its wing, the United States launched psychological warfare and chemical warfare against the local population. A firm sense of white supremacy backed the U.S. program of total war against a people already deemed incapable of being on their own. Secretary of State John Dulles and then-Vice President Richard Nixon, in their 1954 paper, "Taking Up the White Man's Burden," surmised that if the United States did not drum up support for South Vietnam as a bulwark against communism, the fallout would severely diminish America's ability to "save Asia" from its own ethnic forces of anarchy and totalitarianism (Dulles and Nixon 1995: 52).[6] Both Nixon and Dulles recognized early on that the South Vietnamese would attempt to fight for their independence if the United States exerted total control, but they still believed the Vietnamese lacked "the ability to conduct a war by themselves or govern themselves" (ibid.).

There is no definitive date for when the United States entered war with Vietnam, and, depending on who is providing the information, the war could have begun with the United States sending advisors to help the French in 1950, or in 1964 with the Gulf of Tonkin resolution. Either way, for the next two decades, the United States was in some way at war with Vietnam, but this war was concerned with the cultural depictions of the Vietnamese who were, up to that point, a mysteriously exotic unknown population in the "Far East" to most Americans. During the Vietnam War (it was never officially declared a war by the United States Congress), the Vietnamese were represented as impressionable Western supporters but also potential enemies because many American soldiers could not distinguish by sight between friend and foe (Leventman and Camacho 1980). The war was not solely a military enterprise but a "subject-making" event that determined how South Vietnam entered modern history as "a nation without its own history, culture, heritage and political agenda" (Espiritu 2005b: 313). It is assumed that the story of South Vietnam veritably concluded in 1975 with its invasion by joint northern revolutionary forces and the southern-based communist National Liberation Front (Viet Cong). If we take 1975 to be the end of the war, the subject of South Vietnam should be dead or put to rest. But what would speculating about South Vietnam's past mean for postulating its viable *future*? What happens to the history of a war when the outcome and meanings of that war, as well as its designation of winners and losers, were never really settled? A discourse of war that is not caught in the past but always still unfolding in the *now*, Vietnamization's continued existence and geographic memories are carried forth by the South Vietnamese diaspora and refugees displaced by the war.

(South) Vietnamese Refugees in the Diaspora

Returns of War solicits a nod to the melancholic sentiment of not being fully Vietnamese, something felt by many former citizens of South Vietnam given the loss of their homeland. The book moves beyond our common misperceptions of South Vietnam and reveals the complex and often ignored position of the postwar Vietnamese diaspora, whose subjects not only are refugees that have migrated overseas but remain "stateless" when it comes to being South Vietnamese. A number of scholars have studied the memory-making of the Vietnam War and gauged what it even means to be a Vietnamese refugee in the present context of globalization, diaspora, and transnationalism (Espiritu 2014; Aguilar-San Juan 2009; Valverde 2012; Nguyen 2016; Nguyen 2012). These projects refer back to and hint at the South Vietnamese nation-building project but focus more on the refugee experience. My work is more direct and specifically aimed at exploring how the discredited memory of South Vietnam poses a challenge to the manner in which the Vietnam War is remembered and for whom. By focusing on the premises for the founding and loss of the South Vietnamese nation, I am not assigning little importance to the experiences of North Vietnamese or other groups still reeling from the war's effects. My research unscrambles the memory of South Vietnam in the messiness of the current historical moment, throwing the legacy of this ill-fated nation into a continuous play of interpretations to find another way out of what Phuong Nguyen calls refugee nationalism (2017).

The complex reality of South Vietnamese history and U.S. imperial culture are erased by the stereotypical image of the Americans as saviors and the South Vietnamese as helpless subjects and hapless allies. Through a flexible understanding of what it means to *be* South Vietnamese, a paradoxical figure that is co-extensively colonized and colonizer (the South Vietnamese military invaded Cambodia and southern Laos in the early 1970s with the encouragement and sponsorship of the United States), one develops a significant understanding of how "Vietnamese people" are divided, ordered, and classified among the many imaginings of "Vietnam." When we talk about Vietnamese refugees, we should be talking about Vietnamese Americans (the overwhelming majority of refugees found new homes in the United States) and the South Vietnamese diaspora to acknowledge that most Vietnamese who left after the war came from South Vietnam. These exiles continue to hold onto the memory of the RVN even as they adapt to new politico-economic priorities and national identities. Considering the ways South Vietnamese history and memory crop up again within current affairs serves to challenge "South Vietnamese" as a discrete category of geopolitical identity and recognize the irreducibility of this freighted term of belonging, one that can be reworked as a multifaceted object of study deserving of much scrutiny.

For many in the Vietnamese diaspora, their homeland is not some simply idyllic place of ancestral ethnic origin. The Vietnam many remember is South Vietnam, a spatial geopolitical construct born out of the Cold War, one that formally existed only for a short 20 years. This military context shapes the perspectives of Vietnamese diasporic subjects who always consider South Vietnam as the "political unconscious" operating beneath their narratives as displaced peoples (Jameson 2013). One major criticism of diaspora is that the term is much too broad, referring generally to populations strewn about the world away from their ancestral roots, defined by a population's sense of homelessness and desire for return to the homeland. Namsoon Kang (2014) deduces that scholars often miss out on the militarized contexts that caused populations to leave their homes in the first place.

Returns of War writes against the common perception of the South Vietnamese as tragic victims of war, either as innocent bystanders or guilty culprits in their downfall. A focus on South Vietnam and its very politicized diaspora is not meant to bolster South Vietnamese nationalism, but to provide a way to bring nation, economics, identity, culture, politics, and history into play with one another. This book is not a labor of historical revisionism, seeking to inject the perspectives of those overlooked to offer a more "correct" version of history. Such exhaustive work has already been done by many scholars who have documented U.S. historical relations with South Vietnam, all of whom provide the following constants: South Vietnam was put in a bind by American withdrawal; Vietnamization tapered off resources to the war effort and "no military mission since Vietnam has come close to that war . . . in its consequences" (Diehl 2009).[7] A convergence of psychological sensibilities (return is significant for considering trauma) and economic concepts like getting a profit return can be fruitful in unpacking the productivity found in things associated only with negativity and failure. Insofar as the traumatized subject can return to something emotional to make sense of or salvage the past (and clear a path for their future), the future-oriented sense of economic return on past investments suggests a similar course, if one understands how there is a psychology behind economics and an economics behind psychology. When it comes to cultural work of memory, nothing is clear-cut, as there is always a loss in gains, and gains to be uncovered from loss.

The Price of Refugee Memory

If culture allows the United States to represent Vietnamese people in a certain way, it also helps to draw out the unfinished stories of history, introducing unofficial and unrecognized voices of the Vietnamese. Culture can be found everywhere that shared meanings accrue and accrete, particularly in aspects of our daily lives that are far too commonly excluded from the stuff of "serious business" like government or international relations. Through urban ethnography, historical archives, newspaper reports, visual art, oral histories, and literary memoirs, *Returns of War* offers a far-ranging picture of South Vietnamese culture today and a detailed portrait of refugee life that emerges within the shifting gradients of contemporary life. These cultural forms contextualize the propensity to remember the Vietnam War in all its vicissitudes. Looking across culture and memory brings to light the various points of interest and obverse frames of reference through which war "returns" to modern thought. All examples presented herein were chosen because they deal with people trying to soldier on after the war, constructing alternative discourses about Vietnam, the Vietnam War, Vietnamization, and South Vietnam in the early twenty-first century.

Where politics is often considered narrowly, in terms of competing state interests, the politics of culture encourages us to consider symbolic meaning sculpted through our daily interactions, exposing those buried elements and conflicts in society. In this register, the cultural politics of remembering the Vietnam War is "the continuation of war by other means" (Foucault 2003: 15). As cultural critic Lisa Lowe (1996) tells us, culture is the "site of struggle in which active links are made between signifying practices and social structures . . . Where the political terrain can neither resolve nor suppress inequality, it erupts in culture. Because culture is the contemporary repository of memory, of history" (22). Culture acts as the primary medium for grasping the fragmented present and restless past, but I argue it also gives divination to our uncertain futures. The incomplete memory of the Vietnam War, Vietnamization, and South Vietnam forms the harbinger of the unrealized things to come and our lagging sense of what came before. That process of memorialization is made easier due to the great lapse of time, and changing cultural tastes, many decades after the Vietnam War when an older generation is trying to hold onto its fading memories and a new generation is trying to learn more about it. There are costs associated with attaching oneself to a loser nation, and an inherent value that needs to be held onto dearly.

Returns of War: South Vietnam and the Price of Refugee Memory tracks the multi-directional frictions of state power, the economic damages, culture flows, and human insecurities caused by war. The phrase "returns of war" is a play on words, the term cues us to the ways the memory of the past reappears to us, especially in moments of crisis. The pluralistic meaning of "returns" also contravenes the received wisdom of history as a linear progressive movement. *Returns of War* recapitulates the recycled memory of the Vietnam War, marking war's haunting presence in our future-oriented global era. It points to the ways Vietnamese and Americans dredge up the inveterate violence wrought by the landmark event of war in their lives. As much of the research for this book was conducted at the peak of the "War on Terror," which made the U.S. national debt balloon to unforeseen heights, and during the greatest economic slump since the Great Depression, "returns" hints at the pecuniary sense of talking about war in fiscal terms and what kind of profits one can make from major losses, even those from war. Focusing on the "price" of refugee memory shows that historical remembrance can, and often does, take place along uneven lines, where price refers to the sorting and assignment of value, either by refugees themselves or by others. The psychological returns *of* war (memory) is an opportunity to make some economic returns *of* war (capital).

In some sense, the many topics that we will explore are all reconstructive historical projects, all aiming to bring the contentious politics of the past into cultural life today, burdened by the weight of that effort. By assembling an array of texts, images, and documents from the first decade of this millennium, the book builds a unique archive around the ghostly figure of South Vietnam. A "Vietnamized" field of vision helps to see the many returns of South Vietnamese memory and the repetition as well as difficulty of those returns. The book engages with the sticky matter of discussing a country not found on any current official map of the world. In this light, individuals and organizations have retooled this prior sense of the South Vietnamese as mere stooges or imitators of the Americans, the shill of the U.S. military establishment, and a people who cannot represent or speak for themselves. Though many decades have elapsed since the Vietnam War, America's military intercession in South Vietnam triggers thorny and tangled memories that need to be freed from their twisted roots.

As we shall see, the haunting ghost and absent presence of South Vietnam foreground questions of memory and movement within public spaces like urban development, historical archives, ethnic enclaves, and military service. It provides the through-line of my critical appreciation of (and attempts to move beyond) Vietnamization as Nixonian policy and military project of the United States appearing to cede responsibility to proxy forces or allies. For me, Vietnamization is a much more individual endeavor and community-based phenomenon, an ongoing process of giving voice and independence to South Vietnamese people. This personalizing of the political gives traction to the cultural production of memory around South Vietnam as that nation embodies the historical focus of that earlier mission of national self-determination. Using this concept to unfold the case studies gathered in the following chapters, I describe for example elderly refugees in the United States whose memories of the defunct state motivate their need to assert South Vietnamese nationalism in the United States, American archivists trying to incorporate South Vietnamese stories in their historiographies, young Vietnamese American soldiers fighting wars in U.S.-occupied countries like Iraq that resemble another South Vietnam. These case studies serve to "Vietnamize" a U.S.-centric postwar narrative by asking: Who has ultimate power in defining the imaginary and borders of a nation? What official knowledge is made possible? My intellectual project recognizes that South Vietnamese–related stories do and do not conform to the ideological premises of national or cultural belonging; such stories reveal the contradictions and structural injustice beneath the original creation (and propagation) of South Vietnam, the Vietnamese Communist Party silencing of South Vietnam, and the U.S. self-designation as the arbiter of freedom for Vietnamese people abroad and domestically. Some chapters emphasize the ambiguities found in this critique, recognizing that South Vietnamese refugee stories express an ambivalent desire for the continuation of American support, rather than its abandonment. Meanwhile, others are more focused on what happened to the South Vietnamese after the Americans left, recognizing that the Americans are still responsible for the postwar racialization and subordination of South Vietnam.

Returns of War breaks ground in the study of the memory of the Vietnam War and Vietnamese refugees by selecting unique case studies that take stock of the many imaginings and re-imaginings of South Vietnam and what they bode for emerging projects of development, community, nationalism, militarism, and feminism. Taken together, the book's various sites of investigation involve some struggle over representation, making for a tantalizing conversation about ways the arrow of South Vietnam enters people's hearts and minds again, while gaining a better picture of war's trauma within the intransigence of modern life. The following chapters forge a path to a place that has no real beginning or end, setting the stage for the many returns of war.

1

Archival Others

The Vietnamese as Absent Presence in the Historical Record

In the desolate Texan desert stands the beautiful, lush campus of Texas Tech University, located in the city of Lubbock. Tucked away on one side of the school stands the Vietnam War Center and Archive (VNCA), separate from the main library. Upon entering the hallway of the stately building where this site dedicated to preserving the history of the Vietnam War is housed, one is confronted with an impressive visual display: a cowboy figure stands over a cliff facing out toward the High Plains, eyeing the Western expansion of the United States under a sense of Manifest Destiny. This display is courtesy of the school's Southwest Historical Archive, which provides temporary physical space for my current concern, the Vietnam War archive. In the adjacent window display is a hand-illustrated picture of a U.S. soldier in Vietnam facing the opposite direction; this one is overlooking the foreign virgin lands of Southeast Asia, standing at the service of the country's global expansion overseas. Holding the same countenance, the two soldiers are a split image of American empire, twin personifications of the nation—one that calls to mind U.S. soldiers calling Vietnam "Indian country" and how the Indian Wars were the precursor to later wars with foreign nations. Symbolically, these two iconographic figures prompt reflection about "the frontier" myth that animates so much of U.S. colonial culture as well as questions about the public faces of history, what gets remembered, and who or what gets to represent history.

The archive holds a vast trove of documents filled with unknown information. The main public entry point is a giant study room with only a few file cabinets and tables, a noiseless, musty place that belies the archive's humming public activities, community events, and political relationships outside the school. A peaceful and serene mood envelops me as I enter the air-conditioned room, a relief from the searing heat outside. I arrived in pursuit of learning how Vietnamese people are represented, sorted, and categorized in this archive dedicated to the Vietnam War, not expecting to find much more than perhaps a plethora of items dedicated to military missions. Most visitors, I assumed, come seeking information, but I came to find out how that information takes shape within the archive as an ethnographic space, one with transnational boundaries. In this quiet institutional space of learning, I contemplated my family's history while looking up data related to "refugees," "Vietnamese American," or "South Vietnam" on a computer terminal. Depending on the high-profile status or fragility of the materials, I sorted through a portfolio alone, or a staff member physically handed me the files for my sit-down viewing. Interviews with several staff members and a private tour through the physical storage room led me to amazing findings, both in a conceptual and material sense. Soon enough, I gained a deeper appreciation for the Vietnam archive not as a place to simply learn about the past, but as a "living memorial" to a war without peace.

Many scholars have written about the Vietnam Veterans Memorial in Washington, DC, built in 1982 as a controversial piece of national commemoration, both in the way it was built and the way it sanctifies the memory of an embarrassing American war that was too hard to remember due to a lack of consensus about its purpose and value (Griswold and Griswold 1986; Wagner-Pacific and Schwartz 1991). John Carlos Rowe (2002) says that the Vietnam War is "the most chronicled, documented, reported, filmed, taped, and—in all likelihood—narrated war in history, and for those very reasons, it would seem, the least subject to understanding or to any American consensus" (197). Plainly stated, the discourse of "Vietnam" as a war and not a country in the United States has no singular meaning, and its history is defined by a lack of information (during the Cold War, many documents were redacted and shrouded in government secrecy).

For a certain sector of Americans, the Vietnam War morally and financially bankrupted the country with little to gain in terms of national pride; it was a war that had to be forgotten for the sake of national healing, but for antiwar activists, it was a remarkable lesson in humility and a necessary reminder of American imperial hubris. With greater lapses in time and the memory that comes with the passing of time, there is a greater momentum and desire to confront the war's lingering issues head-on, rather than avoid its embarrassing aspects, such as the U.S. treatment of the South Vietnamese or the neglect of the South Vietnamese side of the war's memory.

One potential site through which nations try to remember and work out the war's problematic history is the archive. Housed at Texas Tech University, the VCNA expends much energy to document the experiences of all of those involved in the Vietnam War, preserving the testimony and material record of everyone, from veterans and their families to American antiwar protesters and Vietnamese refugees. Yet, few ever come to archives dedicated to war. While millions of tourists have visited the Vietnam Memorial and the National Archives in Washington, DC, and the ways those sites corral the nation to remember the war and grieve for its dead (Wagner-Pacific and Schwartz 1991; Tatum 1996), the archival repositories of the war have received much less attention. Archives like the one at Texas Tech are far less prominent—and perhaps, for most of us, far less glamorous, or perhaps even banal—but they are equally important spaces for national commemoration and public memory.

While the National Archives in the nation's capital aims to document all facets of the nation's history, as it contains the largest trove of government documents related to the Vietnam War, the VCNA in Texas is the largest standalone entity and archival repository for all aspects of the study of the Vietnam War.[1] It contains the personal belongings, written record, and testimonies of soldiers and civilians during and even after the war. As a site for understanding U.S. history, the archive is not just a physical site or a place of memorialization for a war that shook the core of the country; it is also an axiological site for thinking about national space itself. Within the confines of this state-funded public archive,[2] everything from mementos recovered on the bodies of dead soldiers to audio recordings of Vietnam's communist leaders discussing the impact of the war on their country is included. The archive is blatant in its desire to document all facets of the war . . . and yet there is one noticeable omission . . . the South Vietnamese themselves. Despite archivists' concerns with capturing this "other side" of the historical equation, the full inclusion of America's Vietnamese allies is challenged by the dearth of personal materials collected as much as it is vexed by the political question of how best to represent them. The fact that the South Vietnamese lost the war and lost their country makes them the victims of the Vietnam War, and so their history becomes the "vault of tragic metaphors" (Lam 2007). The South Vietnamese story of independence, translated in the U.S. context as the Vietnamese American refugee story, has become imperceptible, as writer Andrew Lam (2005) reasons, because "our side lost, we became exiles, enemies of history . . . what is epic in one country is inconsequential in another," the South Vietnamese have "no real biographies in the American narrative, no real history. Invisibility, it seemed, was our fate" (30).

In the following, I first give a brief history of the genesis of the archive, recognizing its founding need to preserve the memories and stories of U.S. American veterans, analyzing how the archive serves as a site of memorialization of war. Second, I look at the ways the archive tries to incorporate Vietnamese Americans in its conferences, heritage project, and oral history program. I offer reflections on the stumbling blocks the VNCA encountered in working on and with Vietnamese refugees, and how the institution is at a loss to find a proper place for the Vietnamese within its operations. In doing so, I regard this archive dedicated to an ignoble war as cognizant of the fact that not all historical subjects can be easily immortalized in space and time, and that archives themselves can bear responsibility in shaping the political economy of memory, where refugees are not easily folded into an all-inclusive sense of national history. Upon closer inspection, we discover how the center's efforts to "Vietnamize" its holdings cannot abrogate the peculiar status of the Vietnamese as "archival others" within the U.S. historical record.

Vietnamizing the American Memory of War

As a place for considering the limits of national belonging, the Vietnam Center and Archive finds itself at pains to convert the Vietnamese into "native informants" with information palatable for the U.S. nation-state, while trying not to enfold them into the "intellectual sovereignty" of Western knowledge-production (Warrior 2009). Archival efforts to give historical value to America's former allies, the South Vietnamese, is rebuffed by the ahistorical tendency of the United States to forget them. While the archive contains a rich amount of material documents, ranging from soldiers' personal memoirs to military atlases and equipment donated by American soldiers such as family heirlooms, oral histories occupy a special place in the archive; according to one archivist, individual stories bring into focus "people's views and what they have to say on a personal level."[3] My excavation of the archive speaks to the tunneling of memory, regarding the archive as both a physical space and a polyvalent site of meaning about the war and its people (Yoneyama 1999; Klein 2000; Blight 2002). I add my observations of it alongside interviews with several key members of the staff,[4] which include the archive's founder, the main reference staff member, and director of the oral history project. My findings will make readers privy to the ways archival institutions like the VNCA function as a U.S.-centric enterprise, where public meanings about history are Americanized, even as this very American archive is also undergoing a form of Vietnamization to now include the South Vietnamese perspective, and even globalization to include the North Vietnamese who won the war and now rule over communist Vietnam.[5]

Vietnamization refers to the Cold War policy of Americans arming the South Vietnam military and lending recognition to its foreign allies as independent nations. This military program represented the South Vietnamese as agents and later deterrents of their sovereignty who could not hold onto their own territorial power. In saying that the Vietnam War archive is Vietnamizing itself, I am purposely invoking this problematic geopolitical history—indeed, one cannot, I believe, speak of South Vietnamese people without addressing how they have become historically invisible in the first place—speaking to how certain sources of authority breed forms of power that determine the ways the South Vietnamese people become visible. As I later explain, the challenge in procuring participation by former exiles of South Vietnam is complicated by the fact that some staff members prefer that the archive is isolated from large Vietnamese ethnic enclaves, due to the rabid anti-communist politics that consume the community, as the archive does exchange information with the socialist government of Vietnam, which includes inviting communist officials to its conferences and forums—an unpopular idea with refugees who fled socialism.

Like any scholar researching information, I immersed myself mentally and physically in the archive, but instead of being a neutral researcher standing distant from my object and site of study, my embedded role as an analyst of the archive required me to study physical exhibits and interview staff about the mechanics of archiving and running an archive.

What I learned is that the archive serves as a cultural (and political) medium for transmitting not only history but also memory. Indeed, as the official mission statement for the archive reminds us, there must be a full account of what happened in Vietnam, so future individuals "can study and better understand the people, places, and events of this critical time in history" ("About the Vietnam Center and Archive").

According to the center's mission statement: "The Vietnam Archive stands as a living memorial to all those who played some part in the nation's 'Vietnam experience.' We want to preserve a complete history of the war. To do otherwise would be a disservice to history" ("About the Vietnam Center and Archive"). This early desire to take hold of sometimes unwieldy histories of the Vietnam War and put them into one collection always included the Vietnamese refugee perspective, if at least to provide a more accurate historical view. Studying the archive as a space for the representation of history requires figuring out what materials are contained there, how it's organized, who organizes it, and for what purpose. The Vietnam Center and Archive is today the premier institute in which personal and donated materials from the war are kept, with more than three million pages of scanned material, as well as everything from U.S. military apparel to the clothing of ethnic minorities in Vietnam.[6]

One day in 1989, Professor James Reckner recounts, he was teaching at Texas Tech University when he asked his class of undergraduate students about the Vietnam War and was shocked by their lack of knowledge about it. Most of his students had no idea who General Westmoreland was, despite the notoriety of this controversial public figure as the commander of the U.S. forces in Vietnam from 1964 to 1968. Students' lack of historical awareness inspired Reckner to start an archive to preserve the U.S. experience in Vietnam, culling materials from American veterans he knew in the local area.[7] In 1989, Reckner convened the first meeting of local Vietnam veterans to discuss creating an archive using those vets' personal materials, to show his students. From the start, the archive's founder worked closely with Vietnam veterans, but there were no South Vietnamese organizations or cultural groups in the panhandle region, even though Texas is the state with the second largest population of Vietnamese in the United States, after California, mostly living in urban centers like Austin, Dallas, and Houston. A general information section about the archive found online states:

> The Vietnam Center seeks to provide a forum for all points of view and for all topics relating to Indochina, particularly—but not limited to—the American military involvement there . . . We encourage participation by our former allies in South Vietnam but also offer the same participation to those who supported the government in Hanoi. Similarly, we place equal importance upon preserving records relating to all aspects of the Vietnam War. ("About the Vietnam Center and Archive")

While the center supports the participation of Vietnamese officials, it encourages greater activity from its former allies and friends, the South Vietnamese, many of whom now reside in the United States. The center now includes a Vietnamese American Heritage staff member and a big official endorsement for obtaining more materials, which began in full force in 2008 with a large donation of Vietnamese political prisoner records, including the thousands of state-released records donated from the now defunct organization called Families of Vietnamese Political Prisoners Association (FVPPA), which kept track of refugee family reunification.

This chapter is rooted in an analysis of one specific archive, examining its ideological work and material contents, finding out what it can say about the real biographies and invisibility of the South Vietnamese people. The Vietnam Center and Archive, as both a center of scholarly public activity and an archive of stored materials, presents a fertile source for assessing contemporary archival practices and norms that shape the representation of historical memory. There has been no analysis of the VNCA itself, despite its salience for so many scholars and everyday people who have used its vast resources to construct their own sense of history. The VNCA could be understood as a highly political site involving disputes over the position or role of Vietnamese Americans in relation to what Marita Sturken observes as "the war with the difficult memory" (1997: 122).

But despite the VNCA's genuine desire to consider the Vietnamese and Vietnamese American story, there are stumbling blocks to efforts at inclusion. This remains true, despite the more than one million South Vietnamese who have come to the United States since the end of the war, becoming "Vietnamese Americans" in the process, either through refugee asylum or family reunification. Many of these refugees are viewed as politically conservative and reactionary to all things communist, since many were forced to leave after the United States abandoned South Vietnam under the policy of Vietnamization, which handed over the regime's fate to its people. In wanting to represent their story, the archive presents a possible authentic home for stories about the South Vietnamese, helping to "Vietnamize" the overly Americanized sense of U.S. military involvement overseas. Tracing Vietnamese refugee history as a "constitutive outside" or "invisible inside" of Vietnam War archival work, my research into the archive concurs with the prudent warnings of Laura Kang (2002), who claims that even when an attempt is made to invoice history's past dues, the cultural tension over who can remember the war and who is remembered in the war "calls attention to inaccessibility of the past as self-evident fact" (225). Those of us who believe in the power of the archive may be tempted to believe that once the South Vietnamese experience is documented therein, the South Vietnamese people will secure some fungible form of recognition or value. As Edward Miller and Truong Vu (2009) noted, the "Vietnamization" of Vietnam War studies and American history should be "driven by much more than just a desire to give equal time to Vietnam and the Vietnamese" (10).

As a site of historical memory, the archive provides an opportunity to honor those who served in the war. Photos placed in official newsletters stand out in their customary portrait of former war veterans shaking hands and meeting at the many community events hosted at the archive over the years. In my comprehensive review of the *Friends of the Vietnam Center* quarterly newsletter published over the decades, patriotic language such as "sacrifice," "honor," and "service" was consistently used to describe veterans. The physical archive is already impressive, with floors of materials from the past, but what makes this archive come alive are the many photos selected for commemorative posters, newsletters, and public exhibits that feature stills of war, representing human loss but also the beautiful vistas of Vietnam, or celebratory diplomatic photos of U.S. military veterans shaking hands with Vietnamese communist diplomats. Other photos capture scenes of U.S. soldiers rescuing South Vietnamese refugees from helicopters or leading them through deadly rivers. Sometimes ARVN soldiers can be seen with U.S. soldiers, hanging out in their respective outfits during the war. Ennobling pictures between two allied nations instill a sense of goodwill and cooperation. The images are not meant to be demonstrably divisive or offensive, and there is a noticeable lack of photos depicting gruesome scenes of bloodletting or anything that reflects the South Vietnamese's acrimonious relations with the United States or their need to fend for themselves once the superpower failed to help its allies in their last hour of need. Such visual representations of allies seek to mend the tarnished relations between friends, but the story of the Vietnamese is still wanting.[8]

At the same time, the questions of exchange, value, and labor are also vital, as the archive is one place where cultural capital is created. All archives must in some way continue to justify their existence, especially those found in public schools with limited sources of funding. This push for certain returns on the historical archive produces many community-based projects. Scholars are studying how the work of archiving mediates and determines the process by which subjects come to belong to history and historical institutions as an extension of cultural imaginaries and value-making. Linda Tuhiwai Smith (2013), for example, argues that Western archival practices comprise a system dependent upon procuring "raw" data from colonized populations to propose universalizing views of human science, nature, and virtue to determine "what counts as real" (44). They create a form of intellectual property and sovereignty that only creates scientific "evidence" about a group but does not give more "presence" to them. Vietnamese as archival others do not always count as having "real" presence, standing more in the virtual realm, where virtual denotes something existing "in essence or effect though not formally recognized or admitted" (according to *Merriam-Webster*, 2010). The South Vietnamese are part of the general discourse and memorialization of the Vietnam War in the United States, where they exist almost as an absent presence, one that has been ignored yet whose existence cannot so easily be gainsaid. As James Tatum notes, "The Viet Cong are one thing, the United States' former South Vietnamese allies another. Their omission is more troubling, their absence in American commemorations less easily dismissed" (1996: 637). With strong motivation to remember America's friends, the VNCA presents a valuable space for interrogating the ways that the South Vietnamese experience is constructed for U.S. historical commemoration. How then do the archive's representation of the Vietnam War and its participants frame the way we even think about that war? Considering archives as memorials and economical institutions organized around the exchange and valuation of certain historical objects and subjects, how might the VNCA convince people to reflect upon that war in a way that has resulted in so much controversy?

Originally called the Vietnam Center, the site was established as a place to honor the sacrifices of U.S. Vietnam veterans (the official logo of the archive is the special design of the government ribbon for members of the military who served in Southeast Asia), many of whom were shunned when they first returned home, burned by the negative response of an angry public toward them.[9] In 1990, the Archive of the Vietnam Conflict opened.[10] Soon, the few boxes and files from soldiers expanded to include other items such as military uniforms, music recordings from the war, and other paraphernalia. Recognizing that it had become not just an archive, but an institution of learning, the site officially changed its name to the Vietnam Center and Archive in 1997,[11] with the mission of educating the American public about the Vietnam War. By trying not only to honor those who have been denigrated but also to teach about their experiences, the Vietnam Center and Archive illuminates the difficulty in honoring the besmirched memory of an "unwon war" (Ehrenhaus 1989). Unlike the Vietnam War materials in the U.S. National Archives which store primarily official governmental statistics and bureaucratic memos, the VNCA is more personal in nature. In a letter written to patrons of the center, Reckner set the tone for establishing an archive based on collecting veterans' stories as a means of teaching the younger generation about the personal stakes of war:

> We must work to preserve records of the war; to preserve and honor the memory of those of our comrades who made the ultimate sacrifice there; and we must encourage younger generations to study the American Vietnam experience. There is much to be learned from our missteps there. And our success, too. In the end, I suspect younger generations of Americans will judge those who served in Vietnam much more favorably than have our peers who for various reasons did not serve. (Reckner 1994)

This wistful statement affirms the sacrifice of U.S. soldiers in Vietnam, something not appreciated by those who did not serve and who regard the soldiers in an unflattering light.

Reckner (2004) commented that he believes the Vietnam War was a "necessary" and noble cause for the United States, part of what enabled the country to claim ultimate "victory" in the Cold War. He writes:

> Americans remain divided about Vietnam. Some see in our Vietnam failure a sort of cosmic justice for a nation grown too affluent, too powerful and too self-assured. I cannot accept that view. To me the American effort in Vietnam was a *noble cause* unrealized. I believe Vietnam was a *necessary, extended skirmish* in the global struggle that contributed significantly to the larger *American success in the Cold War*. It was one factor, I believe, in the ultimate defeat of a greater *"evil empire."* (emphasis added)

As a Navy veteran and historian, Reckner brings a robust understanding of the military to the center, moving it beyond a purely academic enterprise.[12] For Reckner, the United States entered a foreign "skirmish" that, despite its losses, was necessary to win the Cold War in the end. This "we-win-even-when-we-lose syndrome," as Yen Le Espiritu (2006a) might describe it, posits the loss of South Vietnam as a necessary sacrifice for Americans to overcome communism. Such "organized and strategic forgetting of a war that went wrong" continues to promote "America's self-appointed role as liberators" for the rest of the world (330). The first prominent visitor to the Vietnam War archive was General Westmoreland, whose public support gave the archive a big public relations boost. He was infamous for saying that "the Oriental doesn't put the same high price on life as does a Westerner" (Davis 1974). We might ask, hypothetically, what does it mean to have those who think Vietnamese people are subhuman entities legitimize the archive?[13]

The archive also contains controversial materials that demonstrate how horribly American veterans viewed the Vietnamese (e.g., eyewitness stories and accounts of soldiers who participated in the My Lai Massacre),[14] but does promote the veterans' heroic service to the country.[15] Many American veterans who talked to Richard Verne, an oral historian at the center, said they regretted the abandonment of South Vietnam, believing "that the United States abandoned an ally. But they also are proud of their individual service [since] they did their duty; they served their country honorably, and they came home and went on with their lives" (Westbrook 2005).

Though the center opened in 1990, the records of Vietnamese Americans were not fully included in the Vietnam War archive until 2006, when the archive received its biggest donation and records from the Vietnamese American Heritage Foundation, which held and released the applications of former Vietnamese political prisoners who immigrated to the United States.[16] The donation was made by the Vietnamese American Heritage Foundation, a nonprofit Vietnamese American organization based in Austin, Texas, which helped former political prisoners to apply for refugee status and settle in the United States between 1979 and 1999. The donation included petitions by former South Vietnamese political prisoners to the U.S. government for refugee status, the first major batch of records related to Vietnamese people for the archive.[17] The Vietnamese American Heritage Project was begun after this major archival donation to address the void of Vietnamese-related documents.[18] With grant funding from the National Historical Research and Publications Commission, the archive was able to hire a full-time Vietnamese American Heritage archivist and staff to collect, preserve, and make accessible materials that provide documentation of the postwar history and experiences of South Vietnamese refugees . The 100,000 applications by political prisoners include many handwritten letters (restricted from public access) written to justify sponsorship in the United States, revealing the stakes involved in the immigration/refugee process.[19]

Including Vietnamese Voices in the Archive

The archive seeks to enliven Vietnamese participation in the oral history project by conducting community outreach, celebrating Vietnamese holidays and festivals, and developing cooperative relationships with Vietnamese American organizations, all the while working with the Vietnamese government. Even though all the staff members and the archive's founder agreed that it is not the job of the Vietnamese to help Americans find "peace and honor" from the war, their involvements will offer a way to heal and to deal with America's national trauma and moral injury, especially in abandoning its South Vietnamese allies. Recognizing the archive's preferential bias toward Americans and the increasing need to "Vietnamize" it as it matured over time, Reckner concluded that, beyond governmental records of refugees, the center needs more direct contributions and personal interest from Vietnamese Americans, which he believes would finally "complete" the archive's documentation of the war. He imagines the archive as merely documenting or recording the Vietnam War experience rather than actively reproducing those larger colonial histories in which this experience is derived. What does the process of institutional inclusion entail? How does the archive include Vietnamese participation? I turn now to speculate on the value of Vietnamese inclusion for the archive, but also its impact by current U.S.-Vietnam relations.

Though Reckner understands why Vietnamese Americans are reluctant to participate in the archival enterprise due to their anti-communist politics, he is still befuddled as to why they would not, as he believes refugees should put their politics aside for the greater good of education and national reconciliation. This push for education against politics works toward the future rather than staying in the past, as Reckner (1994) insists:

> We are building a Vietnam memorial, not for Vietnam vets, but for future generations who will have no first-hand knowledge of the war. In encouraging today's younger generation to study the Vietnam experience, examine the record and arrive at their own conclusions, the Center and Archive offer today's students not only an understanding of our immediate past, but also some basis upon which to formulate more intelligent approaches to America's relations with the world in the years ahead.

The founder's wise statement about the archive's labor spent in memorializing the vets and educating America's youth is echoed by another, where he says the archive's intergenerational mission can also connect generations of Vietnamese Americans, bringing the South Vietnamese elders and their Vietnamese American children closer together. This is a gesture of inclusion that assumes a more positive form of Vietnamization, a form of cultural recognition given to the former allies of the United States that they never properly received from other institutions or wider American society. Reckner is cognizant of the ways other mainstream American institutions fail to memorialize the Vietnamese refugee community, and how they are eclipsed in American historiography, an observation supported by memory studies scholars who examine representations of racialized minorities and the difficulty of finding truth in postwar regimes (Blight 2002; Wilson 2001).

From the mid-1990s, as the archive strengthened its connection with the socialist regime of Vietnam, what happened to the dissident position of so many former South Vietnamese refugees and veterans? Reckner (2002) acknowledges that the South Vietnamese voice is sublimated to the national history and progress of the United States and Vietnam:

> I know such a sentiment will draw cries of outrage from some Vietnam veterans, and from many Vietnamese-Americans. However, we must face realities. The way ahead, in my view, is for those of us who were involved in the war to provide powerful positive images of America to the younger generation of Vietnamese in Vietnam . . . For subsequent generations of Vietnamese-Americans (or Americans of Vietnamese ancestry), I am afraid it may already be too late for the Hanoi government to attract them, with their advanced education and valuable skills, back to their homeland to assist in its development. Over the past 25 years, these sons and daughters of Vietnamese immigrants have become fully integrated into the American mainstream . . . That is Vietnam's great loss. And America's remarkable gain.

This statement shows hope for the idea that Vietnam will recruit those young Vietnamese born in the United States to build its economy, a controversial idea for those older folks who are still opposed to the socialist regime and its human rights abuses. Meanwhile, Reckner believes communist Vietnam has failed to utilize the resources of Vietnamese Americans, many of whom he feels have assimilated into mainstream American culture. Yet, the process of gaining more input from the older generation of South Vietnamese refugees and determining their place in the current order of things remains a challenge.

The center has had difficulty in securing participation and input from Vietnamese Americans in general for numerous reasons: from the geographic isolation—Lubbock is far from major Vietnamese-populated urban hubs, to the financial restraints—it lacks the funding to conduct interviews off-site, to the cultural/linguistic barrier—there is no full-time Vietnamese staff to conduct oral histories. These are among the reasons why the Vietnamese component of the archive is almost minimal.[20] By the same token, there is a reason to maintain a good distance from Vietnamese Americans, as the director suggests this allows archivists to conduct their work "free from outside influences" such as the highly sensitive anti-communist demonstrators that live in "Little Saigon" enclaves. When asked about the serious void of Vietnamese American participants in the archive, Reckner insisted that there was only one possible explanation. He suspects that Vietnamese Americans are resentful of the archive for inviting communists to its annual scholarly conferences.[21] In his assessment, the archive must adopt a neutral stance toward the politics of war to truthfully report history, even if that means inviting communists to speak—much to the chagrin of refugees and activists. Reckner hopes that, in time, Vietnamese Americans can accept the altruistic aims of the archive and respect its decision to invite communist military officers and government leaders. In marking out Vietnamese Americans as reluctant or resistant archival participants, he places the onus on them to step outside their anti-communist politics (though the political nature of inviting these communists is sidelined). As is understood from this statement, archivists need to focus on education and not try to tame reactionary sentiments and politics.

At the same time, the archive is committed to accentuating the "liveness" of its living memorial in the information era. As more historical data and stories are digitized and placed online, what then is the purpose of visiting the physical archive and rummaging through its collections? Though the Vietnam War Center and Archive appears to bear "no political agenda," as it officially states on its website, it still participates in its own political projects. As Jenny Edkins (2003) notes, a compelling question about memory work is not examining what is represented but who "gets to mourn, in what way, and with what political outcomes" (135).

As a site of public education, the VNCA presents a richly evocative place for thinking about the institutionalization of history and the "othering" that happens in the archive. How might the VNCA be viewed not simply as a repository for storing material documents and texts, but also as a place to reimagine the uses of history, that is, as both a concrete place and an "abstract paradigmatic entity"? (Sekula 1986: 17). As a public interface between individuals and society, archives serve an essential role in bringing multiple historical voices and actors into a common space of dialogue that can sometimes be conflict-prone. As Reckner

(1998) makes clear, from the onset, he and the staff have "made it our policy that our former allies, the South Vietnamese, will always have a place at our conferences and in our records; however, at the same time, we work with, preserve, and make available the Hanoi view of events, also". At its annual Vietnam Symposium in 1999, the VNCA invited top-ranking officers from the governments of the United States, North Vietnam, and South Vietnam to present their contrasting perspectives on the war. At this meeting, a general from Vietnam castigated the actions of the United States in the Vietnam War, referring to the "American aggressors," and went on to condemn U.S. support of a "rotten" South Vietnamese administration (Altenbaumer 1999a). James Reckner told the audience "there would be no protesters," an admonishment directed mostly to older South Vietnamese veterans, many of whom are known for protesting Vietnamese communist officials (ibid.).

As a benevolent authority figure, Reckner wished for information to "flow freely and easily," staving off vituperative threats that could threaten the exchange of ideas (ibid.). Yet, this grand gesture fails to reduce the heated emotions behind the anti-communist politics of refugees. For former South Vietnamese exiles, the memories of the Vietnam War feed not into a data archive but into what literary critic Ann Cvetkovich (2003) calls an "archive of feelings," the repository of repressed memories and emotions toward a conflict in which 50,000 U.S. Americans perished but more than 3.5 million Vietnamese lost their lives. Reckner's injunction for civility attempts to equalize the playing field of discourse with the hope not only of resolving differences between South and North Vietnamese, but also of improving diplomatic relations between the United States and the Socialist Republic of Vietnam—an altruistic mission that exceeds the normative role of an archive. Here, the potential value for archives accrued in procuring Vietnamese refugee stories and cooperation is attenuated by the price refugees pay for pushing the anticommunist refugee agenda; archival otherness here is as much political as epistemological.

In its mission to arbitrate peace among enemies, the archive helps preserve communist-related materials and also extends invitations to former North Vietnamese soldiers to speak at its annual conferences, as well as collaborate with and teach state archivists from Vietnam about modern archiving techniques.[22] Better relations between the United

States and communist Vietnam since the end of the Cold War have added to existing problems related to the archive's appeal to many Vietnamese Americans, especially veterans who are adamantly opposed to any form of engagement with a communist country from which they fled. The growing economic power of Vietnam has led the United States to ratchet up better relations with its one-time enemy, despite the dissenting opinions of former refugees who find this symbiosis troubling. Reckner says, "We are in a position to do something auspicious for relations between the United States and Vietnam. Until we have positive relations, we'll never put the war behind us" (quoted in Altenbaumer 1999b). Though South Vietnamese are slotted uncomfortably within a kind of triangle of diplomatic relations, the question remains of where they truly belong and where their value is.

The theme of the archive's 2006 annual conference was the contributions of the Army of the Republic of Vietnam (ARVN), the South Vietnamese forces allied with the United States. This altruistic public form of acknowledgment was matched with the archive's overall desire to present the viewpoint of all warring factions as "a place where former enemies came to make their account of the battles of yesteryear" (Blackburn 2006). The conference's keynote speaker, former ARVN officer Lt. Gen. Lan Lu, was like many Vietnamese Americans initially suspicious of the archive, given its outreach work in Vietnam. Addressing the resistance of South Vietnamese veterans to speak about their experiences, Lu cited language barriers but also shame. Many veterans, he says, are neglected in history, and that neglect mitigates any sense of their historical contributions as an "honor." He opines, "How can I, a man who gets defeated, stand in a position to say that?" After Reckner's retirement, the subsequent archive's director Stephen Maxner continued to reach out to the Vietnamese Americans. Maxner believes that "by coming out and participating in this conference, I think they're [Vietnamese Americans] reclaiming some of their pride" (ibid.). Nguyen Xuan Phong, a senior research associate for the center, claims the archive has not yet successfully reached out to the Vietnamese American community, since former South Vietnamese veterans have a complex relationship with the war that makes it difficult to share their experience.[23] South Vietnamese veterans in tandem with their families were robbed of everything—their country and homes—and the loss remains wrenching: According to Phong, "They [the South Vietnamese] are . . . after three decades, extremely emotional" (ibid.).

In 1998, as made clear by a public announcement entitled "Preserving the South Vietnamese Story," it was evident that archiving Vietnamese stories as a kind of Vietnamization of history was rearing its head again amid the challenging negotiating process by which Americans attempted to give South Vietnamese some form of political autonomy. In that document, the VNCA vowed to redouble its documents related to South Vietnamese people and Vietnamese refugees (*Friends of the Vietnam Center*, 5.2):

> We at the Vietnam Center are increasingly concerned that little is being done to preserve the record of the struggle of the South Vietnamese people during the war. While we find it easy to acquire publications from Hanoi that outline their interpretation of events, such is not the case for the Saigon point of view. Because of this, we are particularly keen to encourage donations of books, articles, newspapers and other materials from South Vietnam, 1945–1975, for permanent preservation. We particularly encourage members of the *Viet Kieu* [overseas] community to consider this problem and how it might be resolved. Without a concerted effort to gather and preserve materials related to South Vietnam, including memoirs of South Vietnamese participants, correspondence, and any records that might have survived, there will be little left for future researchers anxious to obtain a balanced understanding of the war.

This call for remedying the historical absence of South Vietnamese means finding Vietnamese Americans to donate their personal belongings and physical artifacts to the archive. Yet, the tremendous amount of materials forever lost and incinerated during and after the war during refugee flight points to a major absence that will be difficult to fill in the ledgers of history, as history is often defined in terms of the nation-state, but also in the way information is processed and by whom.

Searching for Gooks and the Faceless Friend

The archive collects oral histories from people all over the country who are willing to tell their stories—"matter of happenstance—in this case, word of mouth and connections with veterans' associations short of a more systematic sampling" (Hagopian 2003: 191). Most stories come from veterans who "are proud of their service, are very proud of what they were able to do in serving the country, answering the call and serving with the people whom they served for a worthy cause and they were serving a noble goal and higher purpose."[24] Standard questions asked by interviewers include: "What did you think about the Vietnamese soldiers that you worked with?" and "What did you think about Vietnamization and the decision to pull out of Vietnam in 1973?"[25] These questions led to a conflicting number of interpretations by soldiers about the war and the U.S. abandonment of South Vietnam.

In 1999, the archive publicly launched an initiative that promised to preserve documents related to the South Vietnam republic, and in doing so, to represent an archive that serves the "overseas" Vietnamese rather than just Americans:

> Our goal with this project, quite simply, is to preserve for future generations as much as possible of the record of the Republic of Vietnam. Future generations of overseas Vietnamese, it seems certain, will seek answers to many questions about their ancestors, the role they played in the Republic of Vietnam, and why, ultimately, they came to be *Việt Kiều* (overseas Vietnamese) . . . ultimately, the task must be accomplished by the older generation of Vietnamese, who lived through the traumatic events which shaped, and ultimately ended, the Republic of Vietnam. In this effort, we appeal to the sense of history of the Vietnamese people. We must work to preserve the history of South Vietnam or subsequent generations of Vietnamese who left Vietnam following the war will be condemned to a future without a past. (*Friends of the Vietnam Center* 1999)

Preserving Vietnamese oral histories puts an end to the consignment of the Vietnamese to a future without stories of their own to pass on to their own children.

While community organizations across the country are compiling their own oral history projects in cities with large Vietnamese populations, such as Austin, New Orleans, and Orange County (the UC, Irvine–based Vietnamese American Oral History Project works closely with local refugee communities). The VNCA is trying to build its own archive or at least access these other oral history archives. The archive nevertheless accepts any oral history from Vietnamese who survived the war as well as from their Vietnamese American descendants. Out of 800 oral interviews that have been recorded and/or transcribed and made available to the public online, only 14 of the interviews at the time of my study featured Vietnamese subjects. Key staff members and the head of the oral history project pegged the dearth of Vietnamese oral histories in their archive to the following reasons: (1) the lack of Vietnamese-fluent translators and interviewers; (2) the refusal of many refugees to tell their stories out of fear of political repercussions for themselves and their families in Vietnam; and (3) the geographic isolation of the institution.[26]

Interestingly, most of the interviews in the archive came not from everyday citizens but from former generals, ambassadors, or high-profile public officials of South Vietnam (sharpening the military aspect of the archive).[27] Almost all the interviews touched upon the perennial communist threat and internal problems of managing the South Vietnamese nation after the United States abandoned it. Oral history is broadly considered a valid historical methodology, but can be viewed as biased and sometimes unreliable due to its subjective nature. Amnesia, fear of political censorship, post-traumatic stress, selective or colored experiences based on nostalgia, and language barriers are some of the impediments to procuring an objective or complete account of the past from the word of interviewees. Oral histories nevertheless provide a chief source of information for certain minority groups that have been largely erased from written history. However, the archive does not make any classifying distinction of stories based on participants' race, class, gender, or nationality; instead, the archive categorized interviews based on whether an individual served in the military, with a note of their title or rank, or whether they are a civilian. There is no distinction between Vietnamese and American stories, making it hard for anyone who wants to access Vietnamese-specific oral histories.

The head of the oral history project, Kelly Crager, believes ultimately the main issue facing the archive is the ability to ratchet up more interest from the Vietnamese American community because they are obliged to remember South Vietnam. He reckons there is a slant in the archive's materials toward American veterans that has much to do with how most U.S. institutions recount the war from a U.S.-centered perspective:

We think about the war from the American perspective and as tumultuous as it was and as divisive as it was, and the fact that you know 50,000 Americans died in the war, millions of Vietnamese died in the war from both sides of the conflict, and *many* Vietnamese came to the United States after the war and they are a big part of this, a *very* big part of the story as well in terms of the sacrifice of lives and sacrifice of property, you know the Vietnamese suffered more than the Americans did so we do want to reach out to the Vietnamese American community more and try to include them . . . that's the primary shortcoming in our holding right now.[28]

Beyond its enormous educational value, the emotive payout of including the histories of Vietnamese Americans, says the head of the Vietnamese American Heritage Project, derives from the fact that "all of us need to heal." The director of this project, Ann Mallett, observes the necessity of capturing the refugee story: "The Vietnamese American history is not well-known. It's not very well documented right now. Stuff is now being discovered and part of that, I think, has to do with all that Vietnamese Americans went through as refugees."[29] Distance from large communities of Vietnamese populations hampers the director's expansion of the heritage project, but another complicating element is the fact that she is not Vietnamese. As she put it, "You have to understand, I'm an outsider looking in, trying to learn and understand so a lot of this is what and how I perceive it and the way I'm learning . . . I'm a whitey, I'm an outsider; you have to earn the trust [of the Vietnamese Americans]." That she makes race an operative issue, especially for being head of a program related to Vietnamese heritage, displays a sensitivity to the ways Americans try to speak for the Vietnamese, and how Vietnamese outsider-ness in the archive is matched by the outsider status of Anglo-Americans like Mallett to the community.

While Reckner and other staff members recognized their whiteness vis-à-vis the racialized Vietnamese and the fact that many Americans held deep racial prejudices toward the latter, they recognize that the center is not responsible for managing the language of racial prejudice and its decision not to remove it; therefore, when it appears in materials, like photographs or oral histories, it is understood that the archive is unintentionally preserving and propagating racism, while recording how that language was historically commonplace. In this way, history and archiving are not just representations and processing of dated human events, but signal the human discourse that allows for the distillation of certain ideas and perspectives. While searching the archive's oral history database for stories and documents about Vietnamese refugees, something was amiss. As I quickly learned, "gook" was a key search term. Gook is a derogatory term used by American soldiers for the local people, ally and enemy, during the U.S.-Philippines War (1899–1902), Korean War (1950–1953), and Vietnam War (1955–1975), which reveals so much about the phantasmal place of Asians in U.S. military history, as people not called by their ethnicity or name, but a slur that mocked the childish sound of Asian languages and ethnicities.

The database searches based on keywords like "Vietnamese" or "Vietnamese American" produced photos, interviews, and military records, mostly from U.S. veterans but none from the Vietnamese. Eager to help me upon seeing my initial frustration in not finding Vietnamese-related documents, the archive's main reference archivist, Amy Mondt, suggested that it would be more useful to use the term "gook" as a keyword, especially since most American GIs commonly used racist words like that to refer to the Vietnamese and other Southeast Asians in their interviews. "We don't censor the material," she told me. "It's bad that we're perpetuating that [kind of racist material] but that's what the archive does."[30] You can find gooks everywhere in the archive (though not in official archival publications). Beyond oral histories, the term is used in photographic illustrations with captions (see figure 1.1).

When photos are tagged with the title of "gook" as a way of respecting donors' original language for naming their collection, this creates an interesting situation where the Vietnamese are invisible, except as hypervisible gooks. The main reference archivist was regretful about the centrality and usefulness of "gook" in archival searches, which insinuated the archive's role in perpetuating racism. When I asked James Reckner about the use of "gook" in the archive, he said that it is an unfortunate problem of dealing with problematic human beings; it is wrong, yet the archive's job is not to judge, but to document. He noted that the archive is obliged to consider how racism historically works in U.S. public discourse and America's discourse of "Vietnam," one that for him "evokes more people than war."[31]

Figure 1.1. "GOOKS" Working in Rice Paddies (Photograph VA050928, February 1964–1965, Carl Vogel Collection, The Vietnam Center and Archive, Texas Tech University).

"Gook" marks the epistemological power and knowledge limits through which one can locate the Vietnamese as archival others, despite the good efforts of Reckner and the rest of the staff. Using gook as a key search term, one comes to understand that Vietnamese stories do not have to be physically present in the archive or the oral history program since they are *always* present through the use of this derogatory term. In nearly all oral histories from vets, the Vietnamese—North and South—emerge as gooks. The archive of history in this way mirrors the archival memory of American films and mainstream popular culture. As writer Andrew Lam (2005) observes,

> The three-sided war where North and South [which] fought against one another with the Americans as allies to the South turned into a simpler version in America. In the movies—in the popular imagination—the narrative often told is that of an American protagonist in a foreign land, under siege, fighting all faceless Vietnamese. (31)

Personal testimony from a former American soldier, Edward Feldman, which I found in the archive, sums up this point. When asked by an archivist during an interview who the enemy was in Vietnam, he says without any hesitation: "The enemy certainly is gooks."[32] When another veteran was asked if gook was a term used universally throughout his time in Vietnam:

> You know probably in training it was, but after that the entire time I was in the Marine Corps they were dinks and slopes and gooks and chinks and whatever. It was always—*you* never said Vietnamese, ever, just part of the genre, nomenclature, whatever. My son's an Army Ranger, twelve-year Army Ranger, Sergeant 1st class. He just got back from his second trip to Afghanistan and they have all this ragheads and goat-fuckers, whatever.[33]

Here, the historical usage of gook is synonymous with pejoratives used today in a similarly unpopular manner with regard to Muslim Arabs. Through the unabashed honesty of such interviews, we can suss out the entrenched (archival) history of American racism. While many oral histories from veterans are not as racist as this, the fact that these men can employ such nomenclature with such ease suggests much of their use of the term gook was through speaking with one another, reflecting shifting racial attitudes of the time; some of the men acknowledged that the term could be derogatory, even though they did not believe it was so. A veteran observes the conventional wisdom about the Vietnamese:

> Oh, they were always gooks . . . From everything from boot camp to ITR when you were about to be given a lesson so that they could see the back row, they'd always say, "First two rows down!" and you'd drop to one knee and you'd go, "Kill, kill, kill the gooks!" . . . I didn't think, "This is derogatory," I just thought, "They're gooks." My dad called them gooks; the Korean vets called them dinks. I mean, they were just the gooks because they were oriental. I didn't really think much of, "That's derogatory to them," or nothing, that's just what they were called.[34]

As observed by Viet Nguyen (2002), the Vietnamese "must be dehumanized, derealized, in order to allow for the humanization of the American soldier and the substantiation of his body and, through it, of American ideology and culture" (7). As a normalized racial vocabulary to describe the sometimes indistinguishable faces and names of the foreign enemy (where foe and ally look the same), the gook's morphologies change form through decades of war and war memories.[35] The gook term stitches the experiences of Vietnamese and other groups in a global chain of geopolitical relations. The word has a surprising stamina, both as a historical term and a search term, and thus is a revealing aid in our examination of the "archival other" in the annals of history.

My search for Vietnamese voices forced me to reckon with perspectives of the American GI who fought in Vietnam and only saw faceless gooks. Upon reading the stories of veterans, I was shocked by the unadulterated racism and xenophobia displayed by many of the young soldiers, many of whom did not fully understand the war or region in which they were entrenched. The archive of their stories presents a rich site for dealing with "tension over what should be remembered, how, and in what form" (Sturken 1997: 174). While archives appear devoid of politics, the stories told by many servicemen and their frequent innocuous use of the term "gook" waffles closely to their liberal views of the Vietnamese as helpless "Yellow brothers," many of whom were not the enemy, but allies and civilians. Archival practices and their content then disclose "how difference is established, how it operates, how and in what ways" (Scott 1991: 777).

The archival project of including the Vietnamese and thus Vietnamizing public history cannot fully rectify the historical abandonment of South Vietnam by the United States and the forgetting of the Vietnamese people in the American national psyche. Many refugees no doubt vacated their home countries with nothing more than the clothes on their back, so there will always be an absence of personal materials and documents to write a comprehensive history. Coupled with the refusal or trauma of recounting their harrowing passage to safety and economic struggle to make a living in the United States, it is not surprising that the archive struggles to provide a space for those who have been rendered voiceless and invisible. But what underlines this move to recognize "archival others" is the founder and staff members' desire to symbolically and materially "Vietnamize" the archive and the Americanized memories of the war to recuperate the tarnished legacy of the RVN after the colossal failure of the United States to save this sinking ship. This salvaging of the history of America's misbegotten allies rejects the U.S. Vietnamization military project that consigned the

South Vietnamese to historical oblivion as the archive reconstructs the past to create "a memory of the future" (Krapp 2004: 32), one that finally includes the Vietnamese.

Reading Bureaucratic Paperwork for Narratives

Beyond oral histories, the VNCA's biggest collection of Vietnamese-related documents is the government applications related to the ODP (Orderly Departure Program) instituted by the UN High Commission for Refugees in 1979, which granted asylum status to nearly half a million Vietnamese in the United States.[36] Many of those prioritized were soldiers held in reeducation camps in Vietnam after the war, and their applications make up the largest batch of Vietnamese-related materials in the VNCA, containing the paper trail of applicants seeking exit visas from South Vietnam, along with a flood of letters of support from their sponsors, widows, and children. Those who were successful in petitioning for refugee status arrived on planes and generally had some connection to the U.S. military.

This kind of information represents the bureaucratic obstacle to attaining official recognition as a political refugee in the United States, and it also includes the files of unsuccessful applicants rejected from the program, often for the usual reason that the main applicant has "failed to submit credible evidence to establish he or she spent at least three years in reeducation due to his association with the U.S. prior to 1975" or worked for the U.S. government or U.S. company for *less than* five years. The prerequisite "association with the U.S. prior to 1975" is gauged in the duration of time and material documentation.[37] Many applicants listed the main reason for their detainment in state reeducation camps as "participating in activities against VN communist regime," but they were often denied entry to the United States because their imprisonment by communists was deemed "not related to pre-75 U.S.A. association" (ODP Application File for Dang Minh Tam). This codification of the South Vietnam-U.S. political connection before the Fall of Saigon fails to account for different kinds of political affiliation, providing different standards for evaluating refugees beyond a strictly chronological basis, as many refugees were persecuted for activities after the war.

Within these large dossiers of information, applicants provide data on where they were born, military awards received, names of family members they brought with them, their sponsors and contacts, and certificates of release from reeducation camps in Vietnam. Such official records provide some personal insight and statistics in the immigration process of South Vietnamese. The head of the Vietnamese American Heritage Project finds that these documents tell a story of history analogous to the story of European immigrants who came to America through Ellis Island:

> We kind of call it the Ellis Island of Vietnamese Americans because not only did they lose stuff during the war just through events but then they emigrated, they couldn't take everything with them . . . just from the ones that have shared with me, I don't think they realize how important their stories are 'cause they feel that everyone went through it, it was a hard time for everyone. What's so special about my story? It is special and your kids wanna know and this part of history, you need to save your stories before they're gone.

In this telling passage, the speaker draws on the trope of the immigrant family coming to America to emphasize the significance of having Vietnamese archival material.[38] In this way, she is helping to shift the idea of Vietnamese as archival others (and thus American "others"), participating as a non-Vietnamese person in the economization of cultural memory that allows for historical preservation of community and identity. At the same time, it is an Americanization of the Vietnamese story since Vietnamese came as refugees, not immigrants. Mallett reminded me that refugees in their exodus could not carry many if any personal belongings. This physical loss prevents the archive from attaining diaries, uniforms, medals, letters, and photos, thus minimizing the number of historical objects it possesses.

These documents are primarily the paperwork of technocrats, destined to be filed away in dusty containers, and—after being approved or rejected—never intended to be viewed again. Nevertheless, they also act as vital nodes for the transfer of cultural knowledge about those who eventually became "political refugees" (under the narrow definition put forth by the U.S. Immigration and Naturalization Act of 1965), and they give us a glimpse of those who did not. They tell intricate stories about those former citizens of South Vietnam who eventually became reconstituted into Vietnamese Americans (and those who did not). Viewing the personal files of South Vietnamese soldiers and civilians in this way roots their testimony and state-proctored lives. While refugees are viewed as anyone fleeing the homeland due to fear of immediate harm or persecution, a legal refugee applies only to those able to find success being labeled as one by a government institution, an arduous process requiring the advocacy of outside organizations like FVPPA to convince the U.S. government these South Vietnamese nationals are "worthy" of being saved.

The ODP program represents an Americanization process initiated by the United States, this one designed to release South Vietnamese from captivity. As refugees seeking asylum, applicants were expected to demonstrate their fidelity first to the United States as foreign allies, even though it was the American government which tendered its resignation in 1975 to protect its allies near the end-stage of the war. Desperate stories of family breakups and reeducation make evident the tortured souls of former ARVN soldiers and their need for U.S. assistance, typifying the state of mind of proud allies seeking assistance now as weakened refugees seeking help. Under its oral history project, the archive seeks out oral histories from former Vietnamese refugees currently living in the country, a daunting task of its own, but these refugee applications themselves represent a different kind of oral history through which refugees told their harrowing postwar experiences within a standardized format. Such stories unsettle the assumed binary between fictionality and "evidentiary" forms of writing, between oral stories and the hidden "stories" found in legal paperwork, marking the refugee testimonial as a type of literary genre (Lowe 1996: 156–157). Such documents contain the private confessions that are not always part of "public history."

The application letters demonstrate how the time needed to gain approval for entry as a refugee requires people to move from their former designations as South Vietnamese nationals to their newly acquired status as U.S. resident aliens, though their passports will always list "South Vietnamese" as their birth nationality. In these documents, we can read a dual sense of South Vietnamese displacement, from Vietnam and the

United States. Their failure to certify any "real" connection with the Americans, as I see it, points to the "bad check" or IOU of the United States to back up its South Vietnamese collaborators under Vietnamization, a past pledge or voucher of support held "in trust." The Vietnamization contract, under Richard Nixon, furnished U.S. support to the South Vietnamese to release the Americans of outstanding debts to rescue the throngs of former South Vietnamese soldiers, military girlfriends, civil service workers, and government officials associated with them. As refugees, these former allies must give evidence of what they have done with and/or for the U.S. government, before they are granted the right to enter the nation. In the wake of the refugee crisis, the ODP program is considered a success, especially in terms of family reunification, but this victory can only be so after admitting the historic failure of the U.S. Vietnamization policy. With the South Vietnamese left in the lurch, their great escape from communism required another limited form of American aid and protection as refugees trying to now Americanize themselves.

Insofar as VCNA is in the process of "Vietnamizing" its archive with more oral histories from the Vietnamese Americans, the refugee applications document the burden of proof foisted by former South Vietnamese nationals to notarize their war experiences as legitimate in the eyes of the Americans, despite the paper trail some left behind (many burned their records to avoid persecution by the communists). Some of the personal stories found in these government forms, we can assume, are falsified for the sake of achieving quick asylum status, but what I like about them is that they comprise an alternative space for learning about the South Vietnamese, whose experiences comprise the silent testimony of history's "losers" hankering for someone to hear them out. The ODP files, which contain transcribed paragraphs of interviewees talking to state officials or handwritten notes from soldiers and their families, bear witness to refugees as writers trying to represent themselves as authentic political subjects deserving of magnanimity and recognition by Americans. As archival subjects, they comprise a sizable chunk of the Vietnam War archive, but they do not appear as such, because their stories are buried within uninteresting bureaucratic paperwork. In this way, Vietnamese are absent from view, but that does not mean they are *not* there; their asylum-seeking files provide an alternative source of personal knowledge within the VNCA's larger effort to incorporate more Vietnamese first-person voices.

This virtual condition of being an archival other is becoming more and more identified with digital electronic processes. Though it is a non-profit, the VNCA runs an online database called "Virtual Vietnam" that tries to broaden its cultural capital beyond Lubbock and build its global influence. By making its holdings available for public access in digital format on the World Wide Web, the hope is to make the archive accessible through an online portal with a search engine to access documents without physically coming to the archive building in Texas. The database was created in 2000 through a $500,000 grant from the federal government to scan and digitize its documents (Hagopian 2003: 189). Since 2002, the archive has been digitizing its collection and in the process creating new spaces of representation and modalities for thinking, not only about the changing nature of archival work but also about how archival subjects are repositioned within new informational spaces that disperse meaning about them.

Digitization makes the life stories and images of Vietnamese people available in new cyberspaces, while placing their personal accounts as the "evidence of experience" in desultory fashion (Scott 1991). As more archival content becomes "dematerialized" and flows into global data streams, the archive becomes a more liquid medium, evincing "the ascendancy of transmission over storage" of information, but also the circulation of racially insensitive materials and terms like gook, which cannot be censored owing to the policy of open access (Chow 1993: 174). In this way, history is not simply a representation of human events, but the human discourse that allows for the representation of social experience, however derogatory it may sound.

To achieve even greater digital penetration goals, U.S. archivists share their expertise and materials with their equivalents in the national archives of Vietnam. A pact and memorandum of understanding were formalized during a 2007 visit by a delegation of Vietnam's State Records and Archive Department who came to Texas Tech to participate in digitization training and learning workshops (Maxner 2011). Texas Tech became the first institution in the country to sign an agreement with the Vietnamese government. Part of the reason VNCA has had limited success getting Vietnamese Americans to participate is its binational partnerships with socialist Vietnam, which the Vietnamese Americans frown upon. Indeed, physical distance of the archive from large Vietnamese American communities shields this space, allowing it to perform its daily operations without drawing the ire of anti-communist protesters. Clearly, the geopolitical dimensions behind local archiving practices need to be ironed out, especially as they relate to ways in which refugee communities are to be included. Today, such work in transnational exchange continues as part of our increasingly globalized digital world, but questions persist about the position of Vietnamese Americans, those whose memories and politics related to South Vietnam cannot be neatly integrated into new narratives of multicultural American nationalism and the global community of the digital village. If anything, their absent presence is the filter through which we must understand these issues.

Conclusion

A critical reassessment of the VNCA archive, and its politics of representation help move away from the myth of archival work as being concerned only with fact collection. Through a selective form of archival othering but also what Espiritu (2003) calls "differential inclusion," the VNCA has made great efforts to get a grip on the unwieldy position of South Vietnamese refugees within its operations. Where South Vietnamese refugees and people are the historical excess of America's involvement in Vietnam, I read this archive's efforts to include America's former allies into an inclusive project of research and historical preservation that tries to be objective and apolitical but not ignorant of the political nature of dealing with the Vietnamese, and how the Vietnamization of this archive helps to "rethink thinking" about knowledge production (Spanos 2008). According to Viet Nguyen (2002), the fate of the South Vietnamese for the United States after the Vietnamization project has come to haunt remembrance of the war with the "danger that many American veteran intellectuals can absolve themselves . . . by paying lip service to the 'oppressed' Vietnamese" (112). Such ideas breathe new life into "post-Vietnam fictions," obscuring the conditions that gave rise to U.S. involvement in Yugoslavia in the 1990s and other conflicts (Atanasoski 2013: 94).

During my visit, a new museum was being discussed, to be housed next to the Vietnam War archive. The success and limitations of the

VNCA helped push another archival project focusing on the post–Vietnam War era. Its official mission statement states that the purpose of the archive is to encourage and support "the long-term study and preservation of all aspects of America's diplomatic and military experiences and involvements on a global scale, beginning in 1975 and continuing to the present" (Archive of Modern American Warfare). The year 1975 is important because it marks the Fall of Saigon, and the wars included for consideration include but are not limited to Operation Desert Storm, the September 11th attacks, the Bosnian War, and the wars in Iraq and Afghanistan. It will encompass issues regarding national security and government intelligence, while also centering personal experience of American servicemen and women in the "post-Vietnam era." The "terminal date remains open," archivists say, so long as there are wars with U.S. involvement that resemble the logjam of Vietnam.

Archivists are acknowledging both the starting point and open-endedness of warfare, earmarking the limitless nature of U.S. militarism and the decisive permanent impact of the Vietnam War on it. By inaugurating new archival collections on future Vietnams, this post-Vietnam archive attempts to map the unfolding story of Vietnamized military violence, despite the difficulties of including marginalized perspectives from survivors of the war like the Vietnamese. Overall, the Vietnam War Center and Archive cannot be faulted for its failure to address the archival otherness of Vietnamese people in the U.S. historical record, as this is also a national, cultural, international, and scholarly issue that has yet to be solved. We can recognize still the importance of always trying to listen to marginalized refugee voices, as they are already there in the archive as faceless gooks, waiting to be discovered and heard. In the many returns (to the history) of war, one is not simply visiting a gravesite of the dead, but embarking on many voyages to the unknown place of one's birth. Where institutional archives of history fail, it is here that family stories and personal archives, despite their own silences, can sometimes fill the gaps in knowledge.

2

Refugee Assets

The Political Reeducation of Personal Trauma and Family Bonds

This chapter explores the work of memory for Vietnamese diasporic subjects and how they construct their own archives of memory in the face of historical amnesia, especially by broader American and French society, and how postwar trauma like the kind South Vietnamese soldiers faced in reeducation camps forms the personal basis for understanding postwar family bonds, economic and social. It analyzes Aimee Phan's *The Reeducation of Cherry Truong*, which tells the story of two families that fled from South Vietnam still grappling with the messiness of their war-torn past. The main character, Cherry, attempts to "reeducate" herself about her wayward kin, and while the novel may be read simply as a coming-of-age story, this major fictional work illustrates the ways second-generation subjects must recuperate convoluted histories of war to understand the causes of their own precarious life and uncertain future in a new country, and how they navigate using their given refugee assets. I came to understand the complexity of such issues growing up in a refugee family, where economic deprivation underpinned the debts every member owed to one another—something that incentivized the tradition of filial piety. Such relations became strained as the overriding sense of responsibility overlapped with a sense of people taking too much from one another. At the same, these thick postwar relations of borrowing and giving back, already learned during the war, became the collective assets through which we refugees became reeducated in the politics of survival.

As a story of refugees, Phan's *The Reeducation of Cherry Truong* employs a multiperspectival, nonlinear mode of storytelling to impart the sense of chaos and confusion experienced by those who had left their homeland after the war, unable to form close familial bonds after being dispersed far and wide. An intergenerational story spanning the countries of Vietnam, France, and the United States, *Reeducation* impresses upon readers the mobile forms of belonging and consciousness distinctive to stateless peoples who have been cast adrift in the world. It is very much an Asian American literary text that charts familiar themes of migration, acculturation problems, and culture clashes, generative in approaching Vietnamese diasporic formation broadly in terms of exploring how overseas Vietnamese adapt to new social circumstances, while remembering their South Vietnamese past. *Reeducation* conceptually develops the connection between the filial duty of daughters to their conjugal families and the debt owed by refugees to the host countries, where gendered familial dynamics are a synecdoche for the neocolonial relationship between the refugee and the nation.

Like so many other diasporic writers, Phan stresses the collective pain, anguish, and strength of refugee families striving to stay intact while highlighting the estrangement of family members from one another. The novel opens with a letter from Tuyet, Cherry's mother, written from a Malaysian refugee camp in 1978 to Cherry's maternal grandmother back in Vietnam, explaining why she left her family to follow her husband to the United States. Tuyet pleads the following case: "I tried to find the words, but they would not come. How can you tell your own mother that you are abandoning her? What kind of daughter would do that? I am not that kind of daughter. I will make this up to you . . . your devoted daughter" (Phan 2012: 131). As a sort of reeducation in family responsibility, Tuyet, the former bad daughter, strives to compensate for the mistake of leaving her family. Tuyet's letter demonstrates the need of daughters to be good filial subjects and prop up traditional family structures, a demand that must be recalibrated in times of war. This admission of guilt links the personal actions of individuals to the enduring bonds of family. Tuyet's failure to save her mother leads her to tout the tenets of pious daughterhood, a private endeavor since the letters scribbled by Tuyet were never read by Kim-Ly. Tuyet admits she could not find the words to explain why she betrayed her mother, instead dealing with this guilt in silence. "This is what I struggle with now," Tuyet writes, and she vows to make everything right and honor Kim-Ly from then on. Such carefully crafted words demonstrate the pains of taking to heart the responsibilities of the family.

Offering a political method for situating gendered practices of remembering (and forgetting), *Reeducation* suggests that the refugee memory never simply takes the form of nostalgia or denial of the past but is a constant political negotiation of historical violence as interpreted through past wrongs as well as economic relations between Vietnamese people and Western societies like France, and the former alliance between South Vietnam and the United States. In terms of the refugee economics of memory, the novel raises epistemological and moral dilemmas related to postwar community-building, characterized by the condition of exile from the homeland as well as the active processing of material bonds and demands that came through the war. Recognizing the (child of) refugee as a figure of debt, Phan's reinvention of the term reeducation links the programmatic indoctrination and cultural re-Vietnamization of South Vietnamese political prisoners by communists to the Western pedagogical program to civilize refugees and assimilate their children; this chapter considers the psychic and material debt survivors of war owe to the sacrifices and suffering of others, and the political agency found in that recognition.

Beyond telling another refugee narrative of flight and rescue, *The Reeducation of Cherry Truong* unsettles the normative ideas and narration of the Vietnamese diaspora as one of escape from death and destruction to an apolitical space of democracy and freedom, especially given the ways diasporic communities remain entrenched within nationalist, heteropatriarchal, and capitalist systems of power. The term "reeducation" serves as a useful hermeneutic or method of reading Vietnamese postwar subject formation. Deemphasizing tropes of the "family," "community," or "identity" as the foundations for ontological security, reeducation gestures toward the refugee diasporic subject finding his or her sense of identity as always already linked to inescapable histories of war. Remembering family also means remembering war, and refugee memory work presents a violent memoryscape evoking the camps where many South Vietnamese political prisoners perished as the ultimate "losers" of the war in Vietnam, imprisoned by the victorious communists, and abandoned by the Americans.

What is the logic of the term or process of reeducation that gives it the power to produce contestation against conformist thinking of various kinds? Reeducation camps purportedly turned ARVN soldiers into lovers of communism but turned out to be sites of human captivity. However, the realization of the state's hypocrisy does not solely produce a kind of critical consciousness of power's excesses and abuses, since soldiers knew they were essentially in a prison. The prima facie innocence of the term reeducation—defined as the process of being educated again for new purposes (reform) or resumption of normal activities (rehabilitation)—obscures evil practices (repression). Reeducation was such a personalized endeavor that one of the first exercises for prisoners who were told to report to local schools was to write an autobiography that listed their war crimes against the people and the "debt of blood" they owed to the nation; this practice is documented in autobiographies written by former soldiers, recognizing how one's personal life story is intimately tied up with political control and coercion (Tran 1988: 93). Individuals were punished for being related to a high-ranking official of the South Vietnamese government, which shows that one's blood debt to the nation is tied to the bloodlines of the family. Given that there are fewer stories from wives of these soldiers (or accounts of the women who were soldiers), one could argue that in privileging the male soldier as the central figure of South Vietnamese remembrance, it is women who are the keepers of alternate memories as they provide a less official version of historical events.

To write one's personal autobiography in this context is to always link back to a politically charged history, where information is suspect, where the past is not set in stone, and where there are no true victims. Édouard Glissant (1997) says it should never be accepted that a people are special or exceptional in history. Seeing relations as differentiated but always singular draws the collective past into a kind of "knowledge becoming" that cannot be assessed or isolated but shared as something which "one can never not retain" or "boast about" (1). Titled as a *reeducation* of Cherry Truong rather than a simple memoir or autobiography of the main character, Phan's book echoes on the first level how refugee experience and literature, written in biographical memoir form, must serve an overtly political function. Reeducation as a political form of remembering underscores the historical backdrop to the personal complications of life after the war, but more importantly, the treatment of South Vietnamese people in that period, which must never be forgotten by refugees. *Reeducation* underscores the complications of life after war, as Erin Ninh (2005) puts it, "in which living is not a debtor's prison and one's most cherished wish is not escape," suggesting that the debt one owes to one's history and family need not be reduced to a permanent sentence of guilt but a quiet sense of ownership over the guilty past (159). If anything, it is an asset that one can draw on from the refugee fund/bank of memory. Despite the sinister connotations of reeducation, the novel articulates a flexible poetics of belonging, recognizing that the family can be both a safe place as well as a violent space full of personal wrongs and indignities. As such, receiving one's familial and social entitlements is hard, after so many others have been denied benefits.

For this reason, refugee reeducation is not really an education in the sense of moral uplift, intellectual enlightenment, and social development. It is a term that exists to veil ideology's work upon individuals and society, where reeducation is code for punishment for past deeds and political affiliations. As the source for a kind of refugee "double consciousness," reeducation signifies debt to a higher authority (state, family, society) that makes one free and unfree, bound up to the indeterminacy of the potential future, an unrealized liberation from a past from which one cannot flee. In this way, reeducation enables and disables a proper reading of texts and everyday experience. It invites much discretion toward information kept under the shroud of secrecy and fear of public exposure.

Through the brinkmanship of the U.S. Vietnamization project, which tweaked the American war in Indochina as a "Vietnamese" problem, the South Vietnamese national project was almost forgotten under the humanitarian crisis that was precipitated by the final bow of the southern republic due to the withdrawal of U.S. military forces. Within this image of refugees—their photographed bodies scuttling from homelands and needing rescue at sea—the geopolitical memory of South Vietnam and its military soldiers carries on as the flotsam and jetsam of history, displaced by the static, more searing visage of the helpless refugee. If the rescue of refugees serves to Americanize the narrative of postwar Vietnamese exiles, a reeducation in the history of South Vietnam can potentially Vietnamize this positive U.S.-centric narrative, inserting the ugly geopolitics and forgotten nation that cannot be accounted for.

The haunting or absent presence of South Vietnam (embodied by the reeducated soldier in Vietnam and the reeducated refugee in the West) foregrounds memory, because it brings the piece of history that propels movements to remember what has gone missing, the thing that connects the rupture of war and disruptions of postwar life. Insofar as the fragmented Vietnamese diasporic family serves as the extension of the broken South Vietnamese national family, the refugee autobiography can be a personal genre that reveals political coercion, and literary reeducation (letters, memoirs, etc.) foregrounds familial dysfunction and personal rifts as the expression and by-product of war's legacy. Reeducation as a kind of refugee asset offers a robust conceptual framework and creative device for reading texts, whether fictional or epistolary, a method of interpreting "truth" that cannot find easy solutions in political innocence or emotional catharsis. Through a "Vietnamized" framing of postwar memory work, refugee reeducation reveals the troublesome act of deciphering and representing the postwar experience without flattening what it truly means to be a refugee. Put another way, it conceptually provides the blueprint for diagnosing the limitations as well as possibilities of doing refugee memory work. While harkening back to the terrible abuse of South Vietnamese political prisoners, the novel primarily sheds light on Cherry's own captivity and reeducation in family matters related to life, love, and loss.

Refugee Baggage and the Luxury of Forgetting

Comparable to *The Joy Luck Club* and *The Woman Warrior*, where the uncovering of family secrets is the key formula for telling stories of migrants, Phan's novel bears thematic similarities with those classic Asian American novels and more contemporary ones with a central female protagonist working through secret family histories (Hagedorn 1990; Ng 2015; Lê 2011). In terms of addressing the South Vietnamese gendered condition, her work resonates less, perhaps, with Viet Thanh Nguyen's novel, *The Sympathizer*, which tells the story of a former South Vietnamese refugee and male soldier with torn political loyalties who is unable to connect with others, than it does with Lan Cao's works like *Monkey Bridge* and *The Lotus and the Storm*, which feature daughters dealing with estranged mothers and missing paternal figures, a legal and emotional terrain caused by the wrong moves of the American campaign in Vietnam. Insofar as Phan's protagonist is unaware of the history or machinations of war, she displays the naïve viewpoint of those born after war, who do not quite know what happened at the high level of politics, yet find themselves in dicey political situations.

The Reeducation of Cherry Truong is told in the form of a politicized memoir that merely looks back to the South Vietnamese nation without ever talking explicitly about its overly militarized history. At first, the novel seems to posit an archetypical refugee story based in a very familiar history tracing the Fall of Saigon in 1975 to communism, the mass exodus of refugees, and their resettlement in faraway places like France and the United States. However, this refugee story resists a simple chronological account of exile and despair so typical of many popular commentaries in the United States on the Vietnamese "boat people." Centered on the recovery of hidden family histories and secrets, the novel provides multiple plot threads narrated in such a complicated manner that refugees are depicted neither as noble human beings nor damaged traumatized subjects but as complicated people with both good and bad traits. This complex story begs the following questions, addressed in this chapter: What does it mean to use a politically charged term like reeducation to describe the mental and social development of second-generation youth like Cherry Truong, who never experienced war directly but whose life story remains attached to the history of war and postwar suffering? What lessons are to be learned by utilizing the term reeducation and framing the family story through it? How do individuals cultivate new lives (and privileges) in the face of historical trauma and silence? Who is allowed the privilege of owning or possessing memory? How is dignity maintained under a shameful history of loss, betrayal, and abandonment?

Mainstream academic studies tend to characterize Vietnamese refugees in terms of a cultural "deficit," objects of public sympathy to be adopted and lifted by Westerners, rather than those with assets. By marking Cherry as someone in need of "reeducation," but one who receives higher education, Aimee Phan follows Youngsuk Chae's (2007) recommendation to politicize Asian American literature and recognize the political dimensions and histories behind the economic successes of migrant communities of color. Toward this end, *Reeducation* articulates the "Vietnamese American experience" as something not limited to the cartography of the U.S. nation-state but a transnational economic venture that reminds us of the economic stakes behind the unrealized story of South Vietnam, and the U.S. imperial partnership with France. The author is one of the most celebrated members of a new generation of Vietnamese American writers. Born and raised in the United States, Aimee Phan had to conduct research on her own extended family in France to build enough background material to write her novel. For Phan, the Vietnamese refugee is not a sad, pathetic figure who has to be filled with useful "knowledge" in order to become a productive capitalist worker and citizen-subject, but rather is an always already politicized subject produced through information about their history, something that forces individuals to search for answers rather than depending on institutionalized sources of education about the Vietnam War for example. In an interview for the book, she comments on the novel's purpose in retelling the refugee story differently:

> The younger generation is trying to understand the older generation. People are trying to create this space for history. There's tension and push and pull in how that history gets represented. For me, I really cast Cherry as this detective. She's discovering her family's secrets and trying to understand them. The letters that she's discovering contain what (the family members) are keeping from each other. (Chang 2012)

Although the article from which this quote is drawn is titled, "O.C. Native Writes About Reeducation Camps," the book hardly discusses these specific camps, and talks more about the refugee camps and what families on the outside think about their beloved imprisoned in reeducation camps. In a strange way, the tortured, emasculated male soldiers provide the invisible backdrop for the suffering of women and children within refugee camps and beyond. Seemingly removed from this history as a U.S.-born child, Cherry, as the main "detective," must dig up these secrets to learn about the differently gendered strands of imprisonment and reeducation that have netted her family. The Little Saigon ethnic enclave in Orange County, California, where Phan grew up, provides the setting for understanding the different life opportunities conferred to boys and girls, older generations and their assimilated children, between the haves and have-nots. *The Reeducation of Cherry Truong* tells a story about one person's journey through the past, but it also relays a collective story of how people oppress or hurt one another even if they share the same historical experience or collective trauma. It is a cautionary tale about the pitfalls of memory as well as what or who gets to be remembered.

The novel's title alludes to the notorious reeducation camps created for former South Vietnamese soldiers by the reunification government after the Fall of Saigon in 1975, places of confinement, where thousands of individuals were kept for years, where they were starved, abused, and tortured. Having the word reeducation in the title refuses to forget the violence of authoritarian states, recalling the hypocrisy of institutions of authority to "help" everyday people and citizens. While the novel pays homage to this more historical-political meaning of reeducation, the text itself does not delve too deeply into the actual conditions of reeducation camps. Rather, the camps provide the point of departure for describing the all-encompassing forms of violence encountered by Cherry's family in the West; there is a historical residue of the legacy of South Vietnam and Vietnamization that remains, despite the Westernization of refugees.

The camp is mentioned several times in the novel, as when Grandma Vo discusses the death of her eldest, Thang, and how she had to bribe communist officers to get her son-in-law, Chinh, released from a "correctional facility," where he was being "deprogrammed" from the brainwashing by the Americans (Phan 2012:131). The camps are later mentioned in other flashbacks referencing the trade-offs and compromises made by prisoners in the camps, where strangers were like fictive kin as everyone "had to get along" somehow, despite tensions (26). The "familial" constitution of the reeducation camp provides some explanation for why the structure of Cherry's family appears so much like a camp—where certain members try to outdo and steal from others, passing resources back and forth like contraband, based on notions of who suffered or sacrificed the most and who is most deserving of gifts and perhaps freedom.

The novel sheds light on the racialized gender and class formation of postwar refugee families in France and the United States. Since childhood, Lum and Cherry were treated unequally by their parents, and this gendered divide puts into perspective how Vietnamese boys and girls are both taught to completely obey their families, but girls bear the weight of tradition, carrying less social privilege and less right to challenge their family than their male siblings. Their cousins' relatively egalitarian upbringing in France reveals contradistinctive gender and class systems between two diasporic communities. Rather than privilege the perspective of the South Vietnamese male soldier or men, Phan's story directs attention to the female gaze, the way women see one another as well as the men in their lives. Women are the central figures of postwar historical recall and recollection. As Nathalie Huynh Nguyen (2009) observes, they keep and guard secrets as the main facilitators of their families' reeducation, transmitting the social scripts necessary for collective survival. Reeducation provides the semantic and symbolic grounds for a fruitful discussion of how young women like Cherry must still locate themselves in the war's legacy and all the problems and opportunities it created for her family.

The failure of the United States to protect and deliver freedom to the South Vietnamese under Nixon's effort to Vietnamize the Vietnam War led to the precipitous fall of South Vietnam in 1975. It is here that the American "gift of freedom" to the South Vietnamese refugee, says feminist scholar Mimi Nguyen (2012), became a permanent bad debt, because the framing of the Vietnam War as a "liberal war"—a war to supposedly save and protect the Vietnamese from communism—is distinguished from colonial administration: "Liberalism as an imperial discourse invariably refers to the near future and to a hastened tempo that anticipates, and labors for, the moment in which the formerly colonial other is 'finally' capable of self-government" (45). That more "liberal" way of governing others before they can govern themselves does not involve a chronological sequence of progress based on linear time, but instead integrates two conflicting temporalities, as it "divides development into the normal and the pathological, and orders peoples across the colonial globe according to these measures of presence and potential" (46). For Nguyen, the American "gift of freedom" to the South Vietnamese—first during the war and later as refugees—creates a timeless debt, from which they are unable to escape; it surfaces from those "imperial remains that preclude the subject of freedom from being able to escape a colonial order of things" (5). Freedom is presumed to be an inalienable property of all men, but its realization requires acts of submission by conquered people *to* the will of Americans first as those who intimately know freedom as their birthright and who only can give it to others.

We often like to think that such submission is given freely—that conquered peoples have free will just like the conquerors do—but we know that it is simply not so. Freedom is not simply a universal, inalienable condition inherent to all people, no matter how much we want to believe it is so; rather, freedom exists only as a relationship of power, whether between two people or between two countries. When freedom is used to justify military intervention, even if that intervention is unsuccessful, as in the case of the U.S. Vietnamization of the Vietnam War, the now freed person is still "unfree," colonized in a different way, since the now "liberated" subject has been granted a "gift" from a more powerful authority. The emancipated refugee is thus contracted into a continuous process of subjection (and empowerment) through a debt economy that holds power over "his or her possible desires, movements, and futures" (8). Through the cumulative power of empire's will exercised over time, the gift of freedom is "not the end, but another beginning, another bondage" (20). Nguyen discusses the Vietnamese refugee who over her lifetime must prove her human worth and value to American sponsors, and whose debt to America provides a renewed lease for U.S. imperial expansion. While Nguyen examines this refugee as a figure of debt in a domestic sense, I draw on her to talk about the refugee's material debts as well as assets through reeducation, and how this relates to the transnational and historical matter of South Vietnam.

On "Critical Illiteracy" and the Camp as Ethical Memory

The Reeducation of Cherry Truong gives heft to poignant observations made by literary critic Isabelle Thuy Pelaud (2010) in her major study of Vietnamese American literature. She asks how diasporic Vietnamese identities so freighted with memories of the war "be disassociated from the systems of representation and history of that event without eradicating its legacy" (2). She answers by claiming the war *can never* be dissociated from Vietnamese diasporic identity and that the way one reads Vietnamese American literature and memory is therefore always political in nature (42). The novel brings to life what Pelaud describes as "a deep sense of vulnerability that leads to survival strategies heavy with contradictions that manifest themselves differently along gender and ethnic lines and are heightened by lack of financial resources" (65). The novel demonstrates this by underscoring how postwar "family problems" are inherently "political" because of the splintered conditions of survival set forth by the war and its aftermath. The crushing blow of geopolitical warfare brackets and attenuates postwar subject formation, setting up the kind of shocking experiences later encountered by refugees in their newly adopted homelands. Postwar traumas get passed down through generations, but the forms of war trauma that are disseminated do not often express themselves as holistic narratives of past suffering, but rather as deep silences produced within families still trying to heal from their past. In this way, Cherry's reeducation expresses the Americanized second generation's "postmemory" and absorption of feelings and "Vietnamized" experiences not their own but those of their South Vietnamese parents and kin (Hirsch 2008). Remembering in this context takes shape in terms of how the subject's sense of self is bound up with one's view of life, but also the crucial insights the subject gathers from others, living and dead (Tran 1993).

At a minimum, the novel instructs readers to grasp the manifold ways postwar memories and memory *making* are limited by historical amnesia. It sets forth the project of memory recovery as more than a matter of gaining fluency in reading historical experience but also a matter of what we can call "critical illiteracy" found in the productive failure and "teachable moments" of never fully grasping the diverse experiences of war-ravaged populations. In other words, reeducation postulates the concurrent impossibility of fully reviving or reading the past correctly and the possibility of discovering more information about the past and learning from it.

A critical illiteracy is needed to prevent the desire to turn Vietnamese refugees into transparent subjects of representation, brought into and recognized within the "modern" way of life (Espiritu 2006b). The pedagogical project to rescue and reform refugees aims to "civilize" Third World populations by giving them asylum, transforming these former colonial subjects into modern liberal subjects (Ong 2003). This is inherently a neo-imperialist project to deny them political rights and agency, as many in refugee camps were forced to adopt a white cultural mind-set and Eurocentric standards of family, cleaning, working, dating, and living (Chan and Loveridge 1987). Where the "refugee camp" stands as the spectral double of the political reeducation camp created by Vietnamese communists for South Vietnamese soldiers and officials, the novel contemplates the coupled fates of "freed" subjects and captives, the simultaneity of dwelling in safe harbors of legal protection *and* extralegal "states of exception" in a moment in time when the concentration "camp" is the fundamental paradigm of sovereignty.

For Italian philosopher Giorgio Agamben (1998), terms like "citizen," "refugee," and "stateless peoples" do not fully explain the differential production of biopolitical subjects or how people become subjects of state power/knowledge. In his theorization of the camp as a paradigmatic space for modern governmentality, Agamben claims whole populations are nowadays made vulnerable to the modern state's political calculations. The Vietnamese refugee does not exist in some abstract state of exception, but occupies an array of material spaces defined by the absence or abrogation of law, from war zones to refugee camps to reeducation camps, such that it is apt to say they are both subject to the biopolitical management of "life" by the state but also maintained within postcolonial regimes of death in the way that Achille Mbembé (2003) describes "necropolitics."

Despite the call to respect the racial Other in Western societies as part of a new discourse of multicultural humanitarianism, it is often the case that the immigrant/refugee/asylum-seeker slips easily into the category of the outlaw or criminal, occupying a liminal position within the nation-state, thus needing to be forcibly assimilated into proper forms of cultural citizenship through a coercive naturalization process and curriculum on how to be "American" or "French" (Knight and Harnish 2006). Despite capitalizing on their newfound citizenship status, Vietnamese refugees never really attain true freedoms or the "good life" in Eurocentric white-majority societies as they inhabit a precarious social status and space of exception somewhat analogous to the South Vietnamese national in communist Vietnam. Following Agamben and Mbembé, it becomes necessary to consider the way in which the "camp" serves as a central metaphor for the ubiquitous violence of modern history. Aimee Phan's creative use of the term "reeducation" explicitly injects the politicized practice of torture, killing, and genocide found in "illiberal" pockets of the world like Vietnam into the comforts of Western modernity and national domesticity.

Since the end of the Vietnam War, more than two million Vietnamese along with many other Southeast Asians have left their country and, after being processed in refugee camps, settled in sponsor countries. Today, there are close to four million Vietnamese living around the world in a hundred countries (Pham 2010). While the term "overseas Vietnamese" or *Việt Kiều* came to prominence as a somewhat derogatory description of Vietnamese living outside Vietnam, the connotation of overseas Vietnamese has undergone enormous changes, no longer strictly meaning those exiled from the home country and South Vietnamese refugees but also including those diasporic populations existing within all types of social relations (Dorais 2001).

To approach Vietnamese postwar existence in singular terms such as melancholia, trauma, or assimilation reduces the intricacies of diasporic subject-making to isomorphic affective states. Reeducation provides the critical optics and vocabulary for reckoning with the polyvalence of refugee life absent the wish to erase the many incarnations of the hurtful past for a sanitized totalizing future. It serves as the site of reclamation of knowledge for the survivor, the unfinished contract or bond the living owes to the dead, a call to search for those missing stories not memorialized in official history. As Viet Nguyen observes (2006), Vietnamese Americans as subjects of war are yoked to an ethical memory of the past, haunted by the forgotten and dead, bound to a future without moral salvation and a past without innocence. Thus, while Vietnamese Americans do not always possess what Kim Nguyen (2010) calls the luxury of historical amnesia, they possess other ways of forgetting that can be an economic asset if not a luxury. For Vietnamese refugees and their foreign-born children, the nostalgic remembrance of the homeland recalls raw emotions and insights about what they endured in the homeland under the shadow of war. Nguyen says the refugees' proud desire to "never forget" their history is contrary to their very *need to forget* to relieve the pain of recalling that same history.

Historical amnesia is never about absolute ignorance or forgetfulness; it is a selective partial memory based on the shrewd curation of history, depending on the socioeconomic and personality standing of the person. It denotes an active refusal by people to remember history properly, not just the simple act of forgetting the past. As a mode of survival, historical amnesia transforms what is usually perceived as refugee "lack" of knowledge or emotional baggage left from the war into cultural capital for enduring or succeeding in postwar economies. While many overseas Vietnamese today live in material abundance relative to their counterparts in Vietnam, many diasporic subjects do not have the privilege to forget the war that tore their families apart. Aimee Phan's judicious use of the term reeducation to describe refugee experience defuses the hyper-politicization of Vietnamese diasporic communities under the anti-communist cause, making room for alternate readings of the ways Vietnamese subjectivities come into their own politics not bound to any ideological framework, even if it stands as a tribute to those who suffered under communism. To achieve this venture, the novel focuses on other methods to "imagine otherwise" per Kandice Chuh (2003), the Vietnamese American subject.

The Price of Family Pride and Prejudice

The Reeducation of Cherry Truong tells the interwoven story of two families, the Truongs and the Vos, bound together by a young couple, Sanh and Tuyet, Cherry's parents. Like her debut collection of short stories, *We Shall Never Meet*, Aimee Phan's novel recounts the hardship of families during the Vietnam War and their escape from Saigon in 1975, their challenges in Malaysian refugee camps, and their resettlement in foreign countries. The Truong family includes Sanh, Tuyet, Cherry, and her older brother, Lum, all of whom ended up in the United States, while the maternal side of Cherry's family, the Vos, found sponsorship in France. Grappling with the messiness of her family's past and uncertain futures, Cherry uncovers secrets on both sides of her family and, in the process, learns much more than she bargained for. While the novel may be read as another addition to the genre of immigrant fiction or "ethnic American literature," I draw out some major lessons found in this fictional work to comment on the inherent volatility of refugee writing practices and literary production.

The opening letter by Tuyet to Kim-Vo quickly segues into modern-day Saigon, where Cherry is trying to convince her brother to come back to the states. As a kind of First World "refugee" in exile from the United States forced to return to his homeland—albeit as a rich expat with enormous economic privileges—Lum promotes entrepreneurial efforts to develop French-style residential duplexes and U.S. suburban homes for wealthy Vietnamese diasporans who wish to live in Vietnam. Such projects literally and figuratively insert the "American Dream" and the presence of overseas South Vietnamese (formerly vilified as traitors to the nation) into the newly built environs of free-market socialist Vietnam. Fleeing temporarily to Vietnam to avoid being labeled an academic failure by her parents, Cherry conflates the foreign bourgeois neighborhoods built by her brother with the American suburban environs in which she grew up. "It's Orange County," she says, to which her older brother responds, "No. . . . It's better." On a billboard, she notices a sign with the message: "The Future Site of New Little Saigon . . . The Comforts of America, In Your True Home, Vietnam" (Phan 2012: 295).

In this scene, diasporic imaginaries and desires are superimposed over the globalizing local geographies of Vietnam. The political identity term attached to diasporic ethnic enclaves (Little Saigon) to keep alive the painful memory of South Vietnam is defused by the global phenomenon of Vietnamese refugees returning "home" as elite transplants. This transnational crossing is enabled by renewed diplomatic relations between Vietnam and the United States since the 1990s, and the Vietnamese government's tolerance as well as solicitation of well-off overseas Vietnamese communities to invest in money-strapped Vietnam. Unable to educate himself in the Vietnamese/American Dream with its own subtle form of political indoctrination, Lum finds a more prosperous future in his ancestral land by forsaking his refugee past and minority status as a Vietnamese American, only to exploit his global privileges and status as a U.S. citizen. As Lum sees it, he is a refugee who "escaped" the small enclosure of his family and the provincialism of the Vietnamese American community to reeducate himself in the bourgeois ways of postsocialist Vietnam. Lum's urban planning in Saigon serves as a kind of memory work, overwriting the war's spatial effects on the city by providing a cosmopolitan gentrified diasporic consciousness based on opportunism, materialism, and Westernized notions of industrial progress—a double movement centered on forgetting the problems of "Little Saigon" by reconstituting a better Americanized version of it in the real Saigon, or Ho Chi Minh City as it is officially called in Vietnam.

This prologue posits the Vietnamese diaspora as a confusing network of conflicting desires, where the wish to return to the homeland is fraught with both anguish and hope, mediated by the reeducated diasporic subject's own move to erect new expensive "encampments" in the homeland. It is this neocolonial context of refugee assets turned global capital in which Cherry is visiting her brother Lum, a troublemaker back home in the United States, exiled by his parents and ordered to stay with distant relatives because the parents "thought Vietnam could reshape his perspective, remind him of his humble roots, so when he returned to America, to them, he could have a fresh start" (295). Trying unsuccessfully to convince Lum to return to the United States, Cherry suspects her parents' longings for their eldest son's reeducation was about guilting Lum into leaving the family since "no one can force you from your home unless they make you believe you didn't deserve to be there" (ibid.). Enjoying his newfound life too much, Lum refuses to return to the United States, as he is making a successful living as a planner in Vietnam, a major change from his status as a disappointment back home. Vietnam offers Lum a great future and a steady place to settle down with his girlfriend and child away from the disapproving eyes of his nuclear family.

In *Reeducation*, Vietnamese refugees and their children born outside of Vietnam continue to maintain a connection to the homeland, where Vietnam figures as more than a source for finding one's roots, as it is also a contested political site for negotiating social identity and class in the age of globalization. Lum is a disaffected subject and descendant of the South Vietnamese diaspora, a quintessential loser who comes from a people viewed as the ultimate losers of the war. His incapacity to live up to the middle-class ideals and upwardly mobile values espoused by so many Vietnamese Americans today is transfigured in capitalist-oriented Vietnam, where overseas Vietnamese like him return to colonize, modernize, and reeducate South Vietnamese people on American-style capitalism, a people who were previously reeducated in communism after the war when the government tried to wean the Saigonese off Western capitalist habits. Despite the occurrence of so many types of reeducation, the question remains whether it is possible for diasporic youth to ever escape the encampments of their community and history.

As Nhi Lieu (2011) explains, many Vietnamese Americans have worked diligently to propagate the ideals of the American Dream, resulting in their recognition as a new "model minority" and moving beyond past associations as helpless victims of war or refugees. *The Reeducation of Cherry Truong* ruptures this paradigm of the Vietnamese model minority subject by attending to the differential privileges accorded to individuals. The developmental trajectory of poor South Vietnamese refugees turned prosperous Vietnamese Americans is upset by Lum's "return" to Vietnam after failing to become a model minority in the United States. This allegory of failure and triumph exemplified by the opening montage reiterates Lum's opinion of his U.S.-based co-ethnic community as a closed-minded camp with petty values, whose unrealistic demands for success ironically pushed him to recycle those same demands to maximum effect in Vietnam.

From the 2000s, the novel quickly jumps back in time to the Truong family's escape in the late 1970s as refugees purged from post-reunification Vietnam due to economic and political pressures. Cherry's maternal grandparents, Hung and Hoa Truong, pay for their family's boat passage to a Malaysian refugee camp, where they wait for an extended time for sponsorship, until a wealthy French family, the Bourdains, help them to reunite with their oldest son, Yen, a lawyer now living in Paris. Rather than joining his biological family in France, Cherry's father immigrated to the United States to have a better chance of sponsoring his wife's family, the Vos, who were left behind in Vietnam because Hung did not deliver on his promise to bring his daughter-in-law's family over. It is later discovered that Hung chose to bring his mistress instead.

Though Cherry's family resides in the O.C. and her other family members live in Paris, the separate clans remain in touch, tied together by what anthropologist Nazli Kibria (1993) calls family "patchworking," where uneven family dynamics and gendered kinship forms interact to generate a complex support network for sustaining immigrant households. In these households, survival strategies are intimately yoked to collective debt. For instance, Grandma Kim-Ly's meddling in her family's affairs includes funding Cherry Truong's college tuition through black market investments, cheating other people, and dealing with criminals. Kim-Ly's tough measures to "rescue" her grandson Lum from a life of gambling addiction by making a deal with unsavory street thugs evidences the "dutiful" work of a family-oriented grandma willing to help kin by any means.

In the postwar refugee household, Vietnamese women commonly take on new responsibilities as breadwinners or informal leaders of their families even while they might uphold the traditional gender norms of the heteropatriarchal family system. Vietnamese refugee subjectivity is historically synonymous with the emasculation and trauma of male soldiers. Phan pushes against the male-centered public construction of Vietnamese postwar subjectivity by speaking to the ways families endure and survive because of the power of women. Prideful Sanh, for instance, winds up despondent, working as a school janitor to raise Lum and Cherry, despite his advanced education and fluency in multiple languages, and burdened by the feeling of "leeching off a welfare system" in the United States (Phan 2012: 327). Tuyet, his wife, becomes the decision maker in the family, a leading role initiated when she asked Sanh to marry her to thwart her mother's plans to marry her off to a 70-year-old American soldier, a potential foreign sponsor for the family to help them leave the country.

A women-centered story of sharing family responsibilities and burdens, the novel moves beyond Cherry to follow Grandmother Hoa, described as a beloved, nurturing, long-suffering, and naïve woman. While her abusive husband begins to lose his memory and slip into a debilitating state, she learns to take ownership of the family he had been running with an iron fist. For decades, Hoa allows her children to bear witness as she is taunted, controlled, and physically abused by her tyrannical husband, Hung. She remains the silent, strong female head of household as the Vos move from Vietnam to France with the sponsorship of the affluent Bourdains, to whom Hung says the family should be grateful since "they do so much for the community" (186). While Hoa plays the part of a good wife and mother as tradition would expect back in Vietnam, Hung claims that Monsieur Bourdain was the type of modern Western man he aspired to be. Now, he expects his lawyer son Yen to reach Bourdain's status and thus carry out Hung's Western colonial dreams.

Able to finally delve into her ill husband's office files for the first time without him knowing, Hoa discovers a batch of letters Hung had been keeping private from her all these years, written in French to his mistress, whom Hoa recalled had been on the boat with the family. Interspersed throughout the novel's chapters are personal letters of adulterous love between Hung and his mistress. Hoa does not get angry, accepting the truth of this affair and all those years of abuse she endured from her husband. As she later admits, "the information of his past would be hers, just as his knowledge slipped away. After all these years, she believed she'd earned it" (259). Even though she could not read the letters, just holding and having them as her own personal property felt like small compensation for all the secrets he kept from her. Unable to read French and too embarrassed to ask her children to translate them, Hoa's difficulty reading the letters signal the challenges of translation and literacy. Hoa's lack of education prevents her from accessing a troublesome history that is *her* right to know and own. Meanwhile, her husband always held power through the educational and linguistic privileges accorded to men like him. Hoa quickly realizes the discovery of these letters did not make her any stronger and that, "with his mind half gone, Hung still won . . . because while he was allowed to forget everything he'd done [to her], she had no choice but to remember" (ibid.). Hoa's dilemma shows how the female refugee does not have the luxury to forget *history*. Hung's liberation from guilt and his shameful past forgotten under Alzheimer's is a burden she must bear as someone who cannot *forget*, as she is a woman without the luxury of historical amnesia. Hoa's personal reeducation in her marriage recognizes how she accesses her own refugee reserve of knowledge and capital.

The position of women like Hoa in relation to their husbands finds resonance with the status of sponsored refugees who must always be subservient and grateful to their white patrons. When they first arrived in France, the Bourdains welcomed the Vo family with a toast featuring a patronizing statement indicative of the French colonial attitude and "benevolent paternalism" toward the Vietnamese: "We should have never left you with the communists. We abandoned you then, but we will not do it again. We are honored to help the people of our former colony" (Phan 2012: 94). Hung instructs his family to forget their differences with the French to repay their former colonizer the debt incurred for the freedom they all enjoy now. As Mimi Thi Nguyen (2012) reminds us, Vietnamese refugees bear the weight of the "gift of freedom" that holds them responsible for the "structures of feeling and social forms through which encampment" still regulates their postwar "better-off" lives. Hoa's daughter-in-law, Trinh, likes to speak up against her elders, but Hung tells Hoa to control her foolish speech in front of the Europeans. When Hoa tells Hung that Madame Bourdain talks all the time, he tells her Ms. Bourdain "has an education. She earned her privilege to speak" (Phan 2012: 95). Western education held by white women holds the tongue of Vietnamese women (and men) in check. This high-class education is reserved for whites, while the Vietnamese are consigned to the silenced subaltern position of minorities.

In a family where members do not talk to one another directly about their feelings, the weighty silence that fills Cherry's family life offers little in the way of communal dialogue about what people have endured. Indeed, there is a disjuncture between the openly honest letters written by individuals to significant others and the stilted, elusive manner through which family members verbally engage one another on a daily basis. As one reviewer complained, "Instead of adding layers to the family history, the letters and fractured chronology does more than symbolize the fractured Truong family—it splinters the novel so that no one character or plotline becomes essential, least of all the title character. Phan's family saga has many riches, but it lacks the clear focus" (Kirkus Reviews 2012). However, the book's fractured chronology and shifting narrative voice speak volumes about the disorienting nature of the postwar refugee condition. The family's divided loyalties and identities arise from the fragmented experiences of being displaced peoples, told through a splintered plotline without a neat, one-directional exposition. In this way, *Reeducation* observes the tumultuous reality of diasporic "writing to evoke the past [which] is not always about creativity, nor is it always a matter of choice" (Pelaud 2010: 64).

The experiences of early Vietnamese refugees who migrated to France by "choice" and attained more secure economic positions like the Vos contrast with those of poorer economic refugees who later came to the United States, sponsored primarily by their own family members and often forced to labor in nail salons. Cherry and her brother spent their working-class childhood playing inside their mother's beauty salon, a hub for Grandmother Vos's illicit financial activities, a place where the old matron kept a watchful eye over her family members. Every day this grandma reminds Cherry that the girl has looks, brains, and an education, which she paid for (Phan 2012: 340). This matriarch tells Cherry to always be grateful, never wasting all her gifts by running away from responsibilities like her brother, Lum. Expressed here is a familial economy of debt tied to emotional injury and female virtue. If Cherry wants to honor her family's hardship and struggles, she must work hard on her education, pushing herself to become a successful doctor oriented toward the future, never the past. Yet, the unearthing of family secrets when Cherry visits her grandmother in France gives her the courage to break out of the role of a respectable Vietnamese girl. She receives letters from Hoa and later finds more letters from her grandmother in the United States, and the awful truths contained in these writings reeducated Cherry on how truly dishonorable her family can be.

Receiving Gifts and the Value of a Reeducation

Despite learning more details about her family, Cherry never finds any real satisfaction or enlightenment from reading the many letters written by her mother, grandmothers, grandfather, and father. The bequeathal of these secret writings to her by her two grandmothers (without the consent of her parents or grandfather) symbolizes inheritances from female ancestors, but also the ethical issues of possessing others' private memories. Thus, Cherry's reeducation is not the simple act of reclaiming or relearning the past but offers a vexed interpretative lens for translating, collating, and piecing together fragmented bits of knowledge, all geared toward the question of what this all means for *her* own uncertain future, which echoes the uncertain futures of the South Vietnamese people once the Americans decided to leave Vietnam.

While the book's title, *The Reeducation of Cherry Truong*, suggests the titular character is the main figure of interest, one requiring some personal rehabilitation or acquisition of knowledge, the novel does not exclusively revolve around Cherry, whose story is minor to those of all the other members of her extended family. Acting almost like a fictionalized memoir of the author's own family life, Aimee Phan crafts a successful, academically inclined character able to remember things perfectly, but who would rather use her mental skills to investigate her family's background than practice rote memorization in medical school. Despite having a photographic memory, Cherry realizes that there is no such thing as a "perfect memory," since her own family cannot even remember or account for everything that has happened to them. Cherry is soon starting medical school at the University of California, Irvine, and the family is proud of her career ambitions. However, considering refugee reeducation as a historical and critical lens through which to view the political economy of refugee memory offers an unusual way to think about assimilation that is more materially grounded in theorizing the relation between education and the state. Indeed, it is the lack of real education about South Vietnam in U.S. schools, other than a foreign policy or anti-communist problem, that gives way to refugees being critically illiterate in a country that only sees them as poor, uneducated outsiders who need to be civically reeducated by state civics and American public schools. The refugee family's push for Cherry to become another Asian American "model minority" fulfills the greater capitalist and governmental demand for quiescent, hardworking workers, apolitical, de-racialized ethnic minorities and citizen-subjects living the middle-class American Dream without the stain of the violent pasts.

From the central premise of Cherry being educated in prestigious state universities as the road to happiness, the novel quickly moves into a centrifugal story or political reeducation about the internal strife, conflicts, and affairs of other family members who prove that they are not quiet, obedient types. *The Reeducation of Cherry Truong* is really about the reeducation of Cherry's family in their own history, shuttling and shuffling through their multifarious experiences with one another and the war. It is hard to maintain dignity when all the characters are humiliated in some manner by their own loved ones, and it is a challenge to "save face" and find value under different regimes of blame, shame, and punishment. In the communist reeducation camps, South Vietnamese political prisoners were forced to renounce ties to their own families and incriminate friends in a never-ending game of lies. Yet, the camps made individuals more likely to realize their complicity with institutions of power and their moral obligation to others, who could be friend and/or enemy, collaborator and/or accuser. Secrets could be one's burden or demise, but also could be one's way out to freedom. After a gang shooting accident involving her brother, Cherry falls into a coma, but once she recovers she fails to remember much of what happened to her. Without memory, our heroine's "perfect narration falls apart" and she must call upon others to "take over the story for her . . . [as] Cherry does not trust these fragments [of memory as they] . . . contain perspectives that have been fed to her after the fact, and perhaps they are not her own at all, just other people's opinions, insistent truths" (Phan 2012: 292). Whenever Cherry or her brother would ask their father to describe his experience in the reeducation camps, Sanh would give them little information, as though his memory was a gift to be earned as well as something he wished to hide. For Sanh, the words "reeducation" and "camp" were not a proper translation of the prison in which he was placed, as the two conjoined terms compounded "a lie that still tasted vile in Sanh's mouth" (ibid.).

Though he did not wish to scare his children regarding his tortured past, Sanh realized that the socialist regime's refusal to use the correct term for what "they were doing to soldiers further demonstrated hypocrisy" (320). The victorious government had promised to embrace and reintegrate the country's former traitors but instead meted out punishment, instilling more agony rather than reeducation. Sanh's reeducation consisted of watching others suffer and die without justice. The positive undertone of reeducation denies a cruel reality as the term lies about postwar realities. The impossibility of a "real" reeducation about what South Vietnamese men like him experienced prevents Sanh from divulging information to his American children, who are totally uneducated about the war named after their people. In this way, reeducation serves a double function for Cherry's family: it can evoke a history of violence and simultaneously deny it.

A Black Market of Family Choice

Differentiating between those who might harm or exploit and those who are supposed to protect becomes confusing within the thick interpersonal relations of the family. In the letters written to his mistress, Hung tells her how he envies the youth in France with their "liberated thinking," marrying for love and not following the bonds of tradition or parental expectations (Phan 2012: 262). We see this demand for blind obedience to parents when Kim-Vo, ever the manipulator, tries to arrange the marriage of her teenage daughter to an old American officer who, according to Tuyet, "looked at her and her sisters like they were prostitutes" ready to be bought and sold (ibid.: 350). The frayed relations between the United States and South Vietnam (and the selling out of the latter by the former) is reprocessed at the level of one woman's decision to sell her daughter to an American in order to gain entry to the United States.

Cherry's two grandmothers are two separate character studies. One is a single mother who raised her children using devious schemes, while the other is a cloistered mother and wife who dutifully provides for her family at the expense of her own individual happiness. As two contrasting feminine archetypes, the grandmothers epitomize the refugee will to survive by any means necessary. Cherry's mother, Tuyet, was a rebel against her own mother, but now tries to control Cherry in a repetition of maternal violence/love. The novel is dominated by the voices of female characters whom readers get to know through a third-person view. In a letter written by Tuyet, the rebellious daughter who left her family for her husband finally shows repentance by sponsoring her mother to come to the United States. While her mother is waiting in an Indonesian refugee camp, Tuyet composes a letter with glowing comments about the "Little Saigon" community, which she claims is like "Saigon before the war" or even "better than Saigon ever was" (329). As she writes, "Our years of suffering are soon coming to an end. They have taught me a valuable lesson: families are not supposed to be separated. While our circumstances were dictated by war, we are free to do as we choose in America. Our family shall never be apart again" (ibid.).

Reading these private memos written by her mother, Cherry barely recognized the same strong-willed, domineering woman she grew up with, as the scribbled notes showcased an insecure girl who always gave deference to her mother. Cherry soon comes to embrace her mother as a more complex person rather than a one-dimensional figure of austerity. The letters present a dilemma: "A good daughter would return these letters to her mother" (342), Cherry reasons, but her mother would have been angry at her for taking and reading them in the first place. Cherry wanted to keep them, but would this make her a bad daughter? "After digesting these words—feeling how they scratched at her pride, her heart—Cherry realized that they no longer belonged to her mother" but to her. Her mother's memories were *hers* to possess, Cherry concluded (ibid.).

In her study of the figure of the duty-bound daughter in Asian American literature, Erin Ninh (2005) notes the demands placed on Asian daughters to be both servants and saviors of their families. This female subject in filial bondage speaks to an expression of self that finds "speech only in the borrowed language of misrepresentation" (62). For Ninh, the melancholic "lack" that haunts the Asian American feminine experience generates its own value from the material deprivation and state of debt that remains impossible for the family to repay. The ungrateful daughter who refuses to comport with societal expectations is not simply displaying ingratitude but inhabits "a state of being resistant to the call of debt—the ability to receive without acknowledgment or return" (155). The filial debt owed by the duty-bound daughter to her family/community attempts to create docile gendered subjects, just as refugee/reeducation camps create docile subjects, and just as foreign allies like South Vietnam rely on U.S. foreign aid. In Phan's book, reeducation plays with the twin concepts of family/national debt and family/national duty by allowing Cherry to become aware of her own disciplining as a compliant subject of the family, and the family as duty-bound to the state in the plural sense: the United States, France, South Vietnam, and the People's Republic of Vietnam. *Reeducation* spins an intergenerational story of people learning to juggle and accommodate gendered forms of debt, docility, and duty within asymmetrical social relations and disciplinary governmental structures.

Despite this call to female gratitude, the unruliness of diasporic kinship formation breaks down family relations to reveal slippages in the reproduction of domesticity. As Trinh Minh-Ha (2011) notes, the mother is the proprietor and protector of family knowledge; she holds secrets to maintain the public face of the family. Maternal knowledge offers the word of truth but fails in speech within the patriarchal symbolic order. As Minh-Ha writes: "In the politics of memory, public opinion maintains a reduced conception of memory . . . [but the mother's knowledge is] always opposed to oblivious-ness and identified with the power to recall what has been learned" (103). The silent power of the mother's knowledge to help one to recall what has already been learned is evident in the case of Aunt Trinh, who begins to slowly lose her mind, turned into a deranged religious seeker wandering Paris. Trinh's demented actions are indicative of a strange ailment. It soon comes to Grandmother Hoa's attention that the source of her daughter's psychological delusions and emotional disturbances is the young girl's rape by Malaysian guards during the family's refugee passage—a daily occurrence witnessed by Trinh's young son, who remembers such incidents through his psychosomatic associations with the mother. On certain days, Xuan would be able to vividly recall the pungent smell of the guards, and this memory makes him lose his sense of direction and purpose in life. He would ask:

Was this her memory or his? He felt it was his—he could see, taste, hear, and feel the hopelessness of that night . . . or was it because his mother reminded him of every detail for so many years? He supposed it didn't matter if it was her memory or his. . . . A person could not invent that sort of memory. (Phan 2012: 158–159)

From these episodes of nightly rape, Xuan would remember the way guards directed their lusty gaze toward his mother and sometimes to him, a sexual pedophilic threat thwarted by Trinh, who tried to shield her young child from the men's carnal lust. Mother and son are united in gendered visceral ways through what Yvonne Kwan calls the (re)production of trauma and resilience (2015). The recurring sexual violence of this shared family history leads Xuan's usual photographic memory to fail one day, forcing the rising academic star student to give up on his rigorous French *bac* (baccalaureate) examinations. With no time left to complete an essay for the philosophy portion of this important test, concerned as he was with personal problems, Xuan made no effort to compose a well-considered answer to exam questions such as "Why do we want to be free?" He concludes that while philosophers could ask such lofty questions, delighting in abstract intellectual games, he could not. The apolitical nature of academia fails to recognize the merit of a refugee boy's reeducation in life-and-death matters, which largely come from his vivid experiences in the dangerous licentious spaces of the camp. Xuan resigns to the quiet fact that "he had other subjects to study" (161), refusing to participate in the delicate act of balancing his mental-emotional distress with present professional commitments. In refusing to perform his academic duties, Xuan is not refusing family expectations of success but quietly honoring the life of his mother, thus tackling another important *bac* question: "Must political action be guided by the knowledge of history?" (150). Xuan' political act in resisting the demands of higher education dramatizes the agony and necessity of remembering horrific events and violence made invisible in French history and schools.

Xuan's critical reeducation in what truly matters stops him from equivocating too much over the right response to other exam questions, such as "Is dialogue the path to truth?" when the truth is guided not by verbal dialogue or exchange but by quiet wisdom found in silence (144).

Tapping into his own intellectual and cultural sovereignty, Xuan is the portrait of an anti–model minority subject, exposing the failure of the French public schools to teach him something valuable for his life, resisting the imperatives of a postcolonial reeducation that requires him to fit into white European society by forsaking his Vietnamese history and refugee identity. Xuan thinks to himself, "Memories are hard to quantify and impossible to reason with. People forget all the time and then the past returns, unexpectedly, disturbing the present" (161). Memory then serves as more than a reprocessing or recounting of historical violence tied to national identity but a deeply self-reflexive practice dealing with historical violence due to the collapse of the very production of national identity itself. *Reeducation* incorporates and inculcates men into maternal collective memory and women's experiences with sexual violence. This intersubjectivity highlights what sociologist Avery Gordon (1997) calls "complex personhood" and how all people "remember and forget, are beset by contradiction, and recognize and misrecognize themselves and others" (40).

Conclusion: Learning to Unlearn the Past

Refugeehood is not the static condition of losing nation and freedom but a radical site that fosters a reimagining of those things, as Anh Thang Dao tells us (2012). Acknowledging war diasporas as grounded in the refugee's perpetual move toward potential freedom rather than the outright possession of freedom, one can recognize how the refugee's potential for freedom comes to form what Kaja Silverman (2000) calls the "dispiriting apprehension of the otherness of one's self, and the ecstatic discovery, at the site of the other, of one's utmost 'ownness'" (49). Reeducation as an oblique method of reading postwar refugee experience and writing aims to make sense of the strained circumstances in which people try to "do the right thing" under the wrong conditions. Refugee families carry all sorts of secrets, dirty laundry not usually meant to be aired, and so opening the secret box of history carries both rewards and risks for the subject wanting to be reeducated. The Vietnam War was a major event in which no Vietnamese person was left unscathed, a conflict where there were no clear winners and losers either. This is especially true in Cherry's family, where no one is the absolute victor, yet no one is simply a victim. The reeducated subject is ultimately an indebted subject, chained to the suffering but also the strength of others. Reeducation gives political meaning and urgency to the axiom that everyone must hold one other accountable for their actions, giving an active verb form to and politicizing the remembering of history.

Refugees and their children are never truly free from what happened in the past, and this is all the more reason why a (re)education about South Vietnam and its populace is important in helping individuals learn more about the traumatic effects of war upon their present existence. Despite her parents' disapproval, Cherry suspends her college education to embark on a personal journey piecing together the forgotten parts of her family's history—a voyage that conjures the history of ARVN soldiers sentenced to detention. In the reeducation camps like those where her father and uncles had been sent, convicts had to "rat out" or incriminate fellow inmates by identifying those who lacked a "good education." As a different kind of "prisoner of consciousness," Cherry learns that life means more than getting a good education and feeling bad about the poor, starving children left in Saigon constantly mentioned by her mother. Education is a gift, Tuyet tells Cherry, and in "America, when you improve, you get anything you want" (Phan 2012: 57). Cherry was always encouraged to want this kind of good life by way of higher education, but she never wanted success enough and wonders if this makes her weak or disrespectful to the sacrifices of her parents. Receiving an education fulfills the burden of family expectations, she surmises, but undertaking a reeducation fulfills filial duties of another sort.

The novel concludes with Cherry touring Vietnam with her French cousins, eventually stopping in the scenic Ha Long Bay. She takes with her the secret letters gifted to her by her grandmothers. While Cherry is discussing her poor job prospects with her cousins, a group of young children steal Cherry's letters and scatter them into the water. Though the cousins try to stop them, Cherry could feel her heart growing heavy as the letters sunk to the bay floor, never to be read again. In this dramatic final scene, the youth of Vietnam with no personal attachment to these old refugee letters return them to the great beyond, a timeless place where recovery of history is impossible, but where reeducation is still possible in the void of knowledge made possible by the loss. That loss of an object of memory, combined with Cherry's loss of her photographic memory, is an evocative conclusion or non-conclusion that points to the malleability of refugee memory that remains a project imperfect as that of South Vietnam, a Vietnamization of history project which could never be fully saved by the Americans, destroyed completely by the communists, or salvaged entirely by refugees. Therein lies the political reeducation of personal bonds and family trauma.

A semantically loaded term not easily appropriated in a celebratory manner, reeducation accepts the reality that there exists no true state of refuge from war or proper reparations for war. Inextricable from the history of South Vietnamese political prisoners, reeducation invites the concurrent erasure and exposure of a buried history of oppression. For Vietnamese refugees, the act of passing on war memories to their Westernized children is shaped by silence, amnesia, and ambivalence toward historical truth, but the reproduction of these memories persists through the reeducational work of women and their kin. While Cherry is stuck in the "camp" of her personal journey, others are trapped in ethnic enclaves, gated communities, rigorous universities, profit-driven nail salons, terrible marriages, and so forth, though those places never can be fully compared to the horrors of the postwar reeducation camps. Yet, in those enclosed places where refugees must learn to live, love, and labor again, *The Reeducation of Cherry Truong* provides important clues to the desire for freedom lurking in the closed affairs of the heart, holding true to the feminist mantra that the personal is always political. Indeed, we find out much later that Cherry's name is derived from the French name Cherre. As a Vietnamese American, she bears the heritage of French colonial connection even though she herself grew up not in France but rather in the United States. At the same time, they tell us of the personal battles that occur in the family, a microcosm of the political struggles in South Vietnam and the broader Vietnamese diasporic community.

3

Dismembered Lives

The Fractured Body Politics of the "Little Saigon" Community

This chapter addresses the politics of Vietnamese refugee communities who came to the United States after the end of the Vietnam War. Our entries into this political forum will be a series of anticommunist protests over an art exhibit produced in 2009 by the Vietnamese American Arts and Letters Association (VAALA), and protests by VROC (Viet Rainbow of Orange County) challenging a ban on LGBT people in the annual lunar new year parade in 2012 and 2013. At the center of these conflicts was the meaning of South Vietnamese identity as it is interpreted through Vietnamese American identity, which fueled an outcry against certain protesters as outsiders or agitators. These controversies raised debates about who gets to speak for the Vietnamese American community, but also the diaspora writ large. Refugee body politics as I am terming it not only refers to the specific politics of the national body from which refugees came, but to the re/membered lives of so many refugee groups such as Salvadorans, Haitians, and all those who live with spatial and temporal paradoxes as communities dealing with "new forms of membership, and the work that is entailed in re-assembling groups" (Coutin 2010: 50–52).

All diasporic migrant communities attempt in some way to re/member where they come from, but I argue that they are also dismembered in ways that are not discernible. The story of how Vietnamese refugee politics became a kind of corporal "body politics" must be historically situated in the national body of South Vietnam. In the United States, Vietnamese Americans are most frequently compared to Cuban Americans for their hatred of all things communist and their political conservatism (Herrera 1998; Gibbs and Goodall 2009). Today, these older refugees display what one report calls an unremarkable degree of economic assimilation, which has much to do with the fact that such refugees come from countries of origin with a "common legacy of American military intervention" (Vigdor 2008: 7). Whereas Cuban refugees fled their homeland as a result of U.S. conspiracies against Cuba, once a former U.S. colony, what makes the Vietnamese American case unique is the historic alliance between the United States and its semi-autonomous client state, South Vietnam. To date, there still exist few accounts of Vietnamese Americans' political organizing, and why it is so foundational to Vietnamese American identity (Valverde 2012; Dang 2005). Many Americans attribute the ongoing protests of former refugees to foreign Third World people adjusting to First World democracy, or nostalgic "homeland politics" and anti-communist "red-baiting," a symptom of the inability of "these people" to assimilate into a mostly Anglo-American civil society (Ong and Meyer 2004). I take umbrage with the blanket interpretation of refugee politics, because it fails to consider the dismembering historical and geopolitical processes that separated members of the community from one another. This chapter dissects the anatomical complexities of refugee body politics, as it erupts within Orange County.

Political protests occur frequently on a major scale in southern California, because it is home to the largest number and concentration of Vietnamese in the United States (Do 1999). The ethnic enclave, from an outsider perspective, seems tight-knit, but this view ignores the many forms of symbolic dismemberment and rememberment happening here. The central place of the South Vietnamese soldier and armed forces in the Vietnamese diasporic imaginary is best represented by the Vietnam War Memorial in Westminster, California, which opened to the public in 2003. It features a statue of an American soldier and South Vietnamese soldier standing side by side with an accompanying plaque that casts them as defenders of "freedom and democracy." By focusing on soldiers, the memorial fails to speak to the various discourses of the Vietnamese as foreign allies, immigrants/refugees, racial-ethnic minorities, and Asian Americans "by validating these discourses through the figure of the anticommunist male soldier, [which] renders invisible the rest of the Vietnamese American community" (Nguyen 2005: 27). The desire to reimagine the political, according to Viet Nguyen, needs to be awakened given that there are many who are subordinated in the community and who are excluded or left out of an overly militarized memory of the war and its participants. We can ask then why is the presence of the military so strong in the diasporic imagination? How do former RVN soldiers stand for South Vietnam in ways that exclude others, especially given gendered dynamics and generational aspects of postwar memory?

Dismemberment as a metaphor describes the ways certain communities exclude certain members within communal spaces of living and self-representation. It is a term first attributed to the community psychologist Manuel Calvino (1998), who argues that academic professional fields like psychology tend to be paternalistic, trying too hard to be scientifically objective or politically neutral, without thinking about actual people living in communities, their histories, and their political self-presentation as "dismembered" communities. A community's dismemberment can be counteracted by what artist-scholar Aaron-Taylor describes as the politics of "rememberment," the conscious or unconscious effort to reassemble broken lives into something workable for the future (quoted in McNichols 2010). In terms of remembering those forgotten in history, "rememory" serves, according to Toni Morrison (1991), to take pains to show respect for the "disremembered and unaccounted for" (336). For many Vietnamese living overseas away from Vietnam and after the fall of South Vietnam, the attempts to make whole their experience as refugees often takes shape in attempts to cobble together lost family members as well as a dismantled nation. In their combined efforts to combat dismemberment from the nation-state through rememberment, refugees share a common identity also riven by internal divisions and the memory of "an uprooting, a dismemberment . . . unwillingness to leave their native land" (Tran 1993: 71).

My conceptualization of community dismemberment/rememberment—cultural, political, historical—does not merely reproduce the multicultural refrain of celebrating a community's victory over hardship, but it seeks to comprehend how the refugee experience leads community members to continually become cut off from one another, even as they try to love one another and recall their common struggles. It also reflects the ways in which those detached parts of our lives that separate us from one another also come together into a refugee politics of memory. Dismemberment finds semantic value in its nefarious associations with torture and corporal violence; but it also presents a rich conceptual lens through which to locate justice and solidarity within what appears to be reactionary politics in exile communities, while honoring those geopolitical histories of violence from which people came. Rememberment on the other hand hints at how a former community or fractionalized nation comes together despite the odds, rather than being destroyed altogether. It can refer to the unspoken loss and detachments felt by those who have lost family members and homes as well as aspects of their former selves during or after war. My attention to the dismembering processes at stake in refugee body politics seeks to understand how displaced "stateless" peoples construct or reconstruct their nationalist imaginary without a formal territorial geography to now claim as theirs. A threefold argument is offered in this chapter: (1) Vietnamese American cultural politics around gender, family, art, and identity serve an active creative negotiation of South Vietnam's legacies; (2) postwar community formation exists not as a singular homogenous formation but as a striated gendered struggle over local power and knowledge; (3) diasporic politics shed light on ongoing queer feminist struggles for Vietnamese political agency and community-building.

F.O.B. II: Art Speaks and the Community Responds

The Vietnamese American Arts and Letters Association (VAALA) is an arts advocacy organization based in Orange County. As a community-based nonprofit, VAALA has fostered a number of arts-related programs, presenting educational programs that explore Vietnamese expressive culture, providing a way to open up space for dialogue within the community and around the globe. The "F.O.B. II: Art Speaks" show fueled a public firestorm, attracting hundreds of protesters because it featured artworks that manipulated the design of the South Vietnamese flag (also called the Freedom and Heritage flag by refugees) or replicated the image of Hồ Chí Minh and flag of socialist Vietnam in ways many found disrespectful.[1] F.O.B., which stands for "Fresh off the Boat," was used as the title of the show to repudiate one-dimensional stereotypes about Vietnamese people as newcomers. This linguistic re-appropriation pushes against past constructions of the Vietnamese as unwanted refugees, moving from objects of derision to a people with a strong political voice. One can admire the protesters for shaking up the Asian American "model minority" stereotype of passivity, and while the forms of opposition against VAALA were detrimental and sometimes despicable, an aspect of the protests were also viewed as necessary in exposing the dismemberment of the refugee community.

In January 2009, the F.O.B. II show was scheduled to take place in Santa Ana, California featuring 50 artists working in different artistic media. Most of the art featured was contemporary or postmodern art, expressing the perspective of mostly young artists born after the war. This show attracted considerable media attention as well as arousing fulmination from more conservative sectors of society who found some of the artworks not only communist-inspired but also slanderous toward South Vietnam. While opening ideological blind spots in the work of anti-communism, I also analyze the artworks that garnered the most public interest to peel away the layers of the South Vietnamese historical experience that were not conveyed in U.S. media coverage. Throughout we will explore how art, gender, and anti-communism speak to more than generation gaps, but to incongruent ideas about Vietnamese identity and creative expression (Collet and Selden 2003).[2] In a community with a knee-jerk reaction to anything that smacks of "communism," art still triggers the un-manageable loss of the South Vietnamese nation, that even 40 years later never fails to fan the flames of anger, especially when artists reproduce the hated flag of communist Vietnam or manipulate that of South Vietnam, inviting criticism for two different reasons.

While VAALA does not shy away from controversial issues, F.O.B. II was one of its events where politics was fronted, one in which curators hoped would jar deep reflection and self-reflection. The first F.O.B. Show, held in 2008, contested the perception of all Vietnamese Americans as foreigners or F.O.B.s within mainstream American society. The inspiration for the F.O.B. II exhibit emerged through the fallout from the 2009 "foot spa" controversy. Chau Huynh, an artist and student, painted a foot spa tub yellow, bisected by three bright red stripes in the style of the South Vietnamese flag, constructing an art piece that honors the achievements of her mother-in-law who for many years labored in a nail salon. Certain Vietnamese Americans perceived it as a mocking reference to the beloved flag of South Vietnam, since the foot is the dirtiest part of the body according to Vietnamese custom, and branded it communist propaganda intended to offend the community.[3] Photos of the artwork were published in a local Vietnamese American newspaper, and two editors were fired after protests erupted over the fact that the newspaper even dared to publish the photos.

Using the concept of dismemberment here, a part of the human anatomy serves as a metonym for the remains of South Vietnam and its severed "geo-body" (Winichakul 1994). The artist focused on the foot spa to pay artistic tribute to the physical sacrifices of her ancestors. Meanwhile, her detractors were fixated on the foot as revealing the "dirty" intentions of the piece, singling out the human appendage and misplaced South Vietnamese flag as objects standing outside the imagined wholeness of the South Vietnamese nation and diaspora. Unintentionally conjuring the psychosomatic damage of war, the artist's goal of marking achievement out of historical loss was misinterpreted as butchering and maiming her people's struggle. In this context, the fight over artistic meaning then becomes the political vehicle for understanding the desire for community rememberment, propagating the "value of the heritage that one has received in an undivided form" (Renan 1990: 19).

The fallout from the foot spa incident inspired VAALA organizers to encourage new vocabularies for coming together. As an organized response to the foot spa incident, the F.O.B. II show takes pains to break through political cleavages (communist vs. anti-communist, conservative vs. liberal) and establish more open lines of communication. "We felt this prevailing fear around the Vietnamese community after the foot bath incident," commented Tram Le, one of the show's curators. "I felt the community was on this slippery slope, that we were not progressing toward having open dialogue and being more tolerant of different political viewpoints" (Tran 2009). Both the curators, born in Vietnam and migrating to the United States at an early age, were young enough to remember South Vietnam. Their "dual nationality" helps to expose the war politics carried between the older first generation that lived most of their lives under war and the second generation born in the United States. To challenge the response to Chau's artwork, the show's curators put out a public call for a show featuring artists who could reimagine the political stakes of the community. Refugee history then should not only be connected to anti-communist politics but must spur talk about different opinions on the war and what South Vietnamese means.

Yet, the firestorm that consumed the foot spa incident would also embroil the F.O.B. II exhibit, serving as a lightning rod for further controversy. While the first F.O.B. show six years earlier was not seen as controversial, as the purpose of the show was not meant to be overtly political, F.O.B. II was organized as an act of political solidarity with the foot spa artist (included in the F.O.B. II exhibit).[4] As curator Lan Duong (2009) stated in her essay for the art show's catalog entitled "Vietnamese Americans and the United States of War":

> While war continues in the national and international arenas, we, as a community, must also address the war that burns inside our own borders. I understand that this particular and political form of expression must have a place in American national culture because our voice has often been silenced and grossly misrepresented.

Duong suggests an analogy between large-scale wars which create refugees and the mini-wars erupting within refugee communities themselves. Duong pushes for an understanding of Vietnamese American minority identity that is critical and self-reflective. "If the past is thus reconstructed by Vietnamese Americans to concretize a sense of futurity for themselves within the United States," she writes, it becomes imperative to "investigate the mandates for this elemental passage from past to future" (2012: 184). As the F.O.B. II controversy raged on, the United States was in the final stages of pulling out all troops from Iraq.[5] Recasting political fights within refugee communities as a metonym and metaphor of warfare, Duong lends gravitas to the situation, verifying the ways the local is always global.[6]

A Community of Censorship and Expression

The exhibit was scheduled for January 9–18, and on its second day, the *Los Angeles Times* published an article about the exhibit with an accompanying photograph of the Vietnamese American artist Brian Doan, with two items that anti-communists abhor: the communist flag and Hồ Chí Minh. After being circulated on the Internet, the curators and directors received phone calls and threatening messages that demanded the show be closed. Within the subsequent days, the art exhibit evoked an avalanche of criticism and protests, leading to its premature closing on January 16. Upon hearing about the planned exhibit, Vietnamese

American newspapers, leaders, and organizations built a grassroots campaign through a web of forums to shut down this "communist-inspired" exhibit as they had previously done with other controversial art exhibits in San Jose, Westminster, and elsewhere. SBTN, the local ethnic television network in the local community, and *Người Việt* (Vietnamese people), a weekly newspaper published in Orange County, covered most of the activities on the protest side while also helping to mobilize protesters. While U.S. mainstream newspapers interviewed only the organizers' side, the Vietnamese papers captured the perspectives of VAALA and protesters, including statements from Brian Doan's father and the first Vietnamese American mayor in the United States, Tri Ta of Westminster.

Of three artists who garnered public reproach (I was one of them), the primary target of the political maelstrom was photographer Doan, whose artwork dwells upon central motifs of longing, identity, and desire within contemporary Vietnam and the Vietnamese diaspora. The photograph published was a diptych, or two images juxtaposed next to each other, hinting at what it means to be Vietnamese in all its dislocation, displacement, and disaffection from modern life. The piece distills Vietnamese life in separate locations—Avon, Massachusetts and Thu Duc, Vietnam—portraying two worlds in stark, colorful contrast. The Vietnamese in Vietnam is made incarnate by a young woman sitting at home in a room surrounded by signifiers of modernity such as a cell phone and a quiet portrait of domestic life. On the left, there is a photo of a professionally dressed man, standing alone in the dusky wilderness of the forest, a gothic natural enclosure, brooding and ominous in its presentation of a comfortably middle-class diasporic subject. It is a meditation on diasporic space and time in the cold, alienating foreign environs. Conversely, the woman on the right exists in the homeland seemingly yoked to the socialist past (signified by the bust of Hồ Chí Minh) even as she is chained to a cosmopolitan global future represented by the cell phone. This juxtaposition of color, mood, and artistic subject demonstrates the interlocked yet wildly divergent lives of Vietnamese people since the war.

The political powder keg was about none of that. It was about the young woman's t-shirt, made of the colors and design of the official flag of Vietnam, a singular yellow star centered on a solid red background;

this design has become a common tourist staple for sale through Vietnam. The young woman wearing it is looking away from the camera—out a window, perhaps—while perched placidly next to a gold bust of Hồ Chí Minh. From one perspective, the woman seems to be peacefully habituated to her situation, enjoying the good life bestowed upon her by the Vietnamese socialist state. Seen in this way, she avows—or at the very least, passively accepts—the communists' promise of success and prosperity. But an opposite view is equally possible; the woman is full of rueful longing, mired in the doldrums of house arrest. She wishes to leave her captive immobilized life in Vietnam for a better one. The photograph's furtive meanings are multifaceted enough to elicit such contradictory interpretations.

Despite the ambiguity of the photo, protesters were selective and overly political in their interpretation of this piece, zeroing in on the part of the work most reminiscent of their painful ordeal as refugees, the image of Hồ Chí Minh and the communist flag. In short, they did not read the piece as a whole, but dismembered it, rather than re-membering how the two halves fit together. In interviews, Brian Doan claimed the work is an open commentary on fashion, pop culture, and social life in contemporary Vietnam: "She lives in the communist country, but look at her," he says, "She's looking away, dreaming. She wants to escape Vietnam. Hồ Chí Minh is next to her, but communism is no longer in her. She wants to dream of other things" (Chang 2009a). The woman—possibly interpreted as a symbol of captivity—made Doan appear pro-communist.

Doan's artwork nonetheless generated political heat from two veteran organizations comprised of former South Vietnamese soldiers. These organizations led the protest movement by picketing, with a few individuals holding signs like "VAALA stabs the Vietnamese in the back" or "VAALA does not speak for us." With much of the vitriol focused on the use of the communist flags, such vocal protests triggered memories of war, where those "histories are fractured and retraced" (Lowe 1996: 6). Vietnamese refugee politics then is not a provincial matter about communism but a knotted site for sizing up the meaning of South Vietnam, with one active group engaged in a life-and-death struggle to continue protecting the name of a nation that fell too quickly to enemy forces after the Americans left them. The insularity of the community and refugee gratitude for resettlement in the United States means most protests happen within Little Saigon, and older Vietnamese rarely openly criticize the U.S. government or military.

Recognizing the significance of the South Vietnamese nation for the older generation, a few young Vietnamese Americans inveighed against VAALA out of respect for their elders. *Thanh Niên Cờ Vàng* (TNCV), which loosely translated into English as the youth organization of the South Vietnamese flag, is a group of Vietnamese American youth who fight for human rights and freedom in Vietnam and promote the South Vietnamese nation. Phuc Nguyen, a representative for the organization, said on an online forum that they were not protesting to infringe upon the rights of individual expression, but because displaying the art could be compared to showing images of Hitler in a Jewish neighborhood. As a child of refugees, Nguyen writes: "the symbols you rationalize as art in your exhibit ARE the very reasons why so many Vietnamese Americans are F.O.B.'s." Another second-generation youth said the exhibit is "insulting to Vietnamese women," dividing generations further, degrading the sacred cultural symbols of the people.[7]

Before the opening of the show, protests were already growing outside the exhibit; more protesters arrived even after a contested decision by the VAALA board to close the show down earlier than planned. Controversy exploded, with numerous online bloggers calling Doan a propagandist for socialism. His father, a former high-ranking official in South Vietnam, came out publicly to denounce his son in Vietnamese newspapers and even stopped speaking to him. Such familial disowning and dismembering is symptomatic of the community's own splintering, geographically and politically. The depth of the backlash and the torrent of emotions unleashed—seemingly out of proportion to the thing itself—reveals the depth of resentment among refugees toward communism. The uproar had much to do with the fact that the vets did not think that the Communist flag should *ever* be depicted anywhere, even in art. The presence of Hồ Chí Minh added to the inflammatory power of the t-shirt, considered not so much a common article of clothing but a battle flag.

As the second artist targeted by protesters after Brian Doan, Steven Toly (a Vietnamese American using a pseudonym to avoid being a political target) finds the censorship of people in Vietnam similar to the

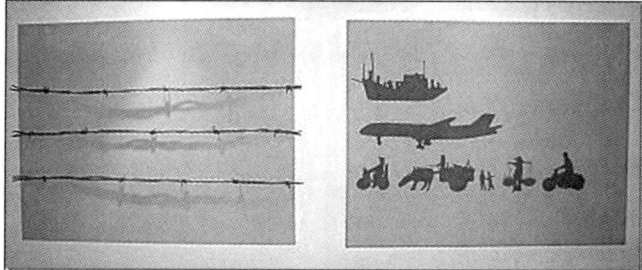

Figure 3.1. *Untitled* and *By Land, By Air, Or By Sea* by Steven Toly (photo by VAALA).

forms of social control exercised within refugee communities where dissenters are suppressed. His piece *By Land, By Air, Or By Sea* depicts the several ways South Vietnamese refugees got out of the country (see figure 3.1). This image of refugee transportation faces an adjacent piece *Untitled*, which redesigns the South Vietnamese flag with the red stripes replaced by red barbed wire, a gesture to reeducation camps. Toly's piece demonstrates how Vietnamese refugee anti-communism is always connected to the historical alliance of the United States with South Vietnam, reflecting a type of "recombinant history" that consummates "Vietnamese historical memory of the American War with images of the Vietnam War in U.S. popular culture" (Schwenkel 2006: 16). This painting makes sense of the reconstitution of South Vietnam in Vietnam America, and how refugees became political prisoners, sometimes of their own making, after the war. The United States plays a leading role in assisting the South Vietnamese in absconding from a moment of unfreedom into another state of unfreedom. In this vein, the American gift of freedom to the South Vietnamese turns into the "gift of barbed wire" (McKelvey 2002). The two pieces, when read together (they are literally placed next to one another in the exhibit), denote refugees moving from one state of war into another; the pieces lay bare the fallout of the U.S. Vietnamization project and the unsolved question of the South Vietnam nation.

Along with Toly and Doan, I was one of the three most controversial artists singled out by protesters and politicians. What angered people was a mixed ink print and oil painting entitled *Super F.O.B. Beauty Queen*, which scrutinized and poked fun at the way the young, attractive

Figure 3.2. *Super F.O.B. Beauty Queen* by Long T. Bui (photo by author).

female refugee body serves as the emblem of the Vietnamese American ethnic economy (see figure 3.2). Inspired by pop and communist propaganda art, this work of satire plays off the ubiquitous use of beauty queen pageant winners to sell commercial products.[8] I wanted to gesture toward the popular use of female iconography to "sell" the merits of South Vietnamese people, where ideas of Asian femininity and ostentatious beauty are tied up in an ethnic political economy marked by mostly male leaders and "the prevalent use of sex to market the diasporic Vietnamese entertainment industry" which often seeks to stimulate the male gaze and phallic "member" (Lieu 2011: x). Despite sometimes muted American ideals, the overall prideful tone of beauty pageants, celebrations, and musical extravaganzas commemorates South Vietnam through pictures of pretty, smiling young women who by default must be staunch supporters of the anti-communist cause (ibid.). In this context, the pun in "re-membering" the nation connects "men's sexed bodies with individual and collective processes of memory" (Jolly 2008: 6).

At one of the exhibit showings, one woman yelled at the organizers for displaying this type of disrespectful "trash." An angry commentator on an anti-communist blog questioned my rationale for the piece.[9] Calumniating my artwork as an attack on the South Vietnamese flag, he found my work "unreasonable," "debased," "immoral," and "evil" by merging the designs of the communist and South Vietnamese flags with images of Viagra: "no matter what your explanation is, it still is an evil idea that is unforgivable. What is it [this image] telling you? The overseas culture is disgusting? Even a young child knows that the overseas Vietnamese community is a thousand times better than the [communist] Vietnam" (*Bài Viết* 2009). *Super F.O.B. Beauty Queen* roiled some individuals by alluding to the power of feminine subversion and authority (it is the beauty queen who holds the bottle of Viagra in *her* hands), gesturing to a new generation of young women shaping cultural image-making despite their own sexual commodification. I hoped to diffuse the seriousness of Vietnamese American political discourse through the subversive power of humor, but my use of the exiled flag, aphrodisiacs, and women's bodies proved explosive and highlights the ways second generations like myself are put in our place as "children."

The public artwork of the male artists like Brian Doan and myself puts to use a prickly gendered discourse on F.O.B. II, even though the exhibit featured an equitable amount of female and male artists. Male artists were the most visible cultural producers, but their work had to be vigorously defended by nearly all women organizers doing much of the hidden labor that supports community events. My artwork sought to unambiguously expose how young women's bodies serve as value-extraction for the commercial propagation and political aims of elderly leaders. One older protester spoke to the organizers, claiming that I showed insolence toward the flag of the RVN, for not designing the *whole* South Vietnamese flag on the woman's sash, even though I intended the unfinished stripes as part of the abstract design of the piece and did not mean to draw the flag and the nation it signifies as "incomplete." Such dismembering interpretations of artwork confront the unflappable view of the South Vietnamese project as incomplete, needing to be finished.

On the Pain of the First Generation

Countering the idea that anti-communists were close-minded and the artist more liberal, Phan Tan Niu, the president of the Federation of Former Republic of Vietnam Veterans in Southern California, told the newspaper that "VAALA should be more open; they can speak louder by apologizing one way or another" (*Người Việt Daily News*). Through publicly circulated comments like this and online petitions, the point was made that the artists were, in fact, the close-minded ones, putting refugees who have already endured so much through more pain. They found the VAALA artists to be "too educated" and "spoiled," refusing to give any acknowledgment or payment to sacrifices made by the war generation.[10] Beyond the street protests, there was a widespread Internet-based campaign against the F.O.B. II show, since online sources have traditionally mobilized dispersed Vietnamese communities (Lieberman 2003). Buzz was generated through weblogs, emails and online letters condemning the show and its organizers. A letter written by Assemblyman Van Tran and signed by other political leaders was sent to the director of VAALA organizers with a request to "discontinue the use of offensive materials." It was signed by the mayor of Westminster city (the commercial hub of Little Saigon which spans all of Orange County) and city council members of several surrounding cities.[11] Tran's request to VAALA to close its show revolved around his South Vietnamese ideas of communist influence rather than issues with free speech, which would make his stance antithetical to American civil rights. In a news interview with the *Orange County Register*, he said: "I don't see it as censorship at all. I don't see it as art. Some of the offensive pieces—it's more propaganda than art . . . I don't see where the creativity is at all" (Chang 2009a).

Unsolicited phone calls made to the VAALA office comprised of older folks came from anonymous individuals who threatened to physically harm the female artists, whom they further demeaned with sexualizing epithets like "sluts." Many wanted the show curators to remove Brian Doan's "offensive" artwork from the show as a display of respect to elders. According to Lan Duong (2012), the women organizers were seen as traitors rather than translators of culture to the outside world, precisely because they pose a historic threat as treacherous subjects in their willingness to counter "the dominant narratives of Vietnamese

American politics, which police the dominant narratives of Vietnamese American politics, which police not only women's bodies but also shape the narratives and rituals of what we are supposed to forget and remember" (181).

In this contestation over national symbols, South Vietnamese iconography provides fertile ground for a cultural politics that tethers feelings of postwar displacement and dismembering to the patriarchal reproduction and re-membering of the RVN. Following feminist scholars, I recognize that the nationalist discourses that occur in the diaspora contain gendered sexist hues because they prop up the human/familial body as a metaphor of the nation, and this corporal symbolism is how patriarchal cultural meanings are validated and reproduced, but they also justify acts of violence and corporal punishment in the name of securing that nation. The through-line of the body-as-nation metaphor is that diaspora must be wedged to filial ideas of the woman as an "unsullied sexual being," enshrined as a totemic figure whose highest aim is to give hearth to bereaved, transplanted groups that have lost their original "home" (Gopinath 2005: 15). Hoping to offer a bracing corrective to the idealized vision of their people as helpless refugee victims or military losers, many South Vietnamese male veterans stake their postwar politics on "domestic masculinities marked through empire" (Ngô 2014: 147).

Anti-communist politics acts as a way of policing the borders of the South Vietnamese diaspora, where national flags are not simply floating political signifiers but the synecdoche for the nation's "imagined community," the touchstone through which nationalism is reproduced, codified, and maintained in the diaspora with rewards given to its purveyors. South Vietnamese nationalism combined with a conservative anti-communist framework provided the raw ideological material and currency for Vietnamese American political organizing, since the first refugees settled in the United States. The F.O.B. II controversy did this by exposing the sacralization of anti-communism as a project based on controlling community members, especially the young who did not grow up under communism and may not care about South Vietnam. According to sociologist Linda T. Võ (2009):

> The Vietnamese suffered from foreign invasions, the civil war, and the aftermath of the war, all of which created internal chasms within families

> and within the nation, and the struggles to survive, escape, and re-create their lives left deep scars. Not surprisingly, these divisions will continue to politicize the first generation, but will also affect the younger generation, even those who want to avoid anything "political" and to establish their own agenda. (97–98)

As in any community, most people are not overtly political, but among these refugees, there is a very loud minority eager to protest the current government in Vietnam. Their efforts take any number of forms: from street protests to boycotting any artist deemed complicit with the socialist regime of Vietnam. Any form of art or representation that dares to offset the candor of anti-communism is considered a betrayal of South Vietnam. For the younger generation, there is a need to refute this form of conservative politics without appeasing or dismissing those who subscribe to the doctrine of *with us or against us*.

Caroline Kieu Linh Valverde (2012), in her study of Vietnamese American politics, finds a single-mindedness that emerges as a natural response to the dismemberment of the diaspora. "At the very core of all the protests lies fear, fear that one's history and experiences will be forgotten and one's suffering will not be remembered . . . The effort to hold on to one truth, history, and experience effectively brings the community to a standstill" (112). However, Valverde is critical of the older generation's response and its impact on the younger generation. She writes: "Can they [younger generations] go away from the shadows of those mostly coming from the first generation with their strong views of what constitutes history and memory? Will the term 'community' ever be seen broadly by the people as holding multiple voices versus only one voice and one ideal?" (Valverde 2009).

F.O.B. II: Art Speaks was another test of that ideal. The ten-day show was VAALA's biggest multi-genre art exhibition to date. At the outset, the curators expected some negative reaction from the public. Featuring 50 artists from a range of backgrounds, the exhibit included everything from installations to poetry to sculpture. Participants were selected based on whether their artwork could "put politics on display" (Tran 2009). A special black room was created for the most inflammatory works, including some pieces that had been banned from Vietnam.[12] Rumblings soon reached such a magnitude that protesters convinced the local Santa Ana police department to close down the VAALA exhibit. Leery of the protests getting out of hand, the city government's injunction for F.O.B. II's closing occurred a day before a planned demonstration with up to 700 participants shepherded by *Người Việt Daily News*.

An emergency meeting led by the Association of South Vietnamese Veterans took place over the subsequent days to "find ways to oppose the [VAALA] organization that exhibited the images promoting the Viet Cong ... and bad mouth our holy flag, the yellow flag with three stripes" (Nguyen 2009).[13] Letters of invitation were sent to Vietnamese spiritual leaders, political representatives, civic and military associations, and the press to join the movement. About 50 representatives from different associations attended this meeting and provided their formal support to protest VAALA.[14] Representatives from this open meeting made a public call for all former soldiers to take a stand against the artists and "would like to call on the community of Vietnamese nationals to fix this problem" (ibid.).

Hai Trieu, a representative from an organization called the Vietnamese military writers group, argued that while VAALA may pretend not to be affiliated with communist authorities, it still plays into the hands of the Communist Party in Vietnam ("Cờ máu, hình Hồ và VAALA tại Nam California"). While anti-communist politics are usually seen as a tactic of vilifying and demonizing people as communists, I read this as indicating the interpersonal nature of Vietnamese Americans politics. The fear of being labeled a communist or "anti-community" led members of VAALA's executive board to step down and pull back from organizing the show, fearing that the anger would boil over into their personal lives.

For many people who are not Vietnamese and/or refugees from socialist regimes, the degree of hostility may seem hard to comprehend. It may seem extreme to most Americans that anyone would protest a picture of a woman wearing a t-shirt, but the depth of this antagonism is exactly what we must reckon with if we are to understand Vietnamese American anti-communism as the natural extension of anti-communist South Vietnam. Protesters object to the very presence of communist symbols, so they would be disturbed by *any* piece of art simply for including either the elements of the communist flag (which protesters nicknamed the "blood flag") or Hồ Chí Minh. They would be even more rankled with anything that glorified communism, so they would not have objected to Doan's art had it shown the same woman burning the flag or expressing *opposition* to communism. At a public meeting where South Vietnamese veterans were invited to meet with VAALA, organizers were verbally accosted, pushed, and manhandled before anyone even uttered a word. Such rudeness can be explained by "cultural" factors, whereby male elders feel superior to the young women, but they also evidence the pronounced effects of war upon postwar refugee interactions.

Artist Vu Hoang Lan designed a poster exhibit, featuring the flags of South Vietnam, communist Vietnam, and a black, undecorated flag. The exhibit was accompanied by a drawing pad, on which visitors could design their own flag as a way out of competing nationalisms, one that recalls the historic fact that South Vietnam was not one monolith, but a site of competing nationalisms (Tran 2006). For some reason, this artist was not met with the same spirited hatred, though he displayed the communist icon. Conversely, Brian Doan, who experienced great hostility toward his work, maintained his rights: "I believe in freedom of speech . . . I have a choice to eliminate some things in my work. But if I'm afraid and do that, the people (who don't like the photos) will win" (Chang 2009a). Ysa Le, executive director of VAALA, concurred: "This was an attempt to get a dialogue started . . . Our intent was not to hurt or offend the sensibilities of our community. We are part of this community" (Barath 2009). Le reiterated that the organization respects and honors all soldiers who have been part of reeducation camps: "We sympathize with the pain of everyone for us and our family also has such painful history" (ibid.).

This gesture of sympathy did not get a positive response from online commentators, who suggested that if Le cared so much, why would she even be displaying insensitive materials. The posters designed with flags of the RVN and photos memorializing the horrors of the communist state resituate the history and nation of South Vietnam as something that is not gone but still very much alive "here" in the United States. While anti-communism is a symptom of the older generation's loyalty to the South Vietnamese nationalist struggle, it also relates to their contemporary need to pass on the mobile dispersed memory of the RVN and to wrangle with whoever opposes this national memory. In their excellent feminist analysis of the F.O.B. II protest, Lan Duong and Isabelle Pelaud (2012) find that refugee politics feeds back into legacies of war, where "Vietnamese American acts of protest are not only tactical but conditioned by historical forces" (251). While Duong and Pelaud focus on the critical gender issues that erupt as result of the traumas and displacement of war, I identify these social forces as a product of U.S. military policies such as Vietnamization, which put the South Vietnamese nation in a bind to arm and protect itself against communist forces, and represent itself as a bona fide nation-state. Without understanding U.S.-South Vietnamese relations, anti-communism is taken as more than the sign of local disruption by war-torn refugee interest groups. By locating the politics of Saigon in the suburbs, they were responding to the fear that communism had infiltrated the O.C., and also "the fear that traditional hierarchies controlling the war narrative had been upended by acculturation in the United States" (Allen-Kim 2016: 167).

City officials felt pressure to close the exhibit and avoid upheaval; the police helped the protesters' cause by arresting the lone man waving the Vietnamese communist flag trying to incense the protesters but leaving the anti-communist protesters mostly alone. Representatives from the city made a call to the exhibit organizers saying they did not want to spend money to dispatch police to monitor the protests. Aside from wishing away the protests, the city's refusal to legitimate the show's right to continue exhibiting the artwork flies in the face of prior actions, since the city managers initially allowed VAALA to organize the show. Meanwhile, VAALA organizers had U.S. reporters on their side saying they helped "protect freedom" and First Amendment American rights.

The show's organizers decided that they would rather shut down the entire show—as a sign of collective support for artistic freedom and integrity—than bow to political pressure and remove the work of a few artists. After the exhibit was shut down, however, someone snuck into the galleries and defaced the artworks with red spray paint. Photos of the vandalized works were posted on the Internet and the defacement was later traced to a well-known anti-communist activist named Ly Tong. Tong, a former South Vietnamese military officer, vandalized Brian Doan's work using women's underwear and a tampon to scrub the photographs. The sexual symbolism of the gesture seemed clear: He sought to degrade the female organizers, even though Tong never fully explained why he did it. At the same time, he undercut an artist's piece, reducing it to mere filth. The fact that the vandalism was carried out by a former soldier of the RVN, and not some random person, says much about the militarized aspects of this personal act of sexual violence. Protesters made and brought their own informal works of art to contest the work on display at F.O.B. II. One protester even brought pictures of a girl in a red bikini wearing the yellow star in a design replicating the socialist Vietnam flag, standing up and urinating into a bust of Hồ Chí Minh. These protesters called their works "real art" to diminish the elevated status of F.O.B. artists. The referential iconography of the Vietnamese female—whether pictured in terms of the commonality (a woman in a t-shirt) or the sexual (a woman in a bikini). If protesters can bring a picture of a scantily clad woman urinating in a toilet, the question of who is being disrespectful to the community seems multi-sided. In her study of Pinay American daughters and their families' regulation of their sexuality, Yen Le Espiritu (2003) recognizes that women are "responsible for holding the cultural line, maintaining cultural boundaries, and marking cultural differences" (172). As Espiritu goes on to say, these norms in terms of cultural authenticity make immigrants morally superior in the face of feeling helpless and invisible as new arrivals in the United States: "Enforced by distorting powers of memory and nostalgia, this rhetoric of moral superiority often leads to patriarchal calls for cultural 'authenticity,' which locates family honor and national integrity in its female members" (178).

An editorial from the *Orange County Register* found Ly Tong's vandalism not only damaging to the artists but also damaging to freedom of speech and expression "which are granted to us by the American Constitution" (Chang 2009b). The article's author also mentions President Barack Obama's inauguration to underscore his point about freedom: "As we celebrate freedom, equality and new beginnings, let us not condone criminal acts of destruction and censorship. We should think about moving forward, not backward" (ibid.). While the United States was galloping toward a democratic multicultural future epitomized by Obama's election, the Vietnamese protesters were portrayed as stuck in the past and acting out from old traumas and internal issues.

There are many threads of gendered and sexual meaning within refugee body politics, which can be confusing because the only artists mentioned in detail are men, a characterization that should not detract from the fact that the curators and organizers of the show were entirely women. At the center of the fight were VAALA's highly educated female organizers, and an oppositional group led chiefly by older and almost entirely male, South Vietnamese military veterans who were incensed by the show's liberal (feminist) attitudes. These veterans fought and sacrificed their lives to protect South Vietnam during the war, and then were imprisoned in reeducation camps after the war; many of them bear a dying hatred for anything related to the Communist Party in Vietnam. On the surface, protesters said they were criticizing the show's support of communism and lack of support for South Vietnam, but what they were really incensed by, at a deeper level, was changing gender and generational relations. This feeling of emasculation by the older military generation can be followed back to the Nixon project to "Vietnamize" the Vietnam War by arming the South Vietnamese militia with the hypermasculine power to organize their own fate and national security, though that was really the cause of their downfall. In a sense, the efforts of the F.O.B. II protesters to "Vietnamize" their newfound American homeland and exert political/spatial control over local refugee communities in the United States can be read as another reiteration of Vietnamization, reflecting the historical effects of the failure of the South Vietnamese nation-building project, and why a defeated group of military men want to assert their power again.

Vietnamizing the Politics of Refugee Anti-Communism

As historian Pierre Nora writes (1989), memory is a community's life in evolution, vulnerable to manipulation, projection, and censorship, while history is an incomplete reconstruction of the past. While history takes form as floating snapshots of what came before, memory helps cleave and binds together the group (8–9). Historical dismemberment caused by war and migration creates tensions within a group and its efforts to reconstruct a singular historical narrative, but the rememory of war and migration holds them in place as a group bound to remember (and live) together.

Anti-communism embodies the first generation's enduring belief that the war is not done, an act of refusal by the war generation to fall off the public radar and slip quietly into the national landscape as another minority or group of immigrants in America. In doing so, anti-communism keeps them and their history alive by producing a kind of "preservation discourse" that maintains their cultural integrity and authority at all costs (Yoneyama 1999: 80). Those who seek to articulate another discourse then must straddle the "line between free expression and traitorous behavior" (Tran 2009). However, it reflects a view of the South Vietnamese business and political elites who easily left Vietnam in 1975 due to their close connections to the U.S. military, rather than the hapless economic refugees who left in the late 1970s and 1980s. In her study of South Vietnamese veteran groups, Thuy Vo-Dang (2005) argues that anti-communism, rather than amplifying the mortifications of some communal past, becomes the vector for "actively constructing a diasporic community for the present and the future . . . for sustaining an identity and community in the present and serves as a pedagogical tool for the younger generations of Vietnamese Americans" (69). Anti-communism is pushed as an all-encompassing community issue for older Vietnamese Americans, though it is driven by those most tied to the U.S. government and South Vietnam. For this reason, Nguyen Qui Duoc (2009), an artist in the F.O.B. II show, accepts anti-communist protests as expressions of people who are presently asserting themselves as "a vocal presence that may offer them a sense of confidence and identity" after losing the war.

This vocal presence found allies in discussion boards and online forums rejecting VAALA for their lack of respect to the community.[15] The director of another local Vietnamese arts organization denounced VAALA organizers, firing off an emailed response to them as "disrespectful cowards" and "presumptuous fools" who think they could "engage" and even teach their forbearers. The open letter written by the director of the Viet Art Center captures this political tension, tying Vietnamese American identity to South Vietnamese refugee pain:

> No matter how young you were when you left VN, no matter if you were born in the U.S., no matter how perfect you speak English, no matter how liberal you try to be, you should not just "recognize, respect, and honor" the pain. You must "feel" the pain. In another word, the pain is in your flesh and blood; the pain is "you"; you are "the pain." You are different from the other non-Vietnamese media reporters, the other

non-Vietnamese artists, the other non-Vietnamese organizations, you are "Vietnamese refugees" and VAALA is a "Vietnamese-American" organization.[16]

Denouncing the VAALA folks while also claiming them to be inextricable members of the community, this Vietnamese American cultural arts leader disapproved of American reporters calling the VAALA organizers "bold and brave" while depicting the protesters as crazy or un-American.[17] Truong's statement at first glance seems to rehash the popular image of Vietnamese as always fighting with one another, a nation in constant civil war. The trope of community-as-family is powerful because it reinstalls traditional norms of being Vietnamese but also the political norm of being South Vietnamese; remembering the war is painful, but it is imprinted in all Vietnamese bodies. Paired with the view of VAALA leaders as being too educated, Truong arrives at the conclusion that one cannot think one can ignore the trauma of the older generation by attaining a college education; there is no escape from the psychosomatic pain of the refugee community. Even if born in the United States, one was still a refugee at heart and forever a "F.O.B." as the history of war is imprinted in one's flesh. She addresses the young generation as integral to South Vietnam's anti-communist struggle rather than as outsiders or observers to that struggle.

Truong considers U.S.-born children to be refugees *beholden* to the demands of the South Vietnamese nation whether they experienced the war or not. At the same time, Truong swiftly brands the younger generation as treacherous subjects, insurgents collaborating with outside communist influences. She "outs" the youth through a politics of shame, forcing them to recognize the primacy of their cultural identity as South Vietnamese subjects. As such, they must always "recognize, respect, and honor" the pain of their people; they must *feel* the pain in their flesh, in their embodied trauma that cannot be forgotten through their First World sense of entitlement or the benefits they gained as American citizens. Her statement makes the case that the refugee is not solely a legal or political designation but a cultural tradition. She turns the remembering of war trauma into a communal rite of passage and directs the attention of Americanized Vietnamese who are out of step with what the elders want them to be. In doing so, she rehearses Walter Benjamin's

(1968) keen observation that "our image of happiness is thoroughly colored by the time to which the course of our own existence has assigned us ... indissolubly bound up with the image of redemption" (254). The significance of Truong's quote represents all refugees as one large communal family, each as a member with their part to play, and if they do not, they will weaken the whole—a whole that must regain their losses after the dismemberment of South Vietnam.

To keep these community members in check, anti-communist youth leaders like Tina Nguyen called out artists for intentionally igniting outrage, seeking fame, telling lies, and ignoring traditional values.[18] Despite the lacerating public response, many F.O.B. II artists never viewed the protesters as the enemy, many of whom were their own family members and friends. While many artists involved in F.O.B. II subscribed to moral precepts based on progressive politics and artistic freedom, they represented not a singular vision of the Vietnamese diaspora but the "art of many Vietnams," as Nora Taylor describes it (2009), as there are many interpretations of what it means to be Vietnamese. Yet, the rememory of South Vietnam and its dismemberment creates blockages in the community agreeing on "where we are going" based on "where we have been" (Duong 2009).

While the United States seems to have largely "moved on" from the Vietnam War, Vietnamese Americans continue to live with the enormity of losing South Vietnam. This burden of remembering South Vietnam has not been well represented in the American media, which focuses on refugees being bogged down by anti-communism. Anti-communism and refugee memory politics are not exclusively Vietnamese; they can be the means for recalling U.S. abandonment of South Vietnam under Vietnamization, a historical device for understanding why refugees are not simply saying they hate communism or want South Vietnam back. Indeed, the push by refugees to constantly "return" to South Vietnam (rather than just a return to the Vietnamese homeland) is a political exercise that attempts to get some returns on their investment in the country that the Americans abandoned. In this way, Vietnamization is not simply an attempt by Americans to restrict concerns with South Vietnam to the Vietnamese, but also a Vietnamese American way of asserting pressure to always remember the American relationship with South Vietnam.

Indeed, where the *LA Times* was responsible for jumpstarting the F.O.B. II controversy, it foreclosed these deeper meanings of Vietnamese political actions. Along with *OC Weekly*, another American major news source based in southern California, it reduced the protest in terms of a Vietnamese American identity crisis to the effects of their harrowing postwar refugee experiences rather than experiences as South Vietnamese people. Although the exhibit's organizers wanted to be sensitive toward the community, they also wanted to bridge the first and second generations. This redrawing of social boundaries was not meant to be construed as a political battle cry, yet in the mainstream news, F.O.B. II was presented as a "test to the community," as the *LA Times* put it, a quote from professor Linda Vinda at UC Irvine that was misinterpreted as a direct challenge to the community (Tran 2009). The situation was not helped by the fact that the *Times* reproduced only one portion of Brian Doan's artwork, dismembering the two-part diptych to broadcast the part with the woman and Hồ Chí Minh, excising the U.S. portion of the portrait to give the impression (whether intentionally or not) that the artwork was only about communist Vietnam.

To add insult to injury, an editorial in the *LA Times* argued that refugees' antipathy for all things communist prevented them from respecting American values like free speech, reiterating the narrative of the United States as the land of the free and Vietnamese as Third World outsiders. Vietnamizing the situation as merely a communist refugee thing, while impugning protesters for their demonstrated lack of Americanization, the article reasons that the passage of time will allow these people to see the wrongs of not conforming to "American traditions of political freedom of expression" (Parsons 2009). "What are some of the signs that an immigrant community has successfully blended into mainstream society?" the editorial asks, and then proceeds to say that the protesters "shouldn't delude themselves: People who would smite the artists and free-speechers have to know they aren't writing an especially appealing chapter in the ongoing American story" (ibid.). The ways the American media portrayed the show is a reminder of how older Vietnamese Americans are still largely viewed as F.O.B.s, castigated for being out of touch with current reality.

Internal standoffs and dismemberment issues in communities are downgraded to cultural assimilation problems, which fails to cut to the histories of war responsible for engendering such "intraethnic conflict" in the first place (Saito 1998; Cohen 1999). By saying the protesters are not writing an "appealing chapter" in the American story, this commits an unintentional act of community dismemberment, as though the experiences of Vietnamese Americans and South Vietnam are not part of U.S. history, rather than remembering the key role of Vietnamese people in that history. For the author who sides with the artists, refugee traumas and anti-communism belong in the past and outside the American nation. Vietnamese refugee stories do not form the core of American experience, only a disconnected chapter of a decontextualized story of American liberal exceptionalism. Such media coverage calls to mind the process I have been describing as "Vietnamization" and the burdens of the South Vietnamese people to fight for their legitimate political claim to exist. We could then consider anti-communist protest as not writing an exposé of the unappealing history of U.S. militarism abroad. Considering it in this way tunes in to the geopolitical contexts from which "local" refugee politics is fomented.

Refugee anti-communist politics appear outdated or disjointed from the politics of today. Such fights are seen as haggling over a passé issue. The main news reporter who covered the F.O.B. II story most extensively offered these comments in the *Orange County Register*:

> While I've written some stories about Vietnamese protests in the past, I don't know the whole history behind the protesters and their concerns. Yet, it seems like they have a lot of power if they can shut down an art exhibit that featured a lot of different kinds of work, much of it nonpolitical, plus get two editors at a local paper fired [the foot bath issue years earlier]. I thought the United States was a place where freedom of speech and expression are protected by the Constitution. But apparently, those rights are not fully protected or respected in certain communities here. (Chang 2009c)

The preceding quote provides a sense that though the reporter can write many stories about Vietnamese cultural politics, he admittedly does so with a poor understanding of those people's history. The author essentially "Vietnamized" the problem of anti-communism, restricted to older South Vietnamese adherents, while he normalized American society as somehow free of problems related to democracy. Another political blogger echoes these statements in harsher terms, labeling the anti-communists as "rabid protesters," finding it "ironic that the same folks in the O.C. Vietnamese community who scream about freedom also practice terrorism" (*Orange Juice Blog*, 2009). This reference to terrorism mutes the historical experiences of those who survived the Vietnam War, marking them as enemies rather than allies of the United States. These statements not only castigate the older generation, but dismember them from the narrative arc of the American story of progress.

In this new dismembering media context, one that repeats the dismemberment of South Vietnam from the United States under the Vietnamization program, I ask what politics means, especially in the way "Vietnamese Americans assert a version of South Vietnam history into U.S. politics, forcing (Vietnamese) Americans to consider the implications of South Vietnamese memories, stories, and bodies on U.S. soil" (Vo-Dang 2005: 76). Anti-communist refugee politics expand upon what Furuya and Collet (2009) define as the "ideological movement to parlay and enforce the symbols and history of the Vietnamese diaspora" against the Communist Party in Vietnam and provide cohesion to the Little Saigon ethnic enclave (191). Insofar as refugee anti-communism also links up to what it means to be Vietnamese in the domestic United States, such politics churns up the cumulative legacy of South Vietnam, beyond a nation consigned to early death under the U.S. policy of Vietnamization policy, making South Vietnamese voices as important in the United States and beyond (Wiest 2008: 276).

While the U.S. media might see this controversy as a conflict between immigrant communities and the demands of U.S. mainstream society, I deem the event as one of dismemberment/rememberment that unravels the separate ties between individual members of those communities. Insofar as many Vietnamese Americans have not moved on from the Vietnam War, as they are still saddled by postwar trauma and an unflagging disgust for communism (a stance that sits at odds with the U.S. government and its willingness to trade with communist nations like Vietnam), I read this shake-up as another instance of Vietnamization in the diaspora's continued fight for the livelihood of South Vietnam in the face of U.S. abandonment and neglect as well as forgetting. The F.O.B. II protest was not about Vietnamese political radicalism butted against

American liberalism; that notion is simple, and not surprisingly, fits well into snappy press coverage. It also likely rings true for an American audience, since it echoes Vietnamization's major selling point which is that the South Vietnamese should be self-reliant, but since they are their own worst enemy, their anti-communism falls into "bad politics." The next section moves beyond the explicitness of anti-communism to highlight how refugees subtly mobilize their abiding commitment to South Vietnam nationalism against queer bodies.

Queering Refugee Politics

Refugee body politics was on display for another controversy, one involving LGBT rights and religion, which took place in the very heart of Little Saigon. For decades, the Vietnamese American community held a parade in Westminster, California to celebrate the lunar New Year, which is considered the most important holiday for Vietnamese. A local controversy involving a ban on queer people, as I show, represents the political nature of mainstream Vietnamese refugee culture, which often shows up in annual parades in Little Saigon commemorating the Fall of Saigon, messages about the enduring legacy of South Vietnam in local festivals, and boycotts of any public figure who does not speak out against communism. The many Little Saigons that dot the landscape are not just cultural neighborhoods, they are political landmines. The Tet parade is hosted and paid for by Westminster city officials as a day to honor the economic contributions of the Vietnamese American community to this once suburban area, but also caters to this politically active electoral demographic. It features many local cultural organizations, but the parade is notable for featuring platoons of proud South Vietnamese veterans, marching in full uniform, flanking military jeeps that roll down the street. The sight, sounds, and signs of wartime Saigon bring to life the raucous violence of Vietnamese military history in the usually busy section of southern California. After many years of operation, parade funding was slashed in 2012 due to budget cuts, and this major cultural event was endangered until it found sponsorship from the Vietnamese American Federation of Southern California, a group that attempts to speak for community interests. With heavy financial backing from many conservative religious Catholic Vietnamese organizations, the organizers made the blank statement that gay people are not representative of the Vietnamese American community at large and were suddenly banned, even though the first LGBT contingent marched for the first time in 2010, in the process queering the usually heteronormative affair with its preference for young beauty queens and male soldiers (Masequesmay 2012).

The new parade sponsors tried to call on cultural tradition to explain the ban: "We respect their choice [to be queer], but this is not our tradition," Ha Son Tran, vice president of the Vietnamese American Federation of Southern California, said before the start of the 2013 parade. Gay rights, he added, are "not like freedom of speech" (Do 2013). VROC (Viet Rainbow of Orange County), an organization that empowers LGBT Vietnamese American youth, protested this exclusion, but parade organizers suggested the group create its own parade or, if they insisted on participating, at least walk behind or before the parade, separated from other groups by 30 minutes. VROC's leader, Hieu Nguyen, responded: "The point is coming together as a community. We're not less than—we're part of this community" (ibid.). Offering their own queer refugee body politics, VROC and its allies fought the decision, and they showed up uninvited to the parade, holding signs like "gay rights are human rights," using the universalizing rhetoric of human rights to find acceptance in a politicized ethnic enclave that has long utilized human rights as an issue to attack communist Vietnam and its potential conspirators, essentially any members who speak out against its conservative mostly Republican leaders. For a community used to constant warfare, the bellicose language of military fighting was invoked when Hung P. Nguyen, a member of the South Vietnamese Marines Veteran Charities Association, said in a newspaper interview with the *LA Times*: "This issue is too new for the community. Don't impose . . . the reaction of the community will be to strike back" (ibid.).

This statement from one of the parade's organizers reinforces the image of a singular refugee community still embattled by secret belligerent forces, one highly sensitive to being weakened internally or attacked by an outside enemy. (In the United States, queer people were often associated with communism, as homosexuality was reinforced during the Cold War–era "red scare" Canaday 2003). The Vietnamese Federation of Southern California sought to keep the torch of Saigonese nationalism alive by rooting out the hidden enemy, finding support from conservative Catholics speaking for a diverse community as one whole. It is the religious fundamentalism of an even smaller minority within this group that sets up political authority based on religion, something reminiscent of the presidency of Ngô Đình Diệm, the first president of South Vietnam, who was controversially accepted as the regime's leader by the United States in part because of his Catholic background, as it was believed that Christianized Asians were more loyal to the West. The military dictatorship suppressed the practices of Mahayana Buddhism, a religion generally ambivalent toward queerness. Though only 7 percent of Vietnamese in Vietnam identify as Catholic, they are a quarter of all Vietnamese Americans, testifying to the power of churches in sponsoring refugees. This sectarian and political background about South Vietnam was missing in the discussions of cultural tradition, family, and religion during the lunar parade event.

VROC lost its bid in court to force the parade organizers to include the group in the event in 2012 and 2013. The main legal question revolved around whether a private organization could ban participants, an action to which the LGBT organizers countered on the grounds that the public lands and municipalities where the parade took place should not discriminate against LGBT people (Potts 2013).[19] Councilwoman Dina Nguyen, one of two lawyers who represented the parade organizers, used the freedoms and liberties found in the U.S. Constitution to defend this exclusionary ban, saying in a public statement, "We respect everyone's First Amendment rights," while Mark Rosen, the other lawyer representing the VFSC, used the cultural argument, adding, the Tet parade is a celebration "to pay respect to the founding ancestors, paying respect to elders, educate youth about traditions, heritage and ceremonial celebration of the new year" (Kopetman 2013). As a cultural event bound to the remembering of U.S. liberal traditions or ancestral cultural traditions, the organizers believed that LGBT politics has "a purpose and a theme that strays and varies from the theme of the Tet parade" (ibid.). This statement affirms the fact that queer exile from families is somehow separate from the sense of exile refugees felt in regard to the homeland.

What seemed to be a domestic issue of gay civil rights involved a geopolitical and historical dimension. Blogger Jimmy Nguyen (2014) connected the fight for freedom, embodied by South Vietnam, to the fight for gay liberation in Vietnamese America.

Figure 3.3. Photo of parade protestors from *OC Register* (November 17, 2013).

After years of feeling they must hide, LGBTs need to be seen in the everyday fabric of Vietnamese American life ... Like so many other refugees from South Vietnam, my parents fled to escape the Communist regime of North Vietnam. My mom and dad wanted a country where they and their children could have freedom and opportunity. My father, who was a judge in South Vietnam, often reminds me that America is the greatest country in the world because, here, you can be and say what you want.

This statement queers the South Vietnamese nationalist project by connecting the queer diaspora of LGBT expunged from the home with the refugees exiled from the homeland; queers without a community or familial home are akin to stateless peoples. Essentially, the blogger flipped the heteronormative traditions and ideals used by South Vietnamese ethnonationalists and conservatives, invoking the legal system of South Vietnam (his father was a judge) and connecting it to American exceptionalism.

This point was made more apparent when VROC protesters held signs that said, "gay rights are human rights," tying the South Vietnamese diaspora's global fight against communist Vietnam based on human rights violations to the international fight against homophobia (see figure 3.3). Just as the Cuban American community is dominated by a conservative political elite, reflecting a whiter, economically privileged class, the pre-1980s cohort that opposed Fidel Castro's communist regime, the Little Saigon community is largely dominated by those business classes and politically connected families who had come from the upper echelons of South Vietnamese society and came before 1975 or immediately after Saigon fell. Both Cuban and Vietnamese Americans are most likely to vote for the Republic Party than their Latinx and Asian American counterparts, and their political conservativism is often attributed by the U.S. media to refugee exile anti-communist politics. A critical attention to history might account for the misogyny and queerphobia, which emanates from "traditional" Confucian Asian cultures, but it speaks more directly to the dismemberment of South Vietnamese culture. While local Vietnamese media outlets were reluctant to support the LGBT protesters, the U.S. mainstream media was strident in making the issue about generational clashes between liberal Americanized youth and "Viet bigotry" (Nelson 2014). The *Orange County Register* published an article with the title, "Vietnamese Americans to LGBT: Don't Join the Parade," as though the whole community was against queer people, the latter seen as radical interlopers erased of ethnicity (Kopetman 2013); this is a polarizing interpretation of outsider-ness reinforced by a post on a popular blog about OC politics with the title: "Gay Protesters Targeting Saturday's Tet Festival parade, in Westminster" (Pedroza 2010). In 2014, federation members again voted to exclude LGBT participation, but after the negative publicity that resulted from the media blitz by VROC and its supporters, a city council meeting in Westminster was created and the federation heads agreed to meet with VROC in "bilateral talks," the operative language of bilateralism evoking Cold War–era treaty conferences like the kind between the United States, South Vietnam, and North Vietnam.

Eventually, parade organizers caved to pressure from a wide coalition of activists, which included major supporters like the Union of Vietnamese Student Association of Southern California and local non-Vietnamese politicians, which included both Democrats and Republicans. While co-chair Natalie Newton put a media spotlight on the issue, expanding news coverage, VROC co-chair Hieu Nguyen convinced car dealerships and businesses to pull out as parade sponsors, which hurt the economic base of the parade. The confusion over how best to address the conservatives, and other internal issues, ended up with Natalie leaving the organization after the TET campaign was over.

Eventually, a Vietnamese American community assembly made up of local representatives voted to allow LGBT people back in the parade. In 2014, it was found that VROC could enter the TET parade again on the condition that they refrain from any public displays of physical affection or display any political uniforms, music, or flags to "keep the focus on those representing the United States and South Vietnam" (CBS News, February 1, 2014). While queers were now accepted as participants in the parade, and tentative members of the community, they were still absorbed into the orbit of Cold War alliances, as the rules of conduct were based on respecting the historic bilateral relationship between the United States and the RVN. The queer contingent became subsumed under the banner of representing "refugees everywhere" and human rights, instead of representing the internationalism of LGBT rights. LGBT participants responded ingeniously to these restrictive codes and recommendations to dismember their sexual identity by constructing a massive multicolored balloon and waving the LGBT-associated rainbow flag, alongside the flags of the United States and South Vietnam. Such actions show that a part of one's sexual identity cannot simply be detached from one's ethno-nationalist identifications. Cast as community outsiders, these activists put the language of LGBT human rights in conversation (or even side by side) with the mobilization of human rights by anti-communist protesters against the socialist state. In this way, they are simply "queering" the presumed heteronormativity of refugee politics and nationalism, and pointing out that all South Vietnamese are potentially queer subjects, never quite fitting into any normal schema of progress. The dismemberment of queers from the South Vietnamese nation can be countered by the rememberment of the fact that South Vietnam is a queer formation that never got a full chance to become a normalized part of the international community or family of nations.

Conclusion

When no "real" returns can be made on a history of loss, as the South Vietnamese nation-state is unlikely to be reinstated anytime soon, Vietnamese anti-communist refugee politics invites responses by those who refuse to see politics in such strict ideological terms. The F.O.B. II show and Tet parade organizers used community dismemberment as a political tool to push out non-conformists, even as such dismemberment addressed the emotional scars of the war and, in the process, revealed the historic meaning behind refugee politics. Efforts at opening the channels of public awareness were agonizing, but such disruptions to community solidarity can be read as creating the ballast through which silenced voices can be heard again within an already marginalized community. The casting of feminists and queers as outsiders to a community is a portable theme across diasporas, especially in those diasporas defined by the need to recuperate masculinity that comes with shame and loss on the battlefield.

How might refugee "body" politics then be read as a form of expenditure striving to unload or unbundle the shame associated with South Vietnam's vaporization as a national body? How might such refugee politics "Vietnamize" and geopoliticize the domestic space of the United States and bring foreign matters of war into the national sphere? How do community responses to efforts to recoup South Vietnamese nationalism—through sexism and queerphobia—attempt to capitalize on its memory of the lost nation as a salvageable thing for the future? Political conflict over the F.O.B. II show and Tet parade epitomizes an unresolved divide between those seeking to redefine traditional understandings of the community against the more entrenched nationalist ideologies that have presided over Vietnamese American politics for decades (Vo-Dang 2005; Aguilar-San Juan 2009). By observing the many cultural wars taking place in Little Saigon communities as an extension of the trauma due to war's dismemberment, but also postwar rememberment, one may wonder whether there is any place to tinker with quarrelsome issues that never find emotional catharsis. Time will not heal all wounds. Forgetting the war is not possible for those who still hold onto the memory of the unforgivable act of South Vietnam's abandonment by the United States and its destruction by the communists. In the end, the younger generation's desire to think about what it means to be Vietnamese American is taken as overstepping and fragmenting the community by members of the older generation. Impulses for intergenerational dialogue are at odds with an imposing rememory of a frazzled, dismembered South Vietnamese nation that does not allow for an easy truce. In refugee communities undergoing demographic and social changes, what defines "Vietnameseness" is becoming elastic and expansive, yet the specter of South Vietnam remains as a sticking point to understand this terminology.

South Vietnamese nationalism has long been defined by the battle against communism. Today, nationalists are facing the rise of newer voices wanting to break out a new mold of diasporic politics and community-based practices. Refugee body politics and the mobilizing memory of South Vietnamese nationalism expose the open wounds of postwar memory, plumbing the profundity of a historical trauma that won't quit. This is a haunted mode of addressing a question about belonging that does not require a full answer but one that must be answered nevertheless, especially by the youth who do not fully understand events that happened before their time. But as the first generation passes on to the next life, the second generation must still wage internal battles within the community, and sometimes they must fight external wars in other future Vietnams on the horizon.

4

Militarized Freedoms

Vietnamese American Soldiers Fighting "Future Vietnams"

Pledging to bring the Vietnam War to a close, Nixon concludes his 1969 Vietnamization speech with a nod toward another "Vietnam" in the future: "I want to end the war to save the lives of those brave young men in Vietnam. But I want to end it in a way which will increase the chance that their younger brothers and their sons will not have to fight in some future Vietnam someplace in the world." (As a "program for the future," Vietnamization disapproved of any more American lives being put in harm's way, as the president warned against the permanent conscription of the country's young into battle.)[1] Before it became a popular metaphor for drawn-out wars, the term "Vietnam" had by 1969 already taken on a life of its own. It was not merely the name of a country, but a concept laden with implications: a signpost for unstipulated future wars fought for America's global empire, a shorthand for costly military operations undertaken without a clearly defined reason. Nixon's reference to brothers and sons adds a gendered familial dimension to the national debt that war occasions; young American men fight and die in the hopes that future Americans do not have to. Unmentioned in this ode to warriors are the South Vietnamese soldiers who had fought and died alongside the Americans; or the possibility that some of those soldiers would someday be Americans of Vietnamese descent. Here we will explore the stories of Vietnamese American soldiers. With their symbolic capital as authentic storytellers or "native informants" about the Vietnam War, Vietnamese Americans hold some premium, even though their perspectives are occluded from mainstream America. As shown later, their narratives compose a dual sense not only of a past Vietnam but "future Vietnams" into which many of them are pulled, a double movement that turns the antiwar mantra of "never again" into "once again."

This chapter processes the thoughts of the second generation, studying the ways those born after a war still deal with or hold onto memories of war bequeathed to them by their parents and by the larger refugee community. For many Americans, the memory of the Vietnam War hews closely to a dulled sense of history that lends itself to historical amnesia and trauma. Jenny Edkins (2003) finds events such as the Vietnam War, though seared in history and historical consciousness, have also been largely forgotten in the American public's mind, since "forgetting is essential because for 'politics' to take place, the way in which the current political structures came into being must be overlooked" (229). In this sense, the "intensely political part of the fight for political change is a struggle for memory" (54). Embodying both the Vietnamese and American perspectives, Vietnamese Americans are "Vietnamizing" the mainstream American experience with the Vietnam War. In this chapter, I ask what young Vietnamese Americans are thinking as the descendants of South Vietnam, many of whom fled from war as children or born as children of refugees but who now participate in U.S. military ventures abroad.

Some questions to ponder: How does the failure of Vietnamization modeled as a sense of both South Vietnamese and U.S. military failures shape narrative strategies employed by Vietnamese Americans in talking about their identity as the children of South Vietnam and American soldiers fighting new wars? Can populations born out of war ever be truly *free* of their malevolent past? How do individuals of the South Vietnamese geopolitical diaspora reconcile their duties to honor, protect, and serve America when America failed to do the same for South Vietnam during the Vietnam War? Through the concept of "militarized freedoms," I can measure Vietnamese Americans' craving for freedom against the backdrop of perpetual warfare. Beyond the Vietnamese American case, however, the pluralization and militarization of freedom pose uneasy, broad questions about how freedom is articulated through multiple voices, and whether freedoms like national self-determination can be truly achieved through violence.

As there are no statistics on the number of Vietnamese American soldiers in the U.S. military, any empirical study of them would be incomplete. Consequently, a focus on personal stories, which are presented here in three distinct bundles, is required. First, I analyze some key quotes in the news media and how the media presents them. Second, I move on to personal interviews I conducted with Vietnamese American soldiers, dissecting the decision of Vietnamese refugees to enlist in the U.S. military as a way to honor their host country. Sitting with soldiers individually for hours on end as they talked about their families and careers, my oral histories with GIs document both their pride and distress in fighting post–9/11 wars in Iraq and Afghanistan dubbed "another Vietnam," revealing their mixed feelings about America "saving" other feckless nations similarly to South Vietnam. I end with a close reading of Quang X. Pham's 2005 best-selling memoir, *Our Sense of Duty: Our Journey from Vietnam to America*, and his newspaper editorials written about the U.S. War on Terror to discuss the creative labor of putting into language the demands of military service, especially when one owes duties to multiple nations and competing national histories. I focus on Pham because his memoir is the only one that has been published by a next generation Vietnamese American vet, it is the most prominent example, and remains quite arguably the most revealing memoir written by someone who can deal with the imaginings of "Vietnam" as a lost homeland and specter of future losing wars.

The stories of the second-generation Vietnamese American soldier were chosen as a case study because they offer a particularly potent lens through which to understand the essential questions of this book. That is because they have links to both the United States and Vietnam, like all Vietnamese Americans, but they are part of the intergenerational struggles within the community. Unlike that community in general, however, they have this specific tie to the U.S. military, bearing a unique vantage point on war and the United States' bedeviled relationship to the Vietnamese people, even though they did not actually fight in the Vietnam War itself. What follows is not a comprehensive study of Vietnamese Americans in the U.S. military, but an exegesis of the delicate, incongruous forms of storytelling that emerge from these culturally hybrid subjects, caught between "America" and "Vietnam," and through which they make sense of their overly militarized lives, and how the concept of militarized freedom acts as a form of negotiation found in dualistic national attachments.

My own personal decision to enlist in the U.S. Army stems from this dual sense of shame and pride, the shame of being a child of refugees, and the pride in being Vietnamese, shame for being a minority in a largely white country, pride as a U.S. American. As an individual within society, my decisions are not my own, they are weighed down by history and politics, circumscribed by the forces that help drive or inspire choices and imbue it with meaning. My taciturn father often brushed off questions about his navy service for South Vietnam during the American War, while my proud uncle conspicuously swirled around his home, parading badges of his military background, wearing the signature maroon army beret he once wore as a soldier of South Vietnam on the anniversaries of the Fall of Saigon. My uncle to this day reminds me why Vietnamese Americans must honor those who fought on the "right side" of the war against the communists, why we must always believe "America is number one," and why we must continue fighting to protect the honor of South Vietnam. These men's muteness and/or fervent dedication regarding a cause that seems no longer relevant impressed upon me the lasting effects of war on those who fought as soldiers on later generations still living under the legacy of that unforgettable war.

For many refugees, forgetting the war meant forgetting the sacrifices of those veterans, suggesting they died in vain for the freedom they so greatly craved. For a people who lost much, the love of nation—both South Vietnam and the United States—is an undying love for freedom and democracy, a love kept as an object of mourning, patrimony, and cultural loss. That fervent love is one reason why, when I was 17 years old, I enlisted in the U.S. Army Reserves. With my brother serving in the American wars in Iraq and Afghanistan, the men in my family served in some soldiering capacity hoping to salvage some honor out of a dishonorable past. While the men spoke loudly or kept their silence about military necessities, the women in the family, from my sisters to female cousins, carried the war stories into the next generation. In writing this book, I am in some ways accepting the call by women to always remember and to care about our family histories, something for me that recognizes traditional gender roles but also their fluidity. The interlocking dynamics of feminine memory work, which I documented in a prior chapter, and masculine military service has, in turn, allowed me to tell my/our collective story.

Owed to Empire: Paying Back War's Past Dues

If Nixon Vietnamized the Vietnam War, he set the precedent for later presidents to Vietnamize other countries. Vietnamization not only pertains to Vietnam but helps to understand the Cold War as well as post–Cold War eras, and America's ongoing engagements with the world from the Vietnam War to today. The script of Vietnamization matched a Cold War realpolitik about the South Vietnamese later applied to groups such as Iraqis, Bosnians, and Afghanis, nations also described as corrupt, helpless, unstable, or "underdeveloped." At a minimum, South Vietnam reflects the inequalities of a global racial order, as much in the present future as it does in the past. In the final calculation, Vietnamization bottomed out in delivering any payoffs or healthy returns on U.S. investment in South Vietnam, leaving Nixon to count down the days before this ticking time bomb imploded. Hedging the risks (and public relations disaster) of losing a war before a reelection year, Nixon wagered a bet on the nation's rigged future by stacking the odds against it. Acquitted from further liabilities, the United States could put the final cost and delinquencies of war onto the backs of its charges. The takeaway of Vietnamization and its other reiterations like "Iraqification" is that, while the walls of old imperial structures might crash, their effects may be long-lasting. The Vietnam War's conclusion as what Yen Le Espiritu (2005a) calls an ending-not-yet-over disrupts the victorious claims of the United States winning the Cold War. In losing its major ally to communism forever, South Vietnam represents one of "those landscapes that were not yet, and might never be, ready for freedom" (Atanasoski 2013: 59). What does it mean to wonder about the "arrested history" and "suspended future" of South Vietnam?

Since the South Vietnamese regime toppled, Nixon's term "Vietnamization" has evolved into a convenient shorthand to describe the precariousness of U.S. "democracy-building" projects in places like Yugoslavia and Iraq (Horowitz 1999; Laird 2005). As with the case of South Vietnam, there was no real victory in these instances of giving people the right to determine their own fortunes. Following the 2003 U.S. invasion of Iraq in a failed search to find weapons of mass destruction, Operation Iraqi Freedom came to a brutal, inconclusive end. The United States left as dazed and bewildered as it had been in Vietnam, not sure of why it committed itself to a zealous cause of terrorist "containment." The catalyst at least was a wish to exact revenge against Iraqi dictator Saddam Hussein, America's former Cold War ally, whose betrayal of the United States spells out the precarious nature of making friends in the declining age of American empire. After several tumultuous years, the American provisional military government disembarked from its project of constructing a "new Iraq," preparing the local people at last for self-rule as an independent democratic state. This new strategy called "Iraqification" required teaching Iraqis to arm and defend themselves against local insurgents with the expectation of the United States parting from this hotbed of political unrest, lest the superpower stay indefinitely as the country's administrative ruler. During this sketchy transition, the *American Spectator* ran the headline: "The Vietnamization of Iraq," where the author of the think piece likened the United States' bungling of the Iraqi War to the mess it created in the Vietnam War:

> "Vietnamization" once meant arming, training and supporting an ally so that it could defend itself and thus relieve Americans of the burden . . . [of] trying to Vietnamize Iraq, Vietnam is not a nation but an outcome. To succeed in Vietnamizing Iraq, they must . . . catalyze the nation's uncertainty into doubt, and then refine public doubts about the war into conviction that America should not fight it, and that the Iraqis must be left to their own devices. (Babbin 2005)

Vietnamization is understood here as a U.S. foreign policy to help allies, but also a neocolonial ideology and discourse that sought to make the term "Vietnam" into a positive outcome of war. It gives the reins of (artificial) power to those colonized subjects turned independent agents in a "Free World" built according to Western standards. It seized on the rhetoric of decolonization, so popular in the 1950s to 1970s—to foster relations of neocolonial dependence between the United States and a people seen as racially inferior. Though the term meant something specific in the case of the American War in Vietnam, the same line of thought contained in Vietnamization prevailed in determining the fate of Iraqis as a people who should solve their own problems without hand holding.

Rather than revealing what the Iraqi people wanted or desired, the logic of Vietnamization translated as Iraqification turned uncertainty about winning a war waged against foreign bodies into a convincing argument that an overloaded global Big Brother can no longer afford to fight in a war best left to his overtaxed friends. The *American Spectator* was in good company, as several newspapers and blogs ran stories about the "Vietnamization of Iraq" as the eruption of an older Cold War history through and against the shrewd, short-sighted visions of modern American warfare. At the height of the U.S.-inspired "War on Terror," news sources regularly printed articles with titles such as "Vietnamization: Enemy Body Counts Make a Grim Return" (Kaplan 2011). News writers correlated the "Afghanization" or "Iraqification" of the U.S. wars in Central and West Asia under George W. Bush as an exit strategy taken from the pages of the Nixon playbook (Diehl 2009; Schram 2010; Kaplan 2011). My main contention is that the conditions set by Vietnamization never expired, as they still linger as the coded militarized history and language for justifying American efforts to fight more wars and make up for Vietnam's loss, but also as a way to make sense of South Vietnamese loss. Vietnamization in this way defines the efforts made by the United States to bequeath freedom to uncivilized nations, but also the preemptive efforts to stem the great loss found in the potential failure of those failed imperial contracts between allies.

We like to believe that the United States has passed through the gauntlet of the Cold War unscathed and has achieved healthy economic returns from the global system thus produced; this vain belief in uninterrupted American progress subordinates historical memory to future advancement. This triumphalism drives down the market value of memory; it suggests that there is little incentive to remember the past—or to engage with complexities and contradictions and faulty fragments of memory at all. Instead, it appears as if the rest of the world has fallen in step with the "American way." Modern wars never truly end with a bang but create a "surplus" of military expenditures. In line with Jodi Kim (2010), I recognize the loose "ends of empire" as igniting the returns of war, generative of new imperial values and rationales. Kim asks how the Western discourse of "Vietnam" circulates ad infinitum through the protracted afterlife of the Vietnam War (196). Popular constructions of an abstract "Nam" as a relic of America's anti-communist Cold War past cloak the failure of the United States to tie up its relations with South Vietnam ("Nam" in Vietnamese means the south). The haunted memory of "Vietnam" as a Cold War flashpoint sneaks up on us again through new "Vietnamized" wars. The United States, I believe, will use the strategy of Vietnamization when it engages in war in the future just as it has done in Iraq. Though we cannot know what it is going to do in the future, I suspect Vietnamization will be a part of future U.S. policy as there are fewer resources to sustain long-term conflicts, but the desire to intervene remains great in order to protect America's global interests and its "friends."

Vietnamization and the Vietnam War are also part of the future for conceiving military service for Vietnamese Americans. In his study of the U.S. Defense Department's heavy recruitment of Latinx into the military, Jorge Mariscal (2005) finds that "the debacle of the American war in Southeast Asia produced a generation of young people wary of warrior masculinities, cheap patriotism, and foreign policy adventurism" (48–49). New generations of Vietnamese Americans, however, are wary of military adventurism not only because of America's mistakes in Vietnam, but because of their own personal ties to South Vietnam. Refinancing this double loss through U.S. military service, these new soldiers broker a valuable sense of personal security tied to nationalism, since the nation-state guarantees a "meaningful conception of personhood" tied to a larger cause, for without a country "the self dissolves into the evanescence of an eternally fragmented present" (Cuevas 2012: 609). Mariscal also warns progressive scholars against becoming too judgmental toward such militaristic zealotry exhibited by racial minorities without understanding that "security for these [working-class] communities comes together at the intersection of limited life chances, concerns about their children's future, and the militarization of the entire culture" (ibid.). Many Vietnamese came to the United States as penniless refugees, and their impoverishment is one reason many join the military—as a form of upward mobility. In this way, soldiering as a form of refugee pride is the overbearing expression of the U.S. military's racialized class-based forms of labor.

In the stories we will explore, military service becomes the means to project moral personhood, refugee pride, class assimilation, and national identity. In the process, these soldiers' confessions and personal admissions try to make sense of their coeval lives as the heirs of South Vietnam's legacy and as dedicated soldiers protecting America's future. For many of them, the irreplaceable loss of family and homeland makes them *obliged* to remember the Vietnam War as a personal debt of honor they must uphold; they are the ones who cannot forget the war, for it bears the name and the pain of their own people. Their acute awareness of the United States' dicey relationship with South Vietnam and the Vietnamization or U.S. abandonment of that war creates a critical stance toward militarism, despite their expressed devotion to military service. I tease out the abstruse ways these subjects negotiate their experiences with the seductions and ideological blinders of U.S. militarism. Similar to Dylan Rodriguez (2010), who plumbs the depths of why Filipina/os are so devoted to the American nation and military, I believe the incorporation of South Vietnamese subjects into U.S. empire transacts a form of permanent debt to former colonial masters, one that prompts thankfulness for receiving freedom from outside protectors but also resistance to intervention from foreigners through a historical memory that "articulates from within the constitutive violent and traumatic rupturing of American conquest and colonization" (48).

Freedoms that are militarized are freedoms given and taken by force, forever bound to the same war powers that conceived it. The muscular sense of militarized freedoms chiseled out of the Cold War is now reposed in new wars that almost repeat the same scenario in Vietnam. Indeed, the Vietnamization of the Vietnam War was one of the first steps by which the United States could engage in global asymmetrical wars, with the Americans in "remote" supervision of enemy territories. For this reason, the "future Vietnam" is necessarily not just Iraq or Afghanistan, but potentially all over.

The Vietnam Syndrome (losing in the Vietnam War) and the Vietnamization Syndrome (loss of South Vietnam to communism) led the United States astray into more wars, however reluctantly, through the need to take over foreign populations and speed up the ascent of those populations into America's global circle of friends. One of those terms that experts and journalists toss around with ease, Vietnamization is both confusing and powerful, a term that explains away the methods by which the shame and enterprise of war get transferred from superpower to ally. To think of a "Vietnamized" war or place as "another Vietnam" without remembering bad U.S. military policies like Vietnamization makes "Vietnam" appear as an abstract thing that revolves around the feelings of Americans, a sign of a self-fulfilling prophecy and harbinger of an inevitable fall from grace. Militarized freedoms, a concept that aptly applies to the question of Vietnamization, is a reminder of the historical past that breaks the abstraction of a U.S.-centered Vietnamization

Syndrome, where freedom is not something to be preserved, protected, potentially lost, or given to others by a superpower, but something that needs to be put into practice through military projects. Of consequence is the realization that there needs to be an inclusion of Vietnamese perspectives. In this way, it might be more apt to use the term Americanization Syndrome with its singular imperial sense of nationalist identity and assimilation of others around the world.

This pattern of conquest and liberation by force is supported by Americans' own historical ignorance about the price of their country's global push for power. As we have seen in the case of my prior discussion of the Little Saigon Community, Vietnamese Americans can be selective or partly skewed in their memory of the past, but those Americans who are not Vietnamese are by and large ignorant of what happened in Vietnam, and why South Vietnam still matters. In historian Thomas Paterson's (1988) estimation:

> Americans are notoriously lacking in an informed historical consciousness . . . Ignorance we know too well, abounds. Americans' understanding of the past is selective and discriminatory. Commemoration often becomes celebration. Negatives, failures, and embarrassments become mere aberrations in the march of progress. And the lesson they draw from such a reading of history is necessarily flawed and misleading. (1)

Americans retain power through a selective remembrance of the past, and they have the freedom to elect or choose certain truths that best fit their narratives. But such distortions give way to a defective reading of history that boosts national self-aggrandizement and shrugs off failures in the Vietnam War as "mere aberrations" in history. The failure of Americans to remember U.S. history in Vietnam and celebrate America's win in the Cold War leaves Vietnamese Americans in the cold.

The historical relationship between Vietnamese Americans and the U.S. military strikes a chord with the racialized experiences of other groups. Filipina/os, Chamorans, Samoans, African Americans, and Native Americans have all enrolled in the U.S. armed services in large numbers, not out of some inherent pride for America or talent for soldiering, but as an outcome of a neocolonial history compelling members of those communities to embrace the U.S. military state.[2] That Filipino/as are well represented in the U.S. Navy, for instance, derives from the long-term effects of U.S. annexation of the Philippines, followed by the recruitment, incorporation, and "forced assimilation" of Filipina/os a feminized labor force used to expand naval operations in the Pacific (Espiritu 2005). The expansionary power of American empire depends on the tacit participation of conquered populations in furthering the project of martial warfare.

Vietnamese are unique in their public recognition as war subjects. Whereas the histories of other colonized groups are not known by many Americans, Vietnamese carry prominence as living reminders of the first military conflict that the United States lost. Despite their general invisibility within U.S. mainstream culture, they are hypervisible as refugees, which gives them some leverage to tell their war stories, even in an ancillary role to American military narratives. Meanwhile, other Southeast Asian groups such as Cambodians are remembered for enduring the genocide of fellow Khmer under Pol Pot's communist regime rather than for enduring foreign invasions by the United States and its attempt to Vietnamize Cambodia by having the South Vietnamese invade their Khmer neighbors (Schlund-Vials 2012). Thus, the Vietnamization of the Vietnam War de-emphasizes how Laotians and Cambodians, along with ethnic groups like Hmong, Mien, Cham, and Kmu, were also affected by the conflict (Um 2005). For the Cham people who are indigenous to the land that we now call Vietnam, the term Vietnamization can mean the long historical process by which Vietnamese people occupied the Cham Kingdom (Ken 2004; Underhill 2014). In contemporary times, Nixon's intent to "Vietnamize" the Vietnam War as a strategy for letting South Vietnamese defend themselves against domestic enemies denies what actually transpired within international affairs, such as the South Vietnamese Army's invasion of Laos and Cambodia with the encouragement of Nixon to sabotage communist logistical bases in the early 1970s. Vietnamization as the United States' enabling of South Vietnamese military aggression not only against the north but Vietnam's neighbors inspired many covert missions to prove the ARVN's mettle, while "buying" more time with U.S. air cover for its allies (McMahon 1999).[3] The invasion of other countries by South Vietnam foreshadows what Vietnamese American troops would later do, assisting the United States to invade countries like Iraq and Afghanistan.

As a whole, it is hard to characterize the population of Vietnamese American soldiers, as they come from all over the country with diverse backgrounds. Little data exist about them and no one knows exactly how many Vietnamese Americans have enlisted since the end of the Vietnam War, or how many are women. The soldiers I chose come from a select demographic: they all reside in California, mostly Orange County, they are generally more interested in maintaining cultural identity, have more ethnic contacts than Vietnamese in other more isolated parts of the country, and are more politically active and organized. They represent Americans who are very in touch with their community. Despite all this, some are older (in their forties), old enough to remember the war, and there are those who are too young to fully remember but who are nevertheless conscious of their (South) Vietnamese-ness and how they are drawn close to the footprints of military history. Thus, they will speak for their overly militarized lives, by which I mean forms of existence primarily defined and shaped by war. Their words do not simply add to the demonology of that appalling American war in Vietnam, but truly "Vietnamize" the conversation to put at center the South Vietnamese refugee perspective. As becomes evident later, soldiers use a vast range of tools—from rhetorical ploys to political calculations to poetic sensibilities—to make sense of the Vietnam War and the U.S. war-mongering on their own terms. If we see the South Vietnamese as down-on-their-luck refugees or victims preyed upon by communists, rather than aggressors in their own right, then that means the image of the South Vietnamese gets frozen in time, suspended somewhere between America's imperial global march toward freedom and its constant returns to war—the Vietnam War and the Vietnamization of it endures as the reminder of U.S. hubris and how military strategies do not always go to plan.

Vietnamese American Soldiers in the News

Today, a twofold Vietnamization process is offered by Vietnam American servicemen who, as I see it, are Vietnamizing America's "Vietnam Syndrome" through their own accounts of their desire to protect their country's freedom, first as repayment for the good life they have been given as U.S. citizens and second, through speculations about how U.S. potential victory in Iraq and Afghanistan will serve as vindication for

South Vietnam's downfall. U.S. newspapers are aiding in that effort by publishing articles with titles like "Vietnamese Americans Repay the U.S. with Military Service," rehashing the common trope of refugees "giving back to America for having provided them safe haven" (Halloran 2005). Prominent in the public eye during the U.S. war in Iraq were men like Commander Hung Ba Le. In an article entitled, "Left Vietnam as a Refugee, Returns as a U.S. Navy Captain," he writes: "My father, my hero . . . was a South Vietnamese Navy commander and his career was cut short because of the war, so I wanted to follow in his footsteps as an officer [in the U.S. military]" (Ward and Bass 2009). In an effort to make up for his father's abbreviated military career during the war, Le seeks to render a kind of historical balance of payment. "We owe a huge debt of gratitude to the United States," another soldier says, arguing that military service is double payment for America's hospitality to two groups: South Vietnamese soldiers and refugees (Tran and Nguyen 2011). Speaking on a CNN television news segment called "Another Vietnam?," Army Lt. Col. Viet Luong, when asked if the United States will lose Iraq just as it lost Vietnam, replies:

> We didn't lose the war from my perspective. People would argue we're losing the war here [in Iraq] . . . we're not losing the war here. But if you ask me as a military man, "Did we lose the war?" Absolutely not. And you know out of the 53,000 U.S. soldiers that lost their lives there; I'm not going to disrespect them by saying we lost the war 'cause we didn't. Okay. But at the same time, we lost the conflict because of all the factors we couldn't control. The will of the U.S. people, the will of the government.[4]

Luong identifies strongly with U.S. Vietnam vets, honoring their deaths by referring to such loss in the first-person plural "we." He also makes an interesting distinction between "war" and "conflict," where war means the *will* to fight, but *conflict* denotes an arena far from the battlefield itself, and the harder-to-wrangle will of the public and of the bureaucracy. Such fine distinctions of terminology work through serpentine language, where Luong's use of the pronoun "we" takes on multiple valances to mean both the South Vietnamese and the Americans. While he states his fidelity to the United States, Luong identifies with the South Vietnamese government, despite its image of incompetence: "The South

Vietnamese leadership as a whole, you can say we're not entirely competent, you know, just like Iraq, if you pick the right people in the right position to run the country of their country, [this] will make a big difference" (ibid.). His identification with the former inept leaders of South Vietnam derives from his cultural identification as a child of South Vietnam, and his cross-cultural identification with the Iraqis. Like many Vietnamese American soldiers, Luong tries hard to validate multiple and sometimes conflicting military enterprises, hoping to defray the human costs of America's overly positive identification with military grandeur.

While actively employed, U.S. soldiers are prevented by law from offering political opinions in public about current government and military policies. On the flip side, soldiers can freely comment on *previous* U.S. actions and "finished" foreign missions. Looping back to Vietnam to comment sideways upon the current state of Iraq/Afghanistan, many of my interviewees expressed an "arrested" form of speech, speaking in an allusive roundabout way about Iraq through Vietnam to evade government censorship. Their linguistic "Vietnamization of Iraq" suggests that oral histories are more than an account of past moments in life but offer a temporally warped political critique of the present. That distinction seems like a useful one to note as soldiers' pluralistic ideas of being free—in the Vietnamese and the American sense—may conflict with the militarized freedom projects advanced by the U.S. government.

Vietnamese Americans often partake in military duties for the United States as a foray into celebrating their "dual nationalities" as Americans and South Vietnamese. Military police officer Thao Thanh Bui displayed this when he raised the golden flag of South Vietnam at his unit in Baghdad (see figure 4.1). Instead of going to the U.S. presses, Bui sent an email to the *Vietnamese Daily News*, a California-based Vietnamese community publication. Speaking for Vietnamese American soldiers scattered far and wide, Thao vows to forever prop up his South Vietnamese heritage, following on the heels of his forefathers in the fight for freedom and democracy, since "we, the younger generation, will never forget what our fathers and uncles have gone through" (ibid.). The U.S. government for the first time allowed the raising of a foreign flag on American military grounds (against the protest of the Vietnamese communist government). A major reason this ritualistic act could be performed is due to the technical fact that South Vietnam is considered

Figure 4.1. Photo of Thanh Bui in Baghdad with U.S. and RVN flags (photo from *Vietnam Daily News*).

a "defunct" country rather than an active one with the power to usurp U.S. sovereignty. The U.S. flag is shown in the photograph flying higher than the RVN flag, recasting South Vietnam in the role of junior ally once again. With this flag raising, Sergeant Thao conscripts his ghost country into the "War on Terror," implicitly placing Al Qaeda in the same category as the Viet Cong. South Vietnamese veterans back home responded heartily: "The Golden Flag is not lost. It is being taken care of by the younger Vietnamese generation wherever they are" ("South Vietnamese Colors Fly in Baghdad, Iraq").

While the mainstream news tended to whitewash the personal stakes of Vietnamese American soldiers in the Iraq War, online news sources and blogs are much more revealing. An Internet article for a popular forum on the war is entitled, "Another Generation's War: Vietnamese American Voices from IRAQ," which features the story of Tino Dinh. For six months, Dinh was embedded with Iraqi soldiers, training personnel and facilitating information swaps between the coalition forces and Iraqi military headquarters. Dinh, a captain in the U.S. Air Force, compares Iraq to South Vietnam, noting that neither country should ever cede ground to terrorizing militias. He says:

> What I believe is that abandoning the Iraqis would be morally irresponsible. We Vietnamese-Americans know this more than anymore. If America withdraws too suddenly, the humanitarian catastrophe would be unthinkable, not to mention igniting chaos in the region. . . . I think it is condescending to believe that non-Western cultures are incapable of developing enlightened, accountable forms of governance . . . the old South Vietnam mirrors that in Baghdad now. Still, this doesn't mean that Vietnamese or Iraqis should abandon the pursuit of democracy. (Thach 2009)

When Dinh was first notified that he was being sent to Baghdad, he initially objected, but once he was stationed there he began to feel a nagging sense of guilt and responsibility for the mission the moment he sensed a reprisal of Vietnamization; he feared that the downgrading of Iraqi military would replicate the hamstringing of South Vietnam. He refuses to capitulate to the logic of Vietnamization in Iraq and argues that the U.S. military must not hastily back out of their commitments to besieged allies, since an American foreign presence acts as an adjudicating force for democracy. Dinh equally avers to the claim that one can have it both ways, saying that other people can do things themselves, but the United States should and can help those people too. He advocates for U.S. military intervention but also for Iraqi national sovereignty.

As figures of double loss, Vietnamese Americans bear national shame two times over—the shame of the U.S. losing and passing off the duties of war to its allies, and the disgrace of the South Vietnamese regime passing away. These two albatrosses create a sickening burden they seek to relieve by taking up arms again in the hopes of defending freedom in future "Vietnamized" U.S. wars as "refugees and survivors to whom a kind of symbolic capital has been endowed . . . [with] supposedly authentic knowledge . . . about the Vietnam War and its aftermath" (Duong 2012: 17). But how does this symbolic capital translate into having the power to narrate wars? What profitable gains or returns on war, if any, are to be had from telling the story as one about Iraq being another

(South) Vietnam? Because Vietnamese Americans are the inheritors of the South Vietnamese legacy, it behooves us to further understand how their life histories sound alarm over the militarized state of the world.

Memories of the Past as Premonitions of the Future

The positive portrayal of Vietnamese American soldiers in the U.S. mass media contrasts with my more extensive sobering interviews with soldiers and my analysis of the novel and newspaper editorials of U.S. Marine Quang X. Pham. These tantalizing news bits are meaningful in exulting the Vietnamese soldier as both the functionary and beneficiary of U.S. empire. In 2013, I interviewed 11 members of varying military ranks and branches with the aim of getting a first-hand sense of their lives beyond the newspaper headlines. Only one of my interviewees was a reserve member and the rest, active-duty soldiers who served in Afghanistan and/or Iraq alongside tours of duty in Europe among other places. Chosen through a snowball effect and personal recommendations, I found a sizeable number of members from the Vietnamese American Armed Forces Association (VAAFA) who volunteered their stories. Though many were contacted through the Internet or in-person, many did not wish to tell their stories, owing to a sense of reluctance with regard to difficult political or family matters. For this reason, my interviewees are a self-chosen group of people more vocal in opinion compared to others, which suggests that there are still more stories to be discovered.

During intimate sessions, I was struck by the many paradoxes and eye-opening disclosures in my interviewees' interpretation of military history and strategies.[5] While many soldiers considered the United States as morally justified in entering Vietnam to fight communism, they also did not like how the it handled the situation, preferring that the United States would have stayed on longer to help the South Vietnamese. Others recognized the imperialist nature of U.S. military intervention in Vietnam. Across the board, all my interviewees believed the Americans should have stuck to their guns and stayed to the end, since these interlopers had already gotten involved in the conflict. Many thought that although the United States had not been successful in Vietnam, a success in Iraq or Afghanistan could avenge all that, *even though* they believed the wars in Iraq and Afghanistan could not erase the gaffes of Vietnam and especially the policy of Vietnamization.

All my interviewees, however, thought Vietnamization was a bad deal, and that the United States underplayed the need for a total military defense strategy for South Vietnam. According to Army Captain Michael To:

> I believe that if South Vietnam had won the war, we would be equivalent to South Korea in most aspects today. But we lost America's support . . . I think the South Vietnamese military did what they could have done by surviving for over two years when the U.S. military pulled out of Vietnam. . . . it was just a matter of time.[6]

Such rationalizing narratives from members of the South Vietnamese diaspora reflect the making sense of past injuries without clear exposition of who was to blame, the United States or South Vietnam. Almost all my interviewees had the following things in common: (1) they had family members who served in the military, especially fathers who fought for South Vietnam; (2) they were all refugees or immigrants sponsored to the United States; (3) their primary reason to join the U.S. military was to give back to their country, though they were also swayed by the educational, labor, and travel opportunities afforded by the military.

According to my interviewees, soldiering allowed them to earn their stripes as "real Americans," exerting their pride in their new country as an expression of the protocols of militarized freedom. While many military servicemen and women adopt the credo that enlisting in the armed forces is the acme of serving one's country, for Vietnamese Americans this sense of national service holds elements of transnationalism that, according to feminist scholar Neda Atanasoski (2006), allow us to tie domestic American multiculturalism and citizenship to geopolitical partnerships. In this sense, the transnationalist masculine desires to procure militarized freedoms for the United States and its allies link up closely to the larger "feminizing" ethos of what Atanasoski describes as "humanitarian violence" or the ways war is used to justify saving others from themselves.

Every soldier I spoke with claims to love the United States, but within that standard statement often lay a sophisticated critique about military histories and freedoms. Hung Tran, a naval commander born in 1979, four years after the Fall of Saigon, says he never knew much about the history of the Vietnam War. He learned from reading on his own that the United States made a deal with China and Russia to halt aid to South Vietnam, setting the country on course to nothing short of failure. Tran found a similarity between the Vietnam War and the many U.S. Gulf Wars in that they present no real winners, even though the United States still stands as a hegemonic power. These wars remain distinctive from each other, however, due to the ideological purposes and political motivations behind them. In Vietnam, he claims the main purpose was to stop communism, but American involvement in Iraq and Afghanistan was aimed at stopping terrorism in order to "spread democracy." In Vietnam, the United States was not successful. Richard Nixon took out U.S. troops, which according to Tran was a good thing, but took out too many soldiers under Vietnamization. He says, "I think they [the U.S.] failed Vietnam. They have not completely supported us [South Vietnamese] all the way. They just decide to not support in financial and weapons and troops and say we're going without you . . . They didn't finish what they started."[7] According to Tran, the United States found its foreign affairs in arrears, and its hand was forced in divesting from South Vietnam. All members of Hung's family suffered because they were South Vietnamese.

There are two primary reasons that war can secure or protect freedom, according to many of the GIs I interviewed. They frequently claimed that they were serving their country to pay their dues for the countless freedoms which many enumerated as part of the bundle of rights accorded to them in U.S. democratic society (free speech, private property, ability to vote, etc.)—rights they believed should be enjoyed by everyone. For Vietnamese Americans, this postulate of giving back to their host country for these freedoms compensates for the loss of freedoms they experienced when the communists took over South Vietnam. Some soldiers consider their service as part of the raw deal and broken promise made between the United States and South Vietnam, a way to patch up a broken geopolitical relationship.

When asked about their military experiences overseas, most of my interviewees provided few details about the "locals," focusing on their everyday work. The many new Vietnam-like wars in Afghanistan and Iraq likewise led soldiers to recognize the "fatal couplings" between Vietnamese people and other communities (Gilmore 2002). Insofar as many of the soldiers I interviewed were employed in support capacities and not ground combat (my younger brother is a rare exception, as a combat engineer searching for bombs and mines), attesting to the military's class-based division of labor where minorities hold mostly service positions; this prevented my interviewees from meeting many locals along the way, but they still made meaningful symbolic connections between their militarized experiences and those of Iraqis and Afghanis. Despite limited contact, the embedding of Vietnamese American subjects in foreign lands can reveal much about the potential for interracial solidarity and cross-cultural politics in terms of how soldiers think about war.

Uncomfortable with divulging much about the nature of his service in Iraq and Kuwait (perhaps also because it takes time for soldiers to emotionally process what they did and what they experienced), navy officer Chuong Nguyen was more at ease talking effusively about the effects of the U.S. Vietnamization policy in South Vietnam:

> In my opinion, I always liked the military and all Vietnamese, whether if you're a communist or whatever the political [ideology] that you're in, if you're Vietnamese you're a fighter and [this has been] proved for a generation and the communist, they happened [to be] on the wrong side. When people fight, they fight hard. The south lost for so many reasons. A small potato of the Cold War and when the U.S. put all the money in the south, some of the money went into corruption like we have right now and so that can be very dangerous, the American public lost their patience so they don't have money to have support for the war and bailed out.[8]

A listener or reader can glimpse the ways Iraq and Afghanistan are described as corrupt regimes similar to South Vietnam, for many reasons, not least of which included the Vietnamization policy that did nothing but turn the American public against American allies and reduced economic aid. At the same time, Nguyen's words strike at the core of the U.S. imperial project and its pouring more money into an unsustainable South Vietnamese government, saying this is just cause for why the United States had to pull out early. When discussing America's possible Vietnamization of the Iraq War, his words were more muted:

> Sometimes people want democracy, but it not gonna happen. Their government may not be the same as us but if you wanna change somebody, it takes generations. Takes years . . . so if America decide to help another country, they gotta be patient, it takes generations to learn the American way. You're gonna expect 10 to 20 years . . . will democracy ever come to Vietnam? People have to make their own choice.

Though Chuong believes the United States cannot always fully help other countries achieve their dreams of becoming democracies, he believes that Americans are correct in trying to assist them. He speaks through many contradictions when he says those foreign people must find their own path toward the future *by way of* America, but people should make their own choices in what to do with their lives. Iraq's fate hangs in the air as does the fate of socialist Vietnam, which is still up for grabs. The United States lost in Vietnam badly due to policies like Vietnamization, but the future of America's allies is dependent upon those people finding *their own* path toward freedom *under* the tutelage of "the American way." The militarized freedoms of nations are wrapped up in the perceived freedoms of individuals. Like Long and Tran, Chuong is very supportive of military service because he believes Vietnamese have been compelled to fight.

Lt. Col. Chris Phan says fighting for America whenever and wherever should be a *time-bound* if not entirely *time-honored* duty of Vietnamese Americans. Born in Vinh Long in 1973, he was raised there by his mother until reunited in 1991 in the United States with his father, a former legal counsel to the president of South Vietnam who fled by boat. Phan didn't know if his father was alive or dead for the first few years since the man's departure because there was no communication with the outside world. Growing up in the United States, he watched military-themed TV shows like *JAG* and identified with John F. Kennedy, who served in the U.S. Navy, who gave him "this sense of duty and desire to serve." His parents disapproved of his decision to enlist, but he tried to make a meaningful career to break into politics. Phan told me that the military can bring a different politics to bear on the wider Vietnamese American community. His younger brother enlisted in Navy Seal training, and as the brother's commission officer Phan signed the paperwork for his deployment, which he felt was like signing his brother's death warrant. But his brother wanted it and Phan supported him, the personal anguish overridden by the call of duty.

Phan became a military lawyer and later deployed to Iraq working for the Navy Seals. He joined a group of Vietnamese American soldiers in California to become the founding president of the Vietnamese American Armed Forces Association (VAAFA). While this fiduciary relationship builds on the debenture that South Vietnamese subjects owe to the U.S. government, it must be remembered also that it is sometimes through war that personal connections are forged, since the military brings far-flung individuals of the nation together. Multiple overseas tours of duty brought the first cohort of Vietnamese American service members to seek each other out and stave off a sense of ethnic isolation found in extended stays abroad. This prompted the creation of VAAFA in 2007 to build a free association of soldiers, bound together by shared ethnicity and occupation. With 150 members spread across the country, the organization has been a network for those who fight for the United States just like their parents did during the Vietnam War.

The freedoms found in the concept of militarized freedoms depend largely on generational and historical perspective. Despite finding synchronicity among the younger generation, Phan describes the cool relationship between VAAFA and the older South Vietnamese veterans' groups still operating in the United States in this manner:

> We definitely maintain our own autonomy; our systems of operation are so much more different. We're much tighter, much more order, rank and file in what we do. We appreciate them but with all due respect, we're very different. The culture's different. The upbringing is very different. We're Americans, make no doubts about that, we're Americans. We just happen to have yellow skin and we speak Vietnamese but the way we operate; we're Americans and *may Bac* [the elders], they're Vietnamese and we respect the heritage but we don't work together because there's no meshing, there's really nothing to mesh about. We learn from each other or we learn from them but we do our own thing.

For younger, true Americans who happen to be Vietnamese, their cultural proficiency in U.S. mainstream and military culture makes them a cut above their elders, who are just too Vietnamese. The historical view of South Vietnamese soldiers as a disorganized fighting force, wracked by in-fighting, is renewed by statements like these from younger generation soldiers who distance themselves from ARVN, but still appreciate them. Thus, the mistakes of war are not just the bumbling of the U.S. politicians but the South Vietnamese soldiers who are not as efficient, because they are not American or Westernized enough. Though he believes there is "nothing wrong with holding to the past" and he himself "was too young to really know the past," Phan does appreciate where the older generation is coming from and that they hurt a lot, and why having "that flag [South Vietnam] fly here means a lot to them . . . because that's where we are from we can't ever forget that."

On the matter of the war in Vietnam, Phan believes it was "a calamity of errors" where the Vietnamese did themselves in. While, he says, the United States failed the South Vietnamese, the latter "should have fought like there's no tomorrow." The ultimate blame for the war effort's undoing belonged to the South Vietnamese who could not imagine that democratic tomorrow:

> I mean was not there so I can't really attest to this but if I'm out of line, I hope that *may Bac* [older uncles] can fix what I say but what I see is we didn't fight like our lives depended on it until it was too late and there is corruption and basically people made it too easy and I think that as much as we can blame the Americans, we were equally at fault.
>
> Had we fought from day one as if our lives depended on it, I don't think we would've been in this predicament. The United States didn't want us to win so basically they were pawning us and trying to keep us at bay. I was really too young to know what went down but it's just discouraging that we had the greatest military power in our corner and we couldn't pull off a victory so something went wrong. I don't know what but something went wrong.

What is notable in this passage is the strong identification with "us/we" Vietnamese and the back and forth for blaming the Vietnamese and Americans for war's calamity. The fact that he was too young to really know what happened does not temper Phan's confidence to fault sides, even though he does defer to his elders to correct him if he is wrong. On the matter of the greatest military power of the world turning over the reins of control to the South Vietnamese, he answers, "I think we relied too strongly on the United States. And we shouldn't have and perhaps we should've . . . I find it discouraging that we blame everybody else except ourselves. So I rather blame ourselves first and if the blame is falsely placed, then blame somebody else but I turn to us first." The question of authentic history and memory is overridden by the soldier's war cry to fight at all costs, even when governments are confused themselves about what to do.

Despite the South Vietnamese having lost everything, there is a demand for them to pay back what they owe to the United States in terms of the many freedoms they gained as refugees fleeing communist Vietnam, which lacks rights to free elections, education, or legal due process, among others. Phan says:

> We owe them [the United States] a debt of gratitude, you can differ with me as far as saying that well if they didn't lose our country, we wouldn't have anything . . . We did lose our country . . . and it gave us the chance to be here . . . we would be outcasted or trying to make a living sweeping streets in Vietnam, so I take my blessings with what they kept in me. Here, I have the liberty to talk and view my points as I see fit and I won't be thrown in prison for it as like being in Vietnam. I think we owe them that much to say, "Thanks for letting us stay here and have a future and we should work for the betterment of the United States."

Speaking in hypotheticals, Phan comments on the price of refugee memory and the debts of refugee gratitude whereby the real possibility of being poor or imprisoned in Vietnam as social outcasts is overcome by the many benefits of being a resettled free person in the United States. A refusal to view Vietnamese as a *resettled* community, but rather an *unsettled* community, as scholar Eric Tang (2015) says, expresses the anxieties of a population unable to squash or mollify its war traumas. There is much confusion, ambivalence, and contradiction in Phan's strong words about patriotism, service, and national debt. But despite sentimental identification with the South Vietnamese soldier as a matter of respect, there is a strong dis-identification with that figure, especially when overemphasizing his Americanness. Chris Phan speaks from a torn position: One the one hand, he wants to blame the United States for actions in Vietnam but cannot, as he and his people have been handed a prosperous American future through the loss of South Vietnam. On the other hand, he wants to fully criticize the South Vietnamese for what they did (or failed to do) in the past, but cannot because he himself is not sure of what really happened and still wants to respect his elders. In this way, the histories of the older and younger generations rub against one another with as much friction as the U.S.-South Vietnam relationship, pointing to the spatial (dis)location and cultural position of Vietnamese Americans as the descendants of South Vietnam.

Long Lam echoes Phan's statements about respecting elders but reserving more space to criticize them for their past failures and nostalgia. Lam's dad served in the Vietnamese Army, left in 1979 as a refugee, and he and his mom and sister came much later in 1990. Sgt. Lam was deployed to Kuwait as a patient administration specialist and returned feeling more open to a better American future. Chiming in on the older generation of ARVN fighters, and how they are saddled with the debts of the South Vietnamese, he says in his particular English level:

> They tend to live with the past and forget the future. The older generation always have opinion about the communists but fail to see the future by encouraging their younger generation to join the military, and get experience in case Vietnam need people like us to rebuild the nation. We cannot learn anything from the older veterans because all they do is fighting among themselves over their differences. We all know the communist regime cannot rule the nation forever, someday it will change, and they will need people with different experiences, more proficient in warrior tasks and combat skill to retrain and reorganize the Vietnamese army to repel all invaders.[9]

When I asked him about the legacy of South Vietnam, he replied, "Nothing, there is nothing left, only the future." For Lam, there is only the memory of a stolen future for a democratic Vietnam under the communists. Though he is critical of his elders, he appreciates the ways they encourage the younger generation to join the U.S. military to gain the technical warrior skills needed for the day when communist Vietnam falls and South Vietnamese exiles can return to their country to reclaim all of it. For Lam, the Vietnam War is not over, and his training in the

U.S. military puts a new twist on the alleged intent of Vietnamization as the U.S. training South Vietnamese soldiers to defend and protect themselves. At the same time, the statements from younger soldiers about their superior knowledge over and above their elders speaks to a certain overbearance that comes with the youths' English language superiority and higher education level and their deftness handling modern American weapons. For Lam, the younger generation of soldiers is more united and stronger, in a better position not only to win back Vietnam but to take control of the future.

Insofar as the War on Terror is a continuation of the Cold War and the Vietnam War, Vietnamese American soldiers are in a unique position to bring that historical connection into light. Lam tells of the challenges of millennials to identify with their elders, even though young and old share a "joint account" in American empire. Lam's genealogical tracing of his family history is not a project to "go back in time" and restore things to order, but processes the mill through which history or many histories can be refined. All my interviewees were born during or right after the Vietnam War, but some were born much later though they still feel the impact of that war. Born in Ho Chi Minh City in 1988 to a Chinese mother and Vietnamese father, Keira Long is part of a generation born decades after war. She came to the United States at the age of 11, joining the Army Reserves a few years later "to do so many things I can and wanted to do."[10] Unlike my male interviewees, Keira faced opposition from her parents since they did not feel the military was right for women. When I asked what she knew about the Vietnam War, Private First Class Keira Long said she did not learn much about it except when she came to the United States. Comparing the similar U.S. involvement in Central/West Asia with Southeast Asia, she responded accordingly, "We're in Iraq and Afghanistan for a while now to give them aid, financial support, equipment. We've been there for a while and that's pretty similar to Vietnam in a way before when we were supporting Vietnam . . . for me, I think it reminds us people of what they fought for." For Long, what holds together different wars is the U.S. support for its friendly allies, a relationship I am theorizing as one based on giving and protecting militarized freedoms. At the personal level, performing military service reprises a gendered "war of maneuver" to elevate the South Vietnamese war veteran and the emasculated Asian male through archetypically "masculine" labor. This invigorated martial masculinity partially explains why men are more encouraged than women to publicly serve in the military.

The passage of time since the end of the Vietnam War allows Vietnamese Americans to find fault with the U.S.-South Vietnam alliance as a Cold War project lacking in real securities with a legacy that remains "in the red," whose invoice or tab continues to run with incalculable costs. Metaphorically speaking, the fight for militarized freedoms is a "joint venture" between superpowers and allies. What for the United States meant the exercise of Americans helping the South Vietnamese under Vietnamization catalyzes an ongoing situation of endless warfare where there are no clear winners. The "War on Terror" places Vietnamese American soldiers in the awkward position of giving freedom to others as duty-bound protectors of the U.S. military state, when their South Vietnamese ancestors and the United States could not win in the Vietnam War. Inderpal Grewal (2014) says that U.S. imperialism masquerading as freedom-giving only works because it draws on the liberal notion of self-help with the humanitarian ethos of helping others when they cannot help themselves, rather than make visible the political project of empire (69). Speaking in a private, spontaneous manner that is not public or easily scrutinized, the Vietnamese American soldiers I interviewed represent the embodiment of militarized freedoms; they speak to the U.S. dilemma of using military force to bring freedom to others, but also the ways those others find their own path to freedom that is highly militarized.

The arguments set forth by Vietnamese American soldiers—that the United States should stay in those places it promises to protect—are arguments both for and against Nixon's Vietnamization policy. These arguments present themselves as critiques of U.S. foreign policies in Vietnam and Iraq/Afghanistan, forwarding the premise that the United States should continue to occupy these territories to spread freedom, but never bail out too soon once it does choose to intervene. Addressing questions about national sovereignty, military occupation, and geopolitical alliances provides a way to reconceptualize Vietnamization as the absent presence of alternate futures for self-governance in an age where wars and countries do not have defined borders.

The American Syndrome: Dealing with the Déjà Vu of Wars

Bringing us full circle back to the Vietnamese American critique of Vietnamization, I turn now to the autobiographical work of well-known U.S. Marine Quang X. Pham to examine the problems of storytelling, where one soldier attempts to construct a different narrative about Vietnamese refugees beyond what Ayako Sahara (2012) describes as an "exceptional rescue effort" by the United States. The opening to Pham's 2005 autobiography, *A Sense of Duty: Our Journey from Vietnam to America*, contemplates the simultaneity of life and death. It begins with the formal military invasion of South Vietnam by the United States at the same time as the author's birth.

> I was born a Vietnamese in an old French hospital six months before President Lyndon B. Johnson ordered thousands of U.S. Marines *into my country*... Saigon is gone—but then again, it isn't... Vietnam will remain a part of me for as long as I live, as will my love for *nước Mỹ* [Vietnamese for the United States]... When I turned twenty I *became an American by choice*. Actually, I was already a by-product, derived from a failed U.S.-backed regime fighting to keep the "dominoes" from falling in Asia... I knew I had to be a citizen in order to join the military as an officer. My childhood dream was to become a pilot like my father. Unknowingly, the pursuit of that dream would enable me to *pay back the rewards of my precious new citizenship* and to seek the truth about my *father's service in a long-ago war*. (emphasis added)

With this introductory vignette, Pham sets upon a personal quest to stake out his claims of home, family, and citizenship within polymorphic cartographies of belonging and memory, a torturous process in which the public act of authorship must draw the line between a soldier's love and hate for the very foreign power that invaded and destroyed his homeland. The ironic punch is that Pham becomes a U.S. citizen "by choice" even though in the same breath he admits he is a "by-product" of U.S. militarism. In a not too subtle manner, Pham unpacks the dense history of American military governance. His writing throughout the book jumps in tone from ironic and flippant to jingoistic and serious, wavering between an anti-war stance and a super-patriotic ethos, hoping to find a choice between militarized freedoms and military necessities.

In this section, I read Pham's story as a prime example of how a younger generation of Vietnamese Americans who came of age after the Vietnam War find themselves at pains to reconcile their "Vietnamized" heritage with their "Americanized" lives. Doing so uncorks the tensions percolating up within Pham's commemorative story to analyze the ways minority U.S. soldiers negotiate the changing memories of American warfare. Despite its cover as a tribute to his country from a proud American soldier and former Vietnamese refugee, the text delivers a mixed message about the United States and about war itself. In terms of narrative voice, Pham hovers between celebrating American jingoism and committing to outright criticism of the United States. His writing tone and literary style are very muscular and hyperbolic, full of bombast if also self-reflective in its emotional vulnerability; cognizant of the ways military training instills an unblinking desire to fight the foreign enemy . . . an enemy that looked like him. Pham opens his memoir with less than kind thoughts about past and present U.S. presidents, congressmen, military brass, protesters, South Vietnamese leadership, and communists in Vietnam. Memoirs are by nature messy and unruly, reveling in the storyteller's personal politics, biases, and mental flaws. Told as a sort of "refugee bildungsroman" or coming-of-age story drawing on classic themes of refugee displacement, alienation, migration, and resettlement, Pham's biography bucks the usual narrative approach to telling refugee stories entrenched in the assimilationist movement from infantilized Vietnamese refugee to adult U.S. citizen.

Pham's retrospective epitomizes the unnerving traumatic experiences of so many children born during the Vietnam War who remain scarred by it. He left Vietnam in 1975 at the age of 10, among the first to leave after Saigon's fall, because of their close ties to the South Vietnamese government or U.S. military. While Pham left Vietnam with his mother and sisters, his father, a South Vietnamese Air Force pilot, was unintentionally left behind and sent to a reeducation camp for 17 years by North Vietnamese captors. Distressed over his father's absence from his life, Pham became determined to enlist in the U.S. Marines to honor the legacy of his missing father, who once fought with the Americans and trained with the U.S. Air Force. Pham found fame as the first Vietnamese American helicopter pilot in the U.S. Marines serving tours of duty in Kuwait (1990–91) and in Somalia (1992–94). His memoir, published a decade later, sought "to give South Vietnamese soldiers a voice" and to help him sort out "refugee baggage" (Le 2007). As a son of South Vietnam, Pham assumes the commanding role of representing a whole generation of veterans unrecognized in U.S. history, but whose stories must be told by someone with cultural capital and fluency able to convey the experiences of these GIs to Americans. He explains, "The United States provided my family a second chance to live in freedom and peace and to get to know each other again; it did not forget about my father and his fellow detainees. And for that we are indebted. This is our story" (13). Though the story of refugees from Vietnam to America seems clear, some clarifying points needed to be made about how that journey is represented. One can spot ambiguity for instance in the various covers and titles for Pham's book.

On the first cover of the book's original printing, the beaming uniformed son is standing next to his smiling, formally attired father; the two men stand equal in the foreground, bridging the space between Vietnam and the United States, uniting the two countries through their love for one another. In the second edition of the book, the cover features photographs of his father during the war and a young Pham (dressed in a baseball uniform to signal cultural Americanization) as well as his family. This version puts Pham's military service in dialogue with that of his father, the image of his family placed farther back. The bolded title "Our Sense of Duty" overhangs the two Pham men while the subtitle "Our Journey from Vietnam to America" hovers above the family photo of Pham, his sister, and mother. Both covers touch upon the powerful bond between men that can symbolize the entire struggle of the family and nation. The title of Pham's autobiography was originally published as *A Sense of Duty: My Father, My American Journey*. In later editions, it was rebranded as *A Sense of Duty: Our Journey from Vietnam to America*. This change reflects the paradox and development of Quang's thinking from his father to his family and community. The decision to change to "my" journey and "my" father to "our journey" can be read as not only including the rest of the family but inviting all South Vietnamese to see their journey in this personal story. This pluralization expands the definition of freedom from a singular process of individual possession to the collective freedoms enjoyed by many.

Such freedoms are hard to convey when bathed in the ignominious memory and besmirched name of South Vietnam. Such pain necessitates rechanneling the republic's shameful history for many like Pham through pride in the imperial might of South Vietnam's former benefactor, the United States. Pham's mother chose to settle in the United States despite having family in France, as she predicted that more opportunities for success existed in the United States and believed that "the French never saw Vietnamese as equals" (96). Coming of age amidst these depictions, Pham claims a true account of "what happened to the South Vietnamese remains in the hands of expatriates" (64). While the South Vietnamese were not treated as their equals, he writes, Americans still embraced the refugees in their country, an act of kindness for which he *must* feel grateful; after all, the United States had treated other Asian groups like the Japanese and Chinese worse. As Pham intones, "In 1975, we Vietnamese refugees were just—refugees. Yet we received better treatment than our Asian-American predecessors and we got out of the camps after months, not years. How could a refugee ever pay back such kindness?" (97).

Recompensing for America's goodwill toward Vietnamese refugees, Pham joined the U.S. Marines to risk his life for the very country that had saved his life. He never envisioned himself as a military pilot before since all the military pilots featured in air shows, aviation books, and films he watched as a child were white. Pham later decided to join the Marines to prove he was more than a helpless F.O.B. washed onto America's shores. While training to become a pilot, Pham often thought about his caged father back in Vietnam and wondered about the patriarch's life in the communist reeducation camps. This missing father figure never left the boy's mind "thanks to the never-ending American nostalgia for Vietnam" (133). Fatherless and living in a foreign country without a male role model, the military gave Pham a sense of the future, even though he saw himself another "faceless minority member" and "perpetual foreigner" (ibid.). Despite feeling a sense of what Anne Cheng (2000) calls the "racial melancholia" from not approximating normative whiteness, Pham proclaims himself an "all-American." This authentic Americanness foregoes any attachment to South Vietnam: "I wanted to be a *real* American because I could no longer be a true Vietnamese, since my country of birth no longer existed" (135). The narrator's incapacity to be a "true Vietnamese" stems from his inability to relate to the country of his birth—South Vietnam. Shorn of his original homeland as a cultural foothold, Pham wholly accepted his assimilation into the American culture, if only to "shed the last threads of bitterness and resentment" whenever the Vietnam War was mentioned (32).

Pham's desires to become a full-blooded American adult male requires disavowing his South Vietnamese heritage. Yet, the author is reminded constantly of his ethnicity in the racist culture of the U.S. military. Despite joining the U.S. Marine Corp, he could not escape the shadow of the war. During training, he was often called "VC" or Vietcong by officers and other Marines, even though he and his family came from the side that fought *with* Americans. Similarly, the Hollywood movie clips and training films shown to trainees reminded him of anti-Asian military racism:

> It became a wash of images of Marines bayoneting and flame-throwing Japanese on South Pacific islands, Communists in Korea and more Communists in Vietnam. Under the dimmed classroom lights, I would recoil while my fellow candidates screamed *Oohhrraahh*! and *Get some*! I did it too to go along with the crowd. This fixation on the Asiatic as the enemy was not the Corp's fault. It was not racism, it was reality, our simulated field training exercises were from lessons learned in the last war, the Corp's experience in Vietnam . . . *Your mission is to destroy the enemy by fire and maneuver and close combat. Fix bayonet! E-tool! Oohhrraahh!*" (149; emphasis in original)

"In Vietnam," Pham claims, "such blind discipline, even in response to illegal orders, had led to atrocities in such places in Cam Ne and My Lai, the latter an Army atrocity. 'Burn all dem hootches! Waste 'em motherfuckin' gooks! Get Some!" (138). Though cognizant of the tangled American logic of warfare and racism, Pham never performs a full assessment of this union, sometimes even making excuses for it, suggesting that Americans had to kill or be killed by the foreign enemy. He often touches upon such delicate issues in a sporadic fashion, owing to his uncertain feelings regarding these matters, thus leaving readers to decipher his own muddled thoughts. Such distortion in the author's point of view evidences a personal approach to politics, a lifelong attempt to finagle the competing cultural narratives that have capped his entire life as a Vietnamese American, even though to his Marine instructors Pham symbolized that loss and shame of the Vietnam War (142).

This statement is followed by one about his father paying *for* the loss of South Vietnam at a prison camp and Pham's paying *forward* his father's loss. One reviewer's blurb for the book described *A Sense of Duty* as "a poignant story of two distant wars . . . but ultimately it is a son's tribute to his father and a way of saying 'thank you' to all in his father's generation who served honorably to defend freedom and whose story has yet to be told" (Berman quoted in Pham 2005a). Despite insipid feelings about his ill treatment in the U.S. military, Pham felt luckier than his father, the latter stuck for many years in hard-labor prison camps in Vietnam without any freedom whatsoever. When his father was finally released from prison and allowed to go to the United States, whose interest he faithfully served, Pham said he "never received a welcome home, veteran's benefits, or a pension" from the U.S. government, even though he expected some type of gratitude (5). Seeking to rid this stigma, Pham writes, "I wanted to relieve him of a loser's guilt, a husband's regret, a father's remorse. Most of all, I wanted him to know that he stood for respectability—for duty, honor, and country" (32).

Oddly, while he wants to remember and honor his father, Pham is ashamed of his father and the men of that generation for losing the war. When he joined the U.S. Marines, he claimed it was a way to honor the South Vietnamese military legacy of his father, Van Hoa Pham, but he also admitted to using it "to walk out from his shadow once and for all . . . by becoming a *real* American through the U.S. Marine Corps" (32). The son is put in a different standing than his father, the latter signifying the disrepute of the South Vietnam military. Unlike his father, who was an ally of the Americans, Pham was a true American, a soldier of a superpower, not a small, lost nation. In this regard, U.S. military service is a rite of passage; where paying tribute to a "failed" parent and "failed state" also requires forsaking those same figures of failure.

Blaming his poor understanding of Vietnam War history, Pham believes in the mythic greatness of America by dint of his own limited knowledge of what happened, especially to ARVN soldiers like his father. Such historical amnesia encourages younger-generation soldiers like Pham to blindly promote the greatness of America as the path to freeing oneself from a horrible Vietnamese past. Pham went to war overseas during Operation Desert Storm to fight for the United States, but his mother worried about Pham joining the U.S. Marine Corps and did not understand his absolute faith in the mission of the Corps. As Pham noticed, "She confessed that the night we left Saigon, she never would have guessed that her only son would go off to war for this country. Neither had I" (171). Blind trust in the U.S. president and senior military leaders led him into war. In the case of Operation Desert Storm, Pham figured the war was about Iraq but also Vietnam:

> *It's not just another job, it's an adventure. See the world, meeting interesting people . . . and kill them . . .* As convincing as the outcome in Kuwait was, no one could have guessed then the long-term effects of not going all the way to Baghdad. But the victory was enough for this nation to finally purge itself of the guilt over the despicable homecoming it had given Vietnam War veterans decades earlier. (188)

In this prescient passage, the writer recognizes the disastrous effects of the United States not pursuing a military endgame *all the way* to victory in Central Asia, a tactic redolent of the strategy in Vietnam. If pursued correctly or to completion, the hope for the United States was that any victory in the "Middle-East" could remedy American misgivings about the Vietnam War. He describes the armed northern communist forces invading the south as being similar to the United States invading the Arab world: "They roared through the South Vietnamese central cities the way the U.S. Marines stormed Kuwait City sixteen years later, then Baghdad a dozen years after that" (20). When the United States emerged from the Persian Gulf victorious over Iraq and Pham returned a celebrated war hero, his South Vietnamese past reminded him of the drawbacks of celebrating temporary military victories. When Pham was invited to speak at a political rally held in Little Saigon, he made the following observation about his homecoming to the Vietnamese American community: "I felt as if I were a U.S. Marine landing in Vietnam. *Déjà vu*" (190). This statement relays a bizarre form of mental dissonance reflective of the "militarized diaspora" of Vietnamese American soldiers, once scattered around the world, interacting again with their fellow refugees back home (Lemarchand 2012). Pham felt like a foreigner or invader, even if his community treated him as a hero. In the South Vietnamese geopolitical diaspora, where the condition of exile does not eradicate the heightened sense of violence that birthed those things, a Vietnamese American soldier can feel like a foreigner to his own people because of his involvement in U.S. military adventurism and estrangement from South Vietnam. Such estrangement follows Jodi Kim's observations about the conflicting geographies of identification resulting from what she calls the "protracted afterlife" of the Cold War. Kim finds that the memory of the Vietnam War, along with World War II, the Korean War, and other American wars in Asia, stirs up mixed feelings even for patriotic individuals about the messy effects of U.S. Cold War militarism; wars always exceed and outlive their historical moment.

As a turning point in the Cold War, the Vietnam War shows us that historical violence never ends in peace but begets further militarized freedoms. This cognitive distance from his own people has much to do with his success as an "American" soldier in Iraq, which affords him a different social status than South Vietnamese veterans who fought with Americans during the 1970s but returned home as losers. An emcee at the homecoming rally (based in the heart of the Vietnamese community in Orange County) asked Pham jokingly, "Now that the lieutenant has returned from victory in Desert Storm, is he ready to fight and win back South Vietnam?" At that instant, Pham realized "the war had not ended for my fellow refugees" (190). The emcee's comment positions Pham as both a fellow refugee and a soldier of South Vietnam, even though he never served as a soldier for ARVN. It pushes out his childhood fantasy of becoming a true American as his mind wanders back to how men like his father worked to fight as an ally of the United States. For his own part, Pham was "off defending freedom (and oil) for America" (202).

The shift in awareness about his position in contrast to his father's nudged him into a greater understanding about the past relationship between the United States and South Vietnam, a growing awareness of which cascades into his sense of U.S. current wars extending the lifeline of the Vietnam War and policies like Vietnamization. As he put it, "For the first few years after his capture, I thought my father was dead. Perhaps from grief, or anger, I couldn't conjure any positive attitudes toward the South Vietnamese. It was easier to blame them the same way we are now pointing fingers at the Iraqis for not holding their own against the insurgents. I could not summon enough strength to deal with my own emotions until my father came back into my life" (10). This dissociation with South Vietnam gave Pham a higher price tag than ARVN soldiers, even if he is perceived as a soldier of South Vietnam.

At a South Vietnamese veterans' reunion where Pham joined his father, the aging attendees peppered the younger Pham with questions: "So Quang, you're flying for the Americans huh? How do they treat you? Better than they treated us?" to which Pham knew the answer to be a resounding "Yes" (241). These statements attest to the trivialized status of America's former allies like the Hmong, locating their dual positionality as what Ma Vang (2012) calls "refugee soldiers," those once assisting the United States in overseas military operations but whose history of service has been forgotten in their rendering as merely refugees needing assistance. (During the Laotian Civil War, the United States brokered the contest between the Lao People's Army and the anti-communist secret army comprised of the ethnic minority Hmong people, trained and aided by the CIA. The success of the Pathet Lao led to the abandonment of the Hmong by the United States and the retribution killing by the Lao communist regime.) The superior treatment Pham received compared to the veteran soldiers of the ARVN reveals lack of respect for America's Vietnamese freedom fighters. This point relates to Pham's general observation of his father's denigrated status pilot fighting for the Americans in "their secret war" but who was shot down and captured by North captors in 1964, only to be recovered later with no honorific tribute from anyone, especially the Americans (7).

The emotional recollection of South Vietnam's demise marks a symbol of Pham's own personal loss, one that became more acute with the death of his father. In 2000, the senior Pham succumbed to lung cancer after lying in a coma that resulted from a massive stroke. Passing a few years before the United States would invade Iraq, the death of the elderly father foreclosed any dialogue Pham wanted to have with this mysterious man who was finally "put to rest with full military honors from a country that no longer existed" (6). The death also posed another challenge to Pham in writing a book honoring this man's legacy. In the hospital, days before his demise, the patriarch's last words mentioned his pride for Pham and his military service, a raw, searing confession which the son found odd. When Pham's father had reunited with the family in the United States, he said very little to his children about his years in reeducation camps. In the weeks after his father's passing, Pham discovered letters his father had written to his son, filled with ideas he felt were important for the book he knew his son was planning to write and publish. He had refused to share memories while he was alive, due to the guilt he felt about his capture and the traumatic experiences of the war and political reeducation (and his lack of English to communicate with his English-speaking son). Pham's letter requires extended quotation here:

> Dear Son,
> You must know how much it means to me when you decided to give me a chapter in your book. It will be written by a former South Vietnamese Air Force pilot in D-English. If it doesn't matter to you what I did was a failure, then I will tell you some stories of the past. . . . This is the only chance to tell about the old days of what I felt, thought, remembered of what I went through to you or anyone else who wishes to know of the past in the Vietnam War.
> Another reason, either simple coincidence or you may call it destiny, is you're in the same Marine unit that I used to fly support for and was rescued by in the early days of the U.S. involvement in Vietnam. What in the hell did I fight in the war for? It was not a war between the north and south. It was part of the Cold War. It must not be forgotten that a war had been going on for 21 years in a very small country at that time with no name on the world map. What I did in the war was a failure, don't you think? Who wants to know about us? No one wants to hear about the Vietnam War no more. (38)

In addition to these scribbled notes, the father also left behind recordings that were being held by a friend, a collection in which Pham found a different, more vocal father. When the interviewer asked his father if all the fighting and bloodshed in Vietnam was worth the price paid by the South Vietnamese people, his father answered candidly:

> When I was fighting the war in Vietnam, I still had many relatives in the north. My wife also had relatives in the north. And my friends had rela-

tives in the north. Both sides had families on the other side. I don't know how the Communists felt. But we [in South Vietnam] knew that we're not going to win the war. We just kept it that way forever until we [would] die. That was it . . . I could not figure out the war, so let's just end it that way. Yeah, we're the losers. But the war must end somehow. The killing has been going on for quite a long time. And now you don't know who the winner is. (257)

Pham did not expect his father to say such words, thinking instead that his father, the victim of communist persecution, would be "gung-ho about how we (the South Vietnamese) could have won, how the United States had abandoned us and how we need to keep fighting communism today" (257–258). Such ambivalence from his father toward the United States shifts the outstanding balance and total costs of the war away from the South Vietnamese. At the same time, the father's refusal to espouse a conservative South Vietnamese anti-communism displays the man's lack of bitterness, something which Pham has not let go. This helped changed the younger Pham's own attitude toward the Vietnam War. The son simply took for granted how his father felt about the communists, probably because that's exactly how most of the other people of his father's generation felt about them. But then, in addition, perhaps Pham's father offers a model of sorts, for how the Vietnamese American community might move beyond its knee-jerk reactions against all things communist and toward a more complex understanding of the world and the war.

For the older generation, the quest for wresting South Vietnam from the depths of history is not simply about valorizing South Vietnamese failure but recognizing its productive loss. The elder Pham's statement exposes the emotional turmoil of an older generation frequently seen as minions of the United States, ARVN soldiers who knew they weren't going to prevail in a war and who required the help of a superpower they were required to love but did not fully trust. This belated and very mixed message from his father informs Pham's own recognition that "no military is perfect" (8).

Despite the prospects of a successful multiyear career in the Marine Corps, Pham left the military to enter civilian life and business. Despite receiving military honors, he always felt like "an outsider constantly having to struggle to fit in, [and] never fully accepted" (236); he even wondered if he earned promotions in the Marine Corps because he was a minority. A return to Vietnam in 1995 to visit family after decades of exile only added more confusion to his split identity. His visit to distant relatives including a half-brother from his father's other marriage fell on the twentieth anniversary of the Fall of Saigon. As he observed, this trip was one of

> unfinished business . . . and new business . . . I went back to Saigon as a U.S. veteran, a Vietnam vet of a different kind. Was it me, the Vietnamese, clinging to old memories? Or was it me, the American, who grew up with portrayals of my homeland from Hollywood directors, politicians, journalists, and old soldiers—all of them foreigners? Or was it both? (243)

The dual sense of wrapping up new and unfinished business depicts a man torn between two places and time periods and reveals his fraught subject-position as a Vietnamese American. The strangest episode occurred later in his visit, when Pham had dinner at his aunt's home with a second cousin in his late thirties who happened to be a major in the People's Army of Vietnam. His instinct as a proud U.S. Marine upon meeting a communist officer was to confront this man, despite the guest's warmth and extension of generosity, but then he conceded that such a reaction was based on the "wrong reason, wrong place, and wrong time" (245). But even as he later enjoyed the time spent with his cousin, Pham still did not have the nerve to shake hands when saying farewell. Leaving Vietnam, he reflected sorrowfully about the place "where policies and policymakers failed miserably, and where brave young Americans and South Vietnamese paid with their lives in a sincere effort to secure freedom for the Republic of Vietnam" (246–247). Pham writes about his send-off from Vietnam again and coming "home" with the badge of honor of being an American: "Life goes on. Once again, I was on a plane heading for a place where I had found a chance to live. This time I was really going home, back to America, as an American" (ibid.). In this part of the book, Pham is documenting something of an identity crisis, as he careens back and forth between various parts of himself. Previously, he felt estranged as foreign "American" among his people, and now he was coming home as an "American," but proudly knowing more about his South Vietnamese side.

The narrator "returns" to his true home, the United States, claiming his rightful place there. This relinquishing of a past Vietnam as a symbolic "home" signals the death of old attachments, even though his association with "Vietnam" as a signifier of future "war" continues to last. He writes of his visit to the nation's capital in bittersweet terms, wanting to thank the United States for saving refugees but also holding tightly to the historical memory of the failures of the U.S. government to save South Vietnam:

> The U.S. Capitol stood in the distance, far removed from military memorials, at the opposite end of the National Mall. The men and women inside that building retain the power to declare and end wars, past and present. I wish more of them could have experienced the effects of war and its lingering wounds. I wish I could someday meet those who voted for President Johnson's Tonkin Gulf Resolution in 1964 and those who torpedoed President Ford's plea in 1975 to help a collapsing South Vietnam. The White House stood in the middle, its occupiers needing to be held accountable for their foreign frays. I shake myself free of the bitterness. "The war had to end. We had been killing each other for so long." My father's voice echoes in my mind. *It's over! Let it go!* Instead, I need to thank Congress for passing the Refugee Act and subsequent legislation that has enabled over a million Vietnamese to live here in freedom. (260; emphasis in original)

Yet, that sense of thankfulness is itself short-lived. Where the book begins with a rankling missive against the United States for annulling ties to foreign allies, it ends on almost the same note: he rages about the horrible ways that U.S. military projects pan out and laments his lack of confidence in this country. There is nothing this former refugee can give back to the United States in its munificence for offering him protection from communism. He feels he cannot repay the United States, but from a theoretical perspective, it implies that no refugee can ever pay back the U.S. government. Equally, there is little to no compensation for his "bitterness" toward that same power in making him and others refugees in the first place. With his father urging him to let go of the past, Pham is still unable to come to terms with living under a cold and ruthless American empire; he realizes that the power that enabled the United

States to save him and give him so many freedoms is the same power that enables it to declare and end wars as it chooses.

Beyond the father-son relationship, there is a gendered mechanism at work in this process of passing on of memory. It was Pham's mother who helped reconstruct and translate pieces of the patriarch's disorganized personal records, which belie the key role of women in making history and reproducing memory. It also uncovers what feminist scholar Cynthia Enloe pares down to the outpouring of "militarized masculinity" generated as a response to the crisis of traditional masculinity and loss of male power in war (Enloe 1993). *A Sense of Duty* offers no apologies or *mea culpas*. Published at the height of the U.S.-led "War on Terror," the book forcefully demonstrates how the history of the Vietnam War turns up again in another military era. Pham's autobiography offers more than a bromide against U.S. military actions, but surreptitiously weaves together disparate wars in a way that cues readers to the repetitious nature of American warfare. His memory of the Vietnam War provides a Vietnamese American perspective to U.S. war-making, one that torpedoes the perception that America's entry into the fray of "other Vietnams" is always innocent and justified due to the militarized freedoms that are pursued as the end goal. Offering a "Vietnamized" perspective that introduces the question of Iraq and Afghanistan, Vietnamese American soldiers are not entering another Vietnam, but another South Vietnam. Pham's account of American empire-building spans from the Vietnam War to the Gulf War and insists upon a consideration of U.S. foreign nation-building in the past and future tenses. While most of the memoir details Pham's military service in the first Gulf War fighting Saddam Hussein under President George H.W. Bush, the book itself was published in 2005 at a time when the United States was caught in the mesh of conflicts in the Persian Gulf, this time fighting the same Hussein under a second President Bush.

While promoting his book, Pham's public stature as a Vietnamese American Marine and published author allowed him a privileged position to publicly criticize the wars in Iraq and Afghanistan which were raging at the time. While newspapers promoted him as a proud American soldier writing about his family (a misreading by the media), Pham for his part used the media and his writings as an early publicity machine for his proposed run for political office, giving a boost to a Republican Party newcomer with an impeccable military service record and immigrant success story. Though decrying U.S. imperialism, *A Sense of Duty* became widely cited in the mainstream media as an example of the major backing of the Vietnamese American community for the U.S. war effort, catapulting Pham into the public eye as a spokesperson for Vietnamese Americans servicemen and civilians alike, even though that was not his intent. As result of this newfound fame, the writer became a frequent commentator in newspaper editorials on Operation Iraqi Freedom and Operation Enduring Freedom in Afghanistan. By narratively linking various wars together, Pham considers American war-making not as defined by singular historical moments but as a repetitious multigenerational process. Pham critiques the way the senior President Bush declared the first Persian Gulf War a decisive success by saying, "By God, we've kicked the Vietnam syndrome once and for all!" (Herring 1991/1992). He is equally critical of the younger George W. Bush, engaged in a longer, more drawn out war in Iraq, but declared "mission accomplished" in finally bringing democracy to Iraq. The jump in time from the Nixon years to the early 1990s to mid-2000s relates back to Pham's argument that wars are often made by the same organizing people and principles, and that we cannot simply declare the "Vietnam era" to be over.

Despite supporting the overall aims of the American military state, Quang X. Pham could not so easily agree with the declaration of victory in the Gulf Wars under the two Bush presidents. The premature assertion that the United States could bury its Vietnam Syndrome was met with skepticism from the refugee soldier who remembered "Vietnam" not as some syndrome of failure needing to be eliminated but as the delirium of experiencing wars without end. These thoughts accord with the insouciance of the United States as an "empire of indifference" with the ability to wage wars based on financial logics of short-term "risk" that enrich America's capitalist barons and political rulers (Martin 2007). The assumption of America's Vietnam(ization) Syndrome as somehow pacified in the Persian Gulf concerns Pham, who is then solicited by news media outlets to write about his country's shady dealings with Vietnamese people. In these scathing editorials, Pham takes to task the current diplomatic-economic trade between socialist Vietnam and the United States, an unholy alliance which he believes invalidates the "inviolable" contract between the United

States and South Vietnam. He also takes aim at early plans by the United States to withdraw from Iraq as a slap in the face not only for Iraqis but also for South Vietnamese people, something that repeats the original sin of Vietnamization. In a 2005 article in the *Boston Globe* entitled "Duty and Deceit," he writes the following: "The rupture between a past forgotten Vietnam and a future Vietnam came to me when I watched as a child the Persian Gulf War taking place . . . Now talk of exiting the war in Iraq has increased. What will happen to the Iraqis who believed in us? Will we let them down too?" In another piece, he writes that the drawdown in the U.S. presence in Iraq is really an excuse for quitting, where "the United States will abandon and betray Iraq as it did South Vietnam" (Kessler and Ricks 2006).

The editorial concludes by mentioning Cuban pilots who came to the United States like his father did, to train for the purposes of reclaiming their homeland from communism.[11] Pham manages to whip up comparable histories of war, splicing together America's "Vietnam Syndrome" from multiple wars resembling Vietnam. This is a corollary to what I am calling an "American Syndrome" or the anxieties felt by colonized peoples haunted by their recurring memories of U.S. acts of aggression against them, which can sometimes be found in tension with their love or respect of the United States. Insofar as the returns of war are also the "returns of the colonized" (Muppidi 2006), Pham experiences a different Vietnam Syndrome than the U.S. government; his is more personal and community-based; meanwhile, he experiences a kind of American Syndrome that connects the dots in the historical sites of U.S. empire and magnifies latent questions about the held-out promises by the United States in terms of delivering so many freedoms to its foreign allies under "future Vietnams."

Addressing a broader reading audience through newspapers, Pham publicizes a fundamental dilemma of empire of the contemporary United States, likening the American letdown of the Iraqis to the ways the United States cheated its Southeast Asian allies through empty promises of salvation, rescue, and liberation. Pham still feels the United States should have expended greater effort to save South Vietnam as it did for South Korea. Stretching the felt loss of his homeland to bear upon feared potential loss of contemporary military conflicts, Pham puts the blame for geopolitical failures squarely on the United States and its propensity to dispense with its allies out of convenience. This stirs up a related question: what debts do South Vietnamese and other groups owe to the United States, when it is the latter that left the former stranded in space and time?[12] Pham's writing creates a passageway between the past Vietnam and future Vietnams by activating a "geopersonal" history, one defined as those personal matters that are geopolitically shaped and spatialized by war. Recognizing that the geopolitical is geopersonal opens our current "geographies of memory" by showing that what seems to be gone or larger than us affects us deeply at an individual or familial level (Hoelscher and Alderman 2004). Pham's autobiography then is an exegesis of "Vietnamized" wars beyond the Vietnam of the 1960s and 1970s, distilling the many "proxy" wars or "secret wars" waged by the United States across the many corners of the earth. Pham raises concerns about the orphaned Koreans, Cubans, Iraqis, and other "allies" cut loose and left defenseless by Americans. His public standing as a Vietnamese American soldier who had served his country in Iraq gave him the pedigree to bring attention to the plight of all those foreign allies. Both a proud spokesman for and loud critic of the United States, Pham's writing concocts a dense "Cold War composition . . . issuing from the globality of the Cold War itself" (Kim 2010: 8). Such invectives against the evolution of the U.S. Cold War encourage the public to consider the unrealized politics of solidarity among disparate nations and to find ways to roll back the American empire's straightforward march to take in stride those "former friends" all over the world who were left out in the cold. Pham's editorials contrast to those news articles about soldiers surveyed earlier.

Pham's critical work comes to blows with his country over the predicament of Vietnamese GIs, both U.S.-born and South Vietnamese, as voluntary soldiers of American empire. He ties their unlucky fate to other soldiers, both foreign and forgotten, who worked for the United States but "didn't fare much better than my father" (ibid.). In a *USA Today* interview for an article entitled "Are We Still Warring over Vietnam" published on the thirtieth anniversary of the Fall of Saigon, the veteran takes an aggressive stance toward America's forgetting of South Vietnam. He writes about how there is no South Vietnamese military voice in the movies or anything in print.

Homing in on the geopersonal stakes of war makes it easier to track Pham's feelings and filiations across world regions. Pham concedes that sometimes those who went through hell and back, whether as refugees or soldiers, cannot forget the horrors they saw. As a child who prematurely "experienced" the Vietnam War and other wars, he believes he must serve the American military as homage to his new life of freedom, even if he resents that impulse. For the former refugee, this is what militarized freedoms truly demand of all of us; a more profound engagement with the multiple wars the United States undertakes in the pursuit of freedom, grappling with the reality that freedom can sometimes be an oppressive commitment to more fighting, especially when the United States has stayed and recommitted support troops and air strikes in fighting terrorist groups like ISIS in Iraq and Afghanistan, despite its "official" pullout in 2012. It seems wars these days never end, but instead they force a return to what was potentially lost.

Conclusion

The thoughts of Vietnamese American soldiers about America's new global wars is powerful, despite their small numbers in the U.S. military. Their colonial heritage reminds us of the South Vietnamese soldiers who once fought for and fought with Americans during the Vietnam War. With the United States engaged in fighting "future Vietnams," which are now here in the present, we can consider again the legacy of the U.S.-South Vietnamese alliance; such failure to remember fully that relationship promotes an abstract type of "Vietnam Syndrome" (as though any war can be exactly like the Vietnam War), which is at odds with Vietnamese Americans' personal sense of losing South Vietnam as well as their "American Syndrome" or sense of U.S. conquest/abandonment. In the final calculus, South Vietnamese are the forgotten allies of the U.S. Cold War empire, and many of them have taken on that broken alliance as their own personal debt, one that cannot easily be paid off or worked down, simply because they are fighting in America's wars as soldiers again.

In his 1972 State of the Union Address, Nixon reminded his fellow Americans that the country was not simply committing to Vietnamizing the war and protecting militarized freedoms around the world (in a limited support capacity) but also bandaging the *wounds* resulting from military violence. As he said, opaquely:

Our commitment to freedom remains strong and unshakable. But others must bear their share of the burden of defending freedom around the world . . . We will help other nations develop the capability of defending themselves. We will act to defend our interests, whenever and wherever they are threatened anyplace in the world. But where our interests or our treaty commitments are not involved, our role will be limited: We will not intervene militarily . . . Once [war] is over, we will do our share in helping to *bind up the wounds* of those who have participated in it. (emphasis added)

Nixon recognized that non-interventionism was elusive because the war is sometimes a necessary evil to achieve freedom. Indeed, one reason the president had to spell out the stakes of his Vietnamization project was because pulling out American soldiers and giving the South Vietnamese the capacity to "defend themselves" did little to induce a true sense of liberation or freedom, both for Americans and the Vietnamese. As Cathy Schlund-Vials (2014) eloquently puts it, the return of wounded and traumatized American veterans and the arrival of distressed South Vietnamese refugees on U.S. soil underscores the fear "that Americans returning and Asians migrating were—by virtue of their inability to forget the past—in fact, 'Vietnamized'" (193). Vietnamization, as a project of giving South Vietnam some symbolic autonomy, can be read as an international "coalition of the willing," where the project of Vietnamization leaves the Vietnamese "charged with the task of nation-building and conflict resolution" (195).

Military wars that have been Vietnamized produce lasting effects, through trauma as well as through new wars of necessity. For some Vietnamese Americans, the inability of their refugee community to free itself from the shackles of the war (or the United States to free itself from Vietnam) compels many of them to discover multiple definitions of freedom, taking up arms to protect American national interests but also those of their South Vietnamese forbearers who exist as "natives of a ghost country" (Vu 2013). What is potentially learned in fighting for both South Vietnam and the United States is that there is no singular freedom, but many freedoms. A pluralistic militarized sense of freedom emerges, most clearly in my interviews between what the soldiers told me "in private" versus the different standards or expectations of soldiers in the public.

For Vietnamese American GIs, theirs is a story of war without completion, not found in history's circle of winners but rather the space of losers, the forgotten. The incompletion of the U.S. Vietnamization project, which cast doubt on whether the United States lost the Vietnam War as South Vietnam assumed full responsibility for losing the conflict, casts a shadow over American overseas military operations and Americans' designated roles as protectors of the Free World. Under the Vietnamization of U.S. global wars since 1975, Vietnamese American soldiers must maintain faith in U.S. support of its friends abroad, but this faith is tested by their personal memory of the original Vietnamization project in Vietnam, something written off as a big loss for South Vietnamese.

Issues of militarized freedoms persist well into the twenty-first century as a result of the problems left unresolved during the twentieth century. The U.S. attempts to recoup the military losses of the past like those of Vietnam through wars in Iraq and Afghanistan, but the Vietnamese American soldiers' participation in these new Vietnamized wars illustrates their complicity in a military that recruits them to risk their lives for a bloody cause that both pains and empowers them. These soldiers stand on the horizon of America's military empire, looking ahead to the future and painfully aware of the past; they are self-willed freedom fighters, caught up in endless American wars resembling that unforgettable war in Vietnam. Through interconnected wars, these soldiers may overcome their historical liquidation as South Vietnamese people, risking their lives as back pay for the past failures and debts of an ill-gotten conflict, even a half century later, providing some returns on war, for themselves, South Vietnam, and the United States.

As new wars rage and wear on, what kind of sustainable Vietnamization project can exist, if any at all? What type of military ideology can people subscribe to that makes sense of their role in America's many untenable wars? What is the role of the Vietnamese American soldier to force themselves, if not others, to reflect upon the Vietnam War's legacies in the new century? These are questions that have no easy answers. The pursuit of freedom is an unsparing war waged on the battlefield of history, swept up in the aching recognition that, while not everyone returns from war to tell about it, some do, and the stories they tell add to the many narratives of loss, confusion, and hope of people in our distressed global times.

5

Empire's Residuals

The Return Migration of Former Exiles to Globalizing Vietnam

Like so many Vietnamese Americans who have traveled to visit or live in Vietnam, Tuyet Nguyen feels a sense of both alienation and familiarity that comes from being part of the "overseas Vietnamese," a category that refers to Vietnamese outside of Vietnam as well as their children. Coming back to the motherland as a child of refugees means carrying certain privileges and pains from the war. Nguyen works in one of the elite international universities established in Saigon, when she first arrived in Ho Chi Minh City, taking residence in this cushy new gentrified part of the city called "Saigon South," with its high-end malls and air-conditioned condos. The area felt sterile, she told me, evoking a less authentic version of "southern California" where she grew up.[1] What was real, however, was the need to chase her "American Dream" abroad, coming to Saigon as part of a more privileged generation of Vietnamese Americans born after the war and taking advantage of rising opportunities in Asia's developing markets, where their First World skills are attractive to globally oriented employers (Nguyen-Akbar 2016). Tuyet is aware that U.S.-born Vietnamese like her possess a huge comparative advantage in cultural capital, in contrast to the locals who earn on average a few U.S. dollars a day, and to their own parents, many of whom left as refugees and started their lives again, usually as penniless adults. My Americanized informant told me that as Saigon began to grow on her and began culturally "Vietnamizing" her again, she never forgets that she is a child of "exiles," and so brings her own Vietnamizing influence to Vietnam as a child of South Vietnamese diaspora, who will never feel totally comfortable in this place she now calls home.

This chapter focuses on two things: First, it considers the economic developments of contemporary Ho Chi Minh City (also called Saigon) as they refract the development spurred by the whirlwind U.S. effort to aid (and finally abandon) South Vietnam to make it a self-sufficient nation. Second, it considers how individuals think about Saigon, historically and contemporaneously. Such individuals include "overseas Vietnamese" who have returned to live or work in the country, southern locals who never left the country, business owners, locals, and foreign tourists. Through the conceptual framework of empire's residuals, I take stock of how Vietnam is thrust in a dramatic course of change, one that brings the country to a rude reawakening to the uncertain global future as much as the international war-torn past.

In a country that has been clocking double-digit growth in the first decade of the twenty-first century, the best economic boom in Asia after China in the 2000s, capitalism has rebounded in Vietnam in less than one generation, and this turbo-charged makeover can be construed as a residual of Cold War empire, a derivative of the exaggerated consumerist military-funded capital introduced by the Americans. As a society embracing capitalism yet still under the control of socialist rule, Vietnam's identity is bipolar, an exhilarating but contradictory hybrid that manifests itself not only through the contradictions of capital but also through culture and history. How then do the social and economic practices in Ho Chi Minh City feed into the production, circulation, and consumption of contemporary Vietnam? Moving beyond touristic sites of public memory like state monuments and museums which have been studied by other Vietnam scholars,[2] this chapter uses as its case study other forms of memory operating in the city with two names, whose protean forms of global commerce bear the trace elements of the imperial past. We are starting our journey, through the realms of both contemporary life and memory of Saigon. That specific focus is helpful because Saigon, in many ways, embodies what South Vietnam historically represented and still represents.

Putting aside the connotations of ruin commonly attached to areas devastated by war, I take up the term empire's residuals to track the *productive* nature of historical and political loss to recognize how a nation's pining for better, brighter times is secured through the remainders and outcomes of inglorious times that came before. Residuals plainly means what is left over when most of something is gone, a term useful for talking about neocolonial postwar relations in a "globalized" moment with few formal colonial empires to speak of. Residuals offers an approach to understanding how cities, regions, and countries change (or do not) over time; it is an approach that does not rely on a classic linear model for studying development, but the continued sales and profit of South Vietnam's past relationship with the United States. Such faith in development, though a product of good intentions, is often inadequate, particularly in the case of "developing" countries in the "global South" like Vietnam, whose industrial growth has been both sparked and impeded by foreign military activities of the West. Where foreign imperialism no longer dominates the concerns of Vietnamese society, at least as it did in prior epochs, my focus on the residuals of American empire in Vietnam is not meant to merely inject the problems of the past into the present, but to suggest how the U.S. war machine and complicated relationship with South Vietnam supply the capital and raw materials for Vietnam's current status as an "improved" nation through its former associations with the RVN.

The term residuals also means royalties due a performer, a financial term more evocative of economic matters than similar words like "residue," "reminder," or "remnant." My use of the term in building this concept of empire's residuals resonates with what anthropologist Ann Stoler calls (2008) "imperial debris" to describe the social waste of wars, which are recycled or repeated over time rather than cleared away. By virtue of their scale, modern empires produce "unfinished histories" that force people to not recall and repeat victimized pasts, but also deal with "imperial effects [that] occupy multiple historical tenses . . . products of the past imperfect that selectively permeate the present as they shape both the conditional subjunctive and uncertain futures" (194–195). For a nation that has lost much through war, an event during which almost every Vietnamese person lost something or someone precious, cashing in on the memory of war would seem to net little benefit. Yet, there are still some proceeds to be made. Despite buzz for the "Vietnam economic miracle," one must still calculate what the residuals produced from the violent "end" of South Vietnam might yield for building the Vietnam and Saigon of tomorrow.

The concept of empire's residuals acknowledges that we are still living in an imperialist age, despite the supposed comity of a "community of nations" after the end of the Cold War. According to philosophers Michael Hardt and Antonio Negri (2000), we now live in "Empire" in a broader global sense with corporations, rich global elites, and First World nations like the United States holding power over the earth's poor in a phase of global development led by the "maturation of the new imperial design . . . built on the ashes of the old imperialisms" (246). Vietnam's pull by globalization, I argue, manifests the residual traces of the Cold War, reminding us how the U.S. efforts to "Vietnamize" the war and turn South Vietnam into a pro-Western capitalist nation turned into a "symbolic center of a whole series of struggles around the world" (280). Vietnamization was as much an economic project as a military one, and it concerned more than South Vietnam, but many developing countries like it.

This struggle for autarky remains operative in our globalized age, when nation-states like Vietnam are technically free of foreign imposition and colonial rule yet must trade and deal with still-powerful nations like the United States. In this most densely populated area of Vietnam, the largest recipient of foreign investment in the country, local boosters and the government like to downplay the imperial history of Vietnam defeating former enemies to drive home the message of its increasing positive relations with once unfriendly nations like the United States, the lone superpower after the Soviet Union's collapse. The neoliberal economic reforms ushered in to Vietnam since the 1980s follow those of the "Washington Consensus" on international trade, which have been ceaseless in their emphasis on privatization, corporatization, and globalization in the developing world. This reflects in part a new American empire inasmuch as the United States exerts its economic power in the world by pushing developing countries to enter new alliances, while voluntarily opening up their labor and consumer markets at a moment in time when the United States wields its power "more through the dollar" (247). In a globalizing world tinged by shades of Americanization, my formulation of empire's residuals follows Hardt and Negri's recognition that the American War in Vietnam was the decisive military moment before the United States assumed the mantle of global leadership. Indeed, Nixon's visit to the People's Republic of China in 1972 meant to diplomatically isolate North Vietnamese in the final year of U.S. troop withdrawal under the Vietnamization program. This move was pivotal in marking that transition from a geopolitical perception of U.S. foreign interventionism abroad to one based on interregional economic cooperation and internationalism. If one were looking for the residuals of U.S.

Figure 5.1. Sign in south Saigon advertising new high-rise condos (photo by author).

empire and the vestigial signs of the defunct South Vietnamese republic in Vietnam today, where would one look? The imprimatur of South Vietnam's prior role as the home base for free-wheeling Western capitalism persists, we might say, in residual form. Because of this, South Vietnam lives on in strange fashion, as a distant shadow of the receding past, but also as an unmovable specter of war haunting the country's speculative future, where the past refuses to desist or sit in abeyance to the utopian impulses and historical amnesia of globalization.

Ho Chi Minh City is rushing headlong toward global capitalism, yet Vietnam's largest city cannot escape its symbolism as the former target of military imperial interests to clutch a new identity as a global magnet for capitalist entrepreneurship. Through a cultural anthropology and urban history approach, this chapter offers some reflections on contemporary Ho Chi Minh City/Saigon as the city reflects its former self as the capital of South Vietnam. A lengthy discussion of Saigon's role as the former base of foreign military operations occupies the first part of this chapter. This section concerns how the U.S. project to "Vietnamize" the Vietnam War made an enormous impact on Saigon's local economy and environment, and how it actually led to the deepening of American/Western ties in this region. The second portion uses interviews with locals, tourists, and expats to grapple with the appearance of and excitement for a "new Saigon" that exists in light of persistent memories of the old one (see figure 5.1).

Saigon's Wartime and Postwar Development

In spring 1975, as the last of the Americans left and the communists declared victory, the new government implemented policies to alleviate crowding in the cities and push people to farming collectives. The Communist Party's efforts to purge the cultural deposit of Americanism clashed with the government's recognition that Saigon's concentration of foreign assets provided a sort of windfall for an "unadventurous industrialization of the country" (Thrift and Forbes 2012, 156). After the Fall of Saigon in 1975, there was also enormous work to be done by the reunification government in "re-Vietnamizing" the southern populace and breaking its addiction to American culture and foreign goods. They found it difficult cleaning up busy streets rife with illicit activities, extricating people from a property-based market of exchange, and confiscating privately owned homes and resettling people into new economic zones to tear asunder Saigon as the fortress of the entitled bourgeois class (Hoang 2010: 35–37). Vietnamese critics penned tracts on the criminality of private ownership, while the communist officials trumpeted a new kind of Saigon under socialism. In 1977, the local government-owned print media announced the end of the old Saigon but suggested that people should not make "a habit of regretting the passing of an artificial glittering Saigon" as "a consumer and commercial city" (ibid.). The new provisional government began to make over the city's image, starting with changing its name to Ho Chi Minh City on July 1976, burying the old designation under the moniker of the nation's beloved revolutionary father. Saigon is used far more often than the longer title HCMC by locals as well as overseas refugee communities who have stuck to this name to preserve their South Vietnamese heritage in the face of the socialist party's erasure of their history. As a result, the usage of the two names feels arbitrary, but their confusion shows the equivocation over the naming of places, the social and historical meanings attached to a place. As Thu-Hương Nguyễn-Võ (2010) writes, Saigon is a "ghostly and nostalgic name in the distant glare of militaristically triumphant name of Ho Chi Minh City... Saigon in its associations with capitalism beckons from the future but only as a ghost of itself in its vanquished past."

A former trading seaport captured by the French colonialists in 1859, Saigon was named the capital of Cochinchina a few years later. Dubbed another "Pearl of the Orient" by the French (along with Laos's Vientiane and Cambodia's Phnom Penh), the city served as an administrative base for "modernized" Vietnamese elites viewed as loyal to the French, but the idea was that these urban elites would be able to always serve French colonial interests. This parasitic relationship ended with the French being ousted by Vietnamese independence fighters and the U.S. entry into Vietnam's colonial war for independence. Hoping to turn the various regional elements of South Vietnam into a functioning polity, the leaders of the South Vietnamese regime working with the Americans ruled from their headquarters in the primary city of Saigon, which also served as the base for U.S. command from 1956 until 1975. The U.S. military occupation of South Vietnam faced enormous public backlash and led to Richard Nixon's Vietnamization program, with expectations of a complete departure of the Americans from the region and the war. Inflated hopes of a Western-style local capitalist economy and a standing army in South Vietnam were allied to a temporary boost in U.S aid to the RVN.[3] As a term specific to war, Vietnamization represented the short-changed dreams of a well-armed, prosperous South Vietnam with a stable government. With fears of the potential chaos that could result from Americans leaving, the ferocity of economic restructuring in the country under Vietnamization showed that U.S. military ventures stimulated national growth in a rapid manner. Vietnamization, in this sense, is not defined as strictly a U.S. policy concerning South Vietnam's political future but an ongoing referendum about fears of the economic development of countries allied with the Americans, regarding what it could be and where it is heading. The decision to "Vietnamize" the war was tied to hope for South Vietnam to exist as a beachhead for the Americanization of Asian political economy, linking Vietnam to a U.S.-led regional system.[4]

As an urbanization project, Vietnamization encouraged the vigorous clearing away of rural areas, pushing villagers into satellite camps around Saigon to disable the brio of communist insurgents assumed to be hiding in outlying hot spots. The policy ironically strengthened American influence in South Vietnam, the latter increasingly dependent on the United States for support, all the while entwining military and civilian life (McCollum 1983). Villages were bombed and villagers relocated close to Saigon, which was spared and insulated from much of the war's fighting, and soon swelled with refugees holding three times the population for which it was suited. The city took form as a "paradise of freedom," the last barrier against communist infiltration while rural hamlets fell. By the end of the war, the population of Saigon had spiked to more than 6 million from an estimated 2 million at the start of the war (Gough 1984: 31). Under Vietnamization, the downsizing of military-related labor seriously affected the incomes of Vietnamese personnel working for the United States but also many auxiliary workers, bar workers, and prostitutes who fed and, in turn, were fed from the U.S. war industry—a black market industry that had injected millions of dollars in foreign aid to grease the palms of the city's rulers and develop this former colonial entrepôt into a modern city. This development project under the war apparatus essentially set into motion unprecedented urban growth that was not sustainable or stable. Through the false guise of Vietnamization as a project of American "benign assimilation," the South Vietnamese temporally "buried their resentments, swallowed their national pride, and surrendered responsibility for their destiny to outsiders . . . [though] the South Vietnamese regarded the American presence as oppressive and stultifying . . . its removal left a void they could not fill" (Herring 2007: 22).

The way that Vietnamization operates in communist Vietnam today (if we can call it that) greatly differs from its original military context, but the two historically distinct projects of letting the Vietnamese people handle their own business are similar in terms of state control over their society. Vietnamization is literally translated in Vietnamese as *Việt Nam Hóa*, meaning the flowering or development of Vietnamese culture and society, which has much broader meaning. However, the forms of cultural Americanization that operated under the guise of Vietnamization were pointed out in the Hanoi-based journal *Vietnamese Studies* published in the final month of the war in a special issue, entitled "U.S. Neo-colonialism in South Vietnam: The 'Vietnamization' of the War." Vietnamese nationalist scholars observed that the close relationship between South Vietnamese and the U.S. cultures that developed under the war will continue to harm the future ability of the South Vietnamese to step away from their addiction to the Americans: "In recent years, although the American GI's have withdrawn from South Vietnam, American culture at its worst remains. The Vietnamization of the war has not put a brake on the Americanization of life and customs" (Hien and Le 1975: 127).[5] Vietnamization was "bearing poisonous fruit" (ibid.), and it would take years to undo, if that were possible, the deep corrosion of South Vietnamese hearts and minds that persists after the American guns and fighter planes have disappeared.

Despite the original intentions of the United States to "Vietnamize" the war, this quote identifies the steadfast influence of American culture in Saigon and its control over local radio and television stations, as well as newspapers, all as part of what he believes is a "cultural Americanization effort" to introduce and permanently impose a "synthetic" foreign culture. In 1975 and perhaps today, the by-products of this cultural Americanization via Vietnamization, which are construed as anti-communist and anti-Vietnamese, include everything from a critical liberal arts education to anti-establishment rock music to cosmetic surgery, from sexual promiscuity to substance abuse. Socialist nationalism and Marxist class consciousness are stunted, as Vietnamization was "designed to mask two attacks against Communism as viewed in the optic of Saigon" by allowing everyday popular culture to "transcend politics" and by allowing people to "enjoy a freedom which knows no bounds" (Hien and Le 1975: 126). As a project of racial assimilation, Ly Chanh Trung denounces the U.S. plan to "transform us and our descendants into a sort of yellow-skinned Yankees" (129).

The revolutionary government formally banned the use of the official name Saigon (except in the case of international airport codes which recognize only SGN), but the denizens of the city and the Vietnamese public still prefer the more colloquial historic name of Saigon. Indeed, the imposed name of Ho Chi Minh City never fully erases the long colonial history of Saigon as an important "contact zone" for merchants and travelers, where a contact zone is a "space where cultures meet, clash, and grapple with each other, often in contexts of highly asymmetrical relations of power, such as colonialism, slavery, or their aftermaths as they are lived out in the world today" (Pratt 1991: 34). Lang and Kolb (1980) suggest that the name Saigon comes out of French colonial times meaning a "tribute of the West,"[6] reminding us that "the urban area now known as Ho Chi Minh City is not then a foreign concept grafted upon the Vietnamese, but rather a normal development of the society which has been greatly influenced by various foreign powers" (13). The Communist Party's attempts to wrestle Saigon away from its "colonial" origins by literally renaming it seeks to drive out the city's many foreign influences and the competing diverse narratives about what it means to Vietnamese. During the war, the Hanoi-based government already took swipes at the Saigonese, refusing to see them as good Vietnamese subjects for being so Westernized. But in the twenty-first century, the urban denizens of Saigon are the new stars of Vietnam, as it is now fashionable in many respects to be wealthy and Westernized in the neoliberal age of globalization (Taylor 2001: 187).

This acquiescing to South Vietnam's pre-1975 cosmopolitan colonial roots also has much to do with the mixed results of the new communist government in erasing the memory of the South Vietnamese republic. During postwar reconstruction, the humble peasant was celebrated by the communists as an important symbolic status for the new nation, while city folks were treated as corrupted people who needed to be sent to the countryside to be Vietnamized and "reeducated" on being authentically Vietnamese again. After the reunification of the country, many northerners were shocked to discover their southern compatriots had more technology and consumer goods than they had ever seen. Upon communist victory, the locus for Vietnamese economic stimulus stayed above the 17th parallel, while the South became a target of social "mobilization" plans (vận động xã hội) to rid the place of the taint of the French and Americans.

Despite the South's obvious economic advantages and material assets for the new socialist republic, this national reprogramming idealized the north as being decades ahead of the South, while the former was construed as backwards. While the peasants of South Vietnam's countryside experienced the worst ravages of war and epitomized the heroic "resistance spirit" of the Vietnamese people, Saigon's urbanites came to embody dysfunctional values. As Phillip Taylor observes, during the 1980s even the southern countryside came to be regarded as a place where under U.S. tutelage "a new modernist consciousness had emerged" (2001: 81). Despite the government's actions to diminish the luster and attraction of this modern orientation, the region's economic productivity has historically served as a pragmatic "resistance" to northern high-minded socialism. In this manner, Taylor argues, a discreet form of warfare was waged by the south against the north, undertaken not through ideological or guerilla tactics but via social activities once considered bad or regressive. Put differently, the communist regime's uptake and doctoring of Saigon's economic success represents the quiet victory of the south over the north, a revolution where capitalism extends to the rest of the country. From this perspective, the "dawning" of Vietnamese modernity might be dated not to emancipation by northern troops or party initiations but to developments in the south. With present-day Saigon spearheading economic breakthroughs, Vietnam's shaky path to prosperity under state-managed crony capitalism evidences the wheeling-and-dealing of a new "spirit of innovation," one that draws on South Vietnam as a historic "crucible of modernity . . . one of the frontline states of the U.S.-sponsored project of postcolonial nation building" (80).

In post-millennial Vietnam, the party's directing of capitalist investment toward global interests is a far cry from the quick-fix schemes promoted during the late 1980s, with its "rapid sense of displacement, disorientation and even moral panic stemming from . . . an economic and political transformation that often seems out of control . . . [with] lost youth, lost time, lost opportunities, ruptured families, victimization, 'falling behind'" (Werner 2006: 312). The reunification government sought to remove many city dwellers (almost 20%) to the countryside to alleviate population problems and reeducate them, while those remaining urbanites were targeted for reeducation as "cities had to be transformed into containers of socialist thought" (Thrift and Forbes 2006: 137). Despite the departure of Saigon's urban residents, many sneaked back into the city without state permission, drawing on the city's history of chaotic entrepreneurship and mobility to regain their economic losses (Lang and Kolb 1980). In terms of Vietnamese pragmatism, "the past is neither idealized nor criminalized" (307); the turn toward capitalism is not an admission of communism's failure or the victory of South Vietnam, but a form of "structural adjustment," one tilting toward greater global integration as a means of instilling national pride and economic stability. This social reordering counts not as a total open embrace of foreign capital and globalization, but a practical solution to the holes of a former command-based economy, and the necessity of taking whatever resources the Americans brought and left in order to retool them toward new Vietnamized ends.

The return of South Vietnam to its capitalist roots became evident after the collapse of Vietnam's domestic economy due to postwar collectivist farming, which led to rapid decline of national GDP (Bhaduri 1977). With the passage of Đổi Mới policies (Renovation) in 1986, the turnaround in government policy to encourage foreign capitalist investment and economic growth at breakneck speed led to a kind of hybrid "red capitalism" that aimed to recoup financial losses and stagnation caused by socialist policies. The pro-capitalist orientation front-loads service-oriented manufacturing jobs characteristic of an export-oriented nation, which has uprooted people from the countryside and herded them into already overcrowded cities, especially Ho Chi Minh City (HCMC). Recent changes in HCMC have caused a shock wave on the appearance, tenor, and feel of Saigonese and Vietnamese life. For a city filled with people making their fortunes alongside tycoons and plutocrats, the story of Saigon today plays out the more dramatic version of South Vietnam's longer track toward economic achievement.

The colonial and capitalist legacy of the "Vietnamized" American war has returned with a vengeance as a material trace of history, influencing the ways communist Vietnam attempts to Vietnamize capitalism. Many country folks touted as model citizens have decamped from their homes to come to the city to learn the new values of capitalism and hopefully to strike it rich as the country continues to privatize its socialist apparatus and put up the nouveau urban rich as paragons of society. The capital of Hanoi must now try to keep up with Saigon, as the latter posts big outputs and economic increases annually compared to the nation's capital. This turnabout of Saigon's fate from a pariah city, once needing to be rehabilitated, to the archetypical modern/global Vietnamese city, stands as a tribute to the forms of international relations and trade ushered in by the Cold War. The returns of the war, I believe, are made possible through the capitalist and social engineering projects that no longer rehash ideas about class inequality, foreign influence, bourgeois ills, and social evils. Rather, they draw on Saigon's imperial roots as a "industrial frontier" to fuel Vietnam's pathway toward international success.

Luring multinational companies and foreign corporate investors to Saigon, Vietnam by the mid-2000s attracted considerable hype as another Asian industrial dynamo, while retaining its special status as one of the five communist nations left in the world. Vietnam was able to incorporate the values of the World Trade Organization and World Bank, neoliberal institutions led by the United States. In this context of "free trade," there is still a symbolic and real payment-in-kind for history (Vietnam is paying back the loans that South Vietnam owed to the United States as part of its deal for normalized relations).[7] The communist regime was willing to amortize the millions of dollars of debt owed by its domestic enemy to its foreign enemy as a condition of receiving new trade deals and integrating into the world economy (Sanger 1997). The struggling Hanoi government balked initially at paying back even the $12 million (out of the nearly $1 billion) owed by the South Vietnamese to the Americans. Despite winning the war, the Communist Party of Vietnam must deal with the financial losses of South Vietnam just to receive basic economic concessions, and so their future depends on the returns made on war and residuals of American empire. From this view, the full throttle of Saigon's bourgeois spirit erupts again, buoyed by an eager socialist regime wanting to paint Vietnam as an appealing place welcoming of global commerce and Westerners.

The Vietnamization of Globalization

Economic development today is keen on revenue-generating remittances from overseas Vietnamese, FDI by businesses, and foreign aid from rich countries, all of which are a boon to the nation's coffers, shelling out the cash and seeding investment capital for the developing nation-state. But development in the country is more than a question of a local and national adaptation to global conditions and forces (what we might call the Vietnamization of globalization), but a re-appropriation of older historical elements. In Vietnam, there is a cross-pollination of two political economic systems—socialist and capitalist—that brings together various elements of history in a new syncretism. This is evident in new, towering buildings and high-end commercial spaces erected upon messy, unpaved streets and ramshackle buildings still coming out of the shambles of war. Newly planned neighborhoods on the outskirts of Saigon remind one immediately of the war, and the economic incorporation of South Vietnam's most extreme provinces can trace their early assimilation during the U.S. modernization effort in South Vietnam, turning it into the most urbanized country in Southeast Asia after Singapore (Douglass and Huang 2007).

At the height of the American occupation of South Vietnam, the planning of Saigon was bound to political imperatives that simultaneously boosted economic trade. Nixon's "forced urbanization" and "de-ruralization" policy, under the auspices of reducing communist infiltration and ramping up Saigon's central military command, turned the region in less than a decade from a mostly rural territory into an urban one with highways, factories, and modern housing (Lang and Kolb 1980). The slapdash aggregation of economic activity around the politicized city in the face of potential communist infiltration contributed to a population explosion in the city that only aggravated living conditions. The subsequent American effort to "Vietnamize" the conflict meant creating an "independent" South Vietnam cohered around a fortified capital of Saigon. Sociologist Ulrich Beck (2000) coined the term "Brazilinization" to describe shantytowns erected next to expensive high-rises in South America's largest economy. But to utilize Vietnamization, one must speak to the term's genesis, when it referred to another course of development during war's duress, when class disparities were first introduced in a major way that established a strong hierarchical relationship between urban rich and poor that made South Vietnam one of the most stratified societies in the world.

The "savage urbanization" fostered in the former capital of RVN under the Americans turned countless destitute people into the necessary sacrifice for modern "progress." This memory of Vietnamization has returned, so to speak, haunting the global expansion of HCMC, which displays its own economic form of creative destruction—even if the overriding military impetus is not there. As Saigon has been the main historic staging ground for Vietnam-American encounters, most of this activity—cultural, business, tourist—continues to happen there.

Globalization raises new issues related to how Vietnamese national interests can be entangled with American security interests (Drummond 2000). It is worthwhile to consider how the globalization of Saigon's economy recalibrates the city's future under the stranglehold of a new world order conceived in the Cold War context, when the United States allowed foreign companies from Japan and Taiwan to penetrate the Vietnamese domestic market and make South Vietnam the center of multinational corporate interests. It may be more useful here to think of the Vietnamese communist nation-state as advancing another kind of Vietnamization project, different from but evocative of the American one, one that puts a good foot forward as a response to new global forces, especially when the United States is again pivoting toward Asia, and Vietnam is now embracing America in the wake of an emerging superpower like China. In 2014, despite human rights concerns, the United States ended its ban on weapons sales to Vietnam to lift maritime security in the region and to boost the two countries' defense relationship. Vietnam's close contact with the United States can provide some flashbacks to the country's prior entanglements with this mighty foreign power, but whose help now seems a necessary evil, even if this creates a structure of dependency that might harken back to the South Vietnamese alliance with the United States (although these relationships are very different in structure and form).[8]

Though globalization is often associated with Americanization in many ways (U.S. companies like McDonald's and Starbucks opened their first Vietnamese stores in HCMC to great fanfare), all countries attempt to create their own version of it (Berndtson 2000). Yet, the disaggregating spatial effects of globalization truncate the geopolitical legacies of war, reintroducing their effects but also drowning them under the trifecta of urbanization (*đô thị hóa*), modernization (*hiện đại hóa*), and industrialization (*công nghiệp hóa*). Here, the floating memory of wartime Saigon can be found within a modern cityscape, helping us observe another "transit of empire" (Byrd 2011).

While not all new developments in Saigon can be attributed to the U.S. war project or its Vietnamization, that military history provides the groundwork for developing associative links between the international aspects of Cold War industries and "postwar" globalizing economies. The boondoggle of making South Vietnam into a Westernized Asian hub in many ways set the wheels in motion for Saigon's current road to financial independence. When the United States disqualified South Vietnam from any additional foreign aid after 1975, despite an initial boost in 1969 when Vietnamization was first implemented, this marked the end of continued South Vietnamese dependency on the United States.

The termination of patronage led to the downward spiral and capsizing of the country in 1975. This sad ending to the troubled short-term,

20-year existence for the country cast a pall on hopes for its future return. Yet, the hope for an affluent, powerful Saigon never perished. The wealth in Saigon today compels a reckoning with "a force that not always bares a proper name" (Stoler 2006). That force, if we wish to identify it, can be called empire's residuals.

The term helps to conceptually discuss what is happening in Vietnam at this moment and lends a name to the architectures of globalization built partially from Cold War political economies. This recognition of the traces of imperial history is important at a time when "the most natural thing in the world is that the world appears to be politically united, that the market is global, and that power is organized through this universality" (Hardt and Negri 2000: 354). The international trading markets and commodity supply chains that the United States introduced to South Vietnam provided a baseline for hyperconsumerism in Saigon. As one taxi driver I spoke with told me, "The stuff the Americans brought over, we've been using ever since."[9] It is necessary then to consider how present efforts by local entrepreneurs, property developers, and expats to globalize Vietnam (and Vietnamize globality) fathoms a South Vietnamese-style capitalist modernity first incubated and encouraged during the war. The foreign bourgeois influences of the south once targeted for extirpation by the communist state now feed into the money-making machinery of get-rich-quick schemes by state bureaucrats and private investors.

The present insistence by various actors to create a prosperous southern economy gleans some part of the original U.S. mission to make South Vietnam and, by extension, the rest of Vietnam a sphere of influence under Vietnamization—even if they do not use that term. To wit, Vietnamization has evolved from its original use to something that today can be used to refer to a variety of things. The term's meaning and use over time remain historically embedded, but the idea of a hypercapitalist (and heavily armed) South Vietnam can be partially observed under a socialist regime more friendly to Western trade, where forms of military-induced capitalism introduced by the Americans are now selectively exploited as well as monitored by the country's political leaders making selective use of Saigon's past to deal with shocks of the neoliberal era.[10] The city's future is entrusted to the guiding hands of regional entities like the Ho Chi Minh City People's Committee, which must reinterpret progress for a local population that is seen as loyal to outsiders. Without necessarily admitting its mistakes of the past or its indebtedness to the Americans, Hanoi's Communist Party must prop up the merits of Western capitalism without releasing its reins of control over South Vietnam and its unruly people.

For now, the Saigonese are the models of globally oriented Vietnam, a remarkable shift from an earlier "anti-urban bias" when communists viewed the city's populations as rapid "consumers" of American culture living in a "parasitic metropolis" (Gainsborough 2003). As the historic "capitalist frontier" of Vietnam, Saigon took global form when the Americans tried to connect the city to other nodes in U.S. global military networks (Dacy 1986). South Vietnam developed much faster (and continues to do so) than other parts of the country for this reason. Today, the Vietnamese government divides the country into three key economic zones (KEZs) in the north, central, and south. Yet, the southern region is responsible for 70 percent of the country's export revenue, and Saigon's airport alone accounts for two-thirds of Vietnam's flights (*Business in Asia*, June 8, 2013). To say Saigon is the economic engine of Vietnam is an understatement.

As one of the sprawling mega-cities springing up in Asia, Saigon gets repurposed in elastic ways that are unpredictable. A consideration of this "global war city," as I have explained elsewhere (Bui 2016), needs to be situated with respect to local and international histories that both encouraged and stunted its growth. For example, the failure of Saigon to be seen as a "global city" like New York, Seoul, or London has much to do with the geopolitical meddling and protracted warfare that hindered cities in the Global South from reaching the status of a "world-class" city, even though it is the richest province in Vietnam. With its capital of Saigon leading the charge, the south stands tall again in the economic race between two halves of the country. Currently, Ho Chi Minh City and Hanoi are rushing to finish their metro-system projects to relieve congestion in their cities. The northern trains are built by Chinese companies, which attest to the socialist connections between Hanoi and Beijing, but this rail system has suffered from a string of high-profile accidents that have put in doubt its safety or viability (Tatarski 2017). By contrast, the southern railway project, which has been free of accidents, is headed by Japanese conglomerates with involvement from the French,

Italian, and South Koreans. This suggests South Vietnam's economic prowess, close ties with Western nations, and finesse in urban planning and civil engineering. These local rail systems represent global-local configurations that are not seemingly tied to war, even though a closer look would reveal something more.

Insofar as southern Vietnam's economic rise signifies the motility and volatility of new global engagements, it also creates the avenues for what Lisa Yoneyama (1999) calls "mnemonic detours," where individuals "traverse not only urban surfaces but also the geopolitical boundaries of the nation-state" (114). Such detours of historical memory, if read within the framework of empire's residuals, refamiliarizes the relationship between what Scott Laderman (2009) describes as global imperialism and global commerce, two things inextricably linked during the Cold War. By speaking of globalization as a moment to ponder the imperial foundations of the present, Laderman believes this again directs the focus on history and politics when everything seems to be all about the economy and trade. Through the residuals of empire framework, we can understand how development rubs up against what Walter Benjamin (1968) described as the "empty, homogenous time" of global capitalism "filled by the presence of the now" (261). But the push and pull force of globalization, if observed carefully, can reveal the multiplier effects of a prior moment in time that was not just concerned with violent destruction, but cosmopolitanism, wealth-building, and cultural novelty.[11] One example of empire's residuals are the products created by former refugees who had left the country but now return to make their mark on the homeland.

The Return(s) of the South Vietnamese Refugee

While there are no reliable numbers for how many former South Vietnamese refugees have returned to Vietnam to live or visit, the impact of the Việt Kiều or "overseas Vietnamese," as the communist state calls them, cannot be ignored. In 2012, Vietnam ranked seventh in the world for foreign remittances or money sent from overseas communities back to the home country. The 4.5 million Vietnamese living abroad accounted for nearly 70 percent of all foreign investment in Vietnam since 1991; this capital is used primarily for business, while only 6 percent of all money was for gifts to relatives. Monies from South Vietnam's refugees has been the major source of economic development, according to a deputy director of the State Bank's HCMC branch (*Tuoi-TreNews*, June 8, 2013). In 1994, when the United States lifted its trade embargo on Vietnam, many returning refugees were viewed with suspicion. As Vietnam ramped up its desire to attract foreign investment in the early 2000s, communist leaders were quick to say that "the ex-refugees are among Vietnam's greatest assets," and they are welcome, but do not bring back any bad blood as "we don't want Việt Kiều who want to fight the war all over again" (Ly 2003). They have been granted privileges enjoyed by nationals, like access to real estate (they can own property but not the land which in name belongs to "the people" and is managed by the state). An estimated half million have returned for work or pleasure or to retire, bringing in technology and skilled knowledge, thus keeping this region's economy humming and giving positive returns on their postwar exile, considered a negative in the aftermath of the war (*VietnamNet Bridge*, January 24, 2011).

Though Hanoi is the political center of Vietnam, Saigon possesses cachet as the economic capital of the country since this is where most of these former refugees originate. Urban commercialism here assigns new meaning to a popular old expression, "ăn bắc, mặc nam," which literally means, eating like a northerner and dressed like a southerner. This phrase points to a dual paradoxical form of national identification, where one must internally embody communist ideals, carrying them in one's heart, but externally must maintain a well-kept appearance as a modern capitalist. In other words, one must feel poor and know the hunger of the working classes, but must also look stylish and lavish. However, this ideological demand is far less effective for overseas Vietnamese, who are not easily compelled to follow state mandates.

For the South Vietnamese refugees who left, many have returned to Vietnam to find better opportunities in their former homeland. For members of the postwar diaspora, original memories of the homeland are now being radically augmented or altered by their return after years of absence; these former exiles turned transnational elites carry out another reimagining of Vietnam and Saigon by doing so (Carruthers 2008). Some return with a specific post-1975 "immigrant bubble" mentality, carrying the ethos, customs, and thinking of the time in which they left, but after decades of absence, they may feel out of place in or distant from Vietnam. Others, however, feel comfortable returning, finding it necessary to reinstate that old memory of Saigon and assert it to recall their personal history.

Dinh Q. Le is a Vietnamese American who works and lives in HCMC as a visual artist. After leaving Vietnam as a refugee, Le came back as one of the earliest returnees when Vietnam slowly opened up to "foreigners" in the mid-1990s. Though he claims he lost his Vietnamese identity when he left, he believes that, by returning and staying, he can reclaim his South Vietnamese identity, ironically in the place where the nation of South Vietnam has been vanquished. In a sense, Le is "Vietnamizing" (and being Vietnamized) in his homeland, bringing a diasporic South Vietnamese political consciousness and cultural sensibility that still holds a torch for the past despite government censorship. As he explained to me:

> When my family escaped southern Vietnam in 1978, we left everything behind, including our identity as Vietnamese. When I returned to Vietnam to live in the mid-1990s, collecting, and learning the cultural histories that are embedded in the objects I found, was a way of reclaiming my heritage, my identity ... The continued systematic erasure of the history of southern Vietnam by the current government, the lack of analysis of our cultural resources, strict governmental control of the flow of information, and the self-censorship that is so deeply ingrained in current Vietnamese society have together led us to a point at which we know very little about either who we were or who we are. There is an urgent need for expressions of collective memory freed from restraint; many people are actively engaged in building these narratives—I chose to do so through art.[12]

For Le, both his politicized art and his residual status as a South Vietnamese national can potentially run afoul of or invite mistrust from government officials who monitor his activities at every turn, as I have seen in censored exhibits of his. As the former refugee explains, the appeal of living here is because "Saigon has always been Westernized, a cosmopolitan city and I think when the country reopened again, Saigon sort of reverted backed to its original old self before 1975 but it's all new and different now than before 1975. I think the attitude hasn't changed." Saigon carries potential for change, according to him more than Hanoi with its "provincial mind," because Saigon is open to everything due to the American influence during the war. All things considered, Le is of two minds when he claims that Saigon is reverting to its old self before 1975 while *also* looking "all new and different." Today, Le is one the hottest artists in Vietnam and Asia, whose work has been featured in many countries, making him a figure of the global contemporary art scene. For the artist, however, the "southiness" of his Vietnamese identity cycles back to HCMC's roots in American capitalism; the fast-forward movement of the city toward global modernity can be read alternatively as a way for the Vietnamese, Le believes, to distance themselves further from the gutted pain of the war. Saigon then is a kind of palindrome, whose very name references a capitalist future that can be read backwards through the history of war (and the future imagined during that time).

The return(s) of the refugee, building on the residuals of empire, reflect a major shift away from a Vietnamese diasporic refugee identity structured around pure hatred of communists and a vow not to return to Vietnam until it is free from tyranny. For those who left as young refugees, their political identity is centered on the simultaneous pride for being Vietnamese, American, South Vietnamese, and a global citizen (Carruthers 2008). For those former castaways, the old Saigon is largely gone, but the new one has not replaced the former one entirely. Alex Hoa is a returnee who left Saigon as a teenager with his family in 1979 but later returned to settle permanently in Vietnam and build a new life, despite believing he would never come back to his childhood home:

> I did not come back looking for the past. I'm Saigonese in that way. It's different than Hanoi where people remember their history. We [Southerners] are concerned with making a living and the future. After 1975, there were not supposed to be any capitalists. It was unimaginable. Now, we have billionaires living in Vietnam.[13]

Taking me to his childhood homes and current haunts, Hoa told me that though people think history is represented by war-themed museums, it can also mean what economic values people carry with them and how they reflect certain ways of doing things in the past. As a television producer, Hoa is one of many refugees from the diaspora returning to HCMC, offering their human capital as former South Vietnamese nationals and U.S. citizens to Vietnam's mixed economy. Hoa brings technical abilities and education from the West, identifying himself not as an "expat" or foreigner living in another country, but a "returnee" who is changing Vietnam as much as Vietnam is changing them. The government that once condemned these refugees as traitors now actively woos and courts them.[14] The government in Vietnam today uses less truculent rhetoric to describe those who left the country to win them back, creating new forms of transnational exchanges and trade regimes (Small 2012). The American War in Vietnam was highly destructive but also generative in creating new global networks and linkages. My discussion of the concept of empire's residuals hypothesizes that some people do in fact profit from the social outcomes of war and residuals of empire, creating their own sense of value within new economic circumstances to get ahead in life, but also find their roots.

Overseas Vietnamese are returning to their homeland in increasing numbers. Many of these visitors are the children of South Vietnamese refugees or refugees themselves, who bring an infusion of capital but also shape the new social reality and perception of Saigon (Earl 2004; Truitt 2012, 2013; Speece 2002). Meanwhile, locals as part of the emerging middle class of Saigon are caught between living for themselves but also existing for the communist party-nation, and thus they "may feel materially secure, but sense a broader ambivalence to their prosperity" (Leshkowich 2012: 97). Ambivalence toward middle-class status in a developing communist country can be more acute for overseas Vietnamese Americans, many of whom already come with higher incomes and certain First World entitlements and rights that, along with a U.S. passport and currency, give them the ability to freely travel across borders with relative ease.

This new sense of liberating Saigon and opening it to the world is reflected in my interview with Kynam Doan, a young property developer who left the United States to work in Vietnam for major real estate business, designing hotel-like residential spaces in Saigon. As he told me, Vietnamese Americans like him can see the potential of Saigon, despite the red tape that surrounds local development.[15] He explains his situation this way:

> My parents questioned why I would come back because it's the reverse from what they did. They couldn't understand why the children they left with to find better opportunities would come back. They don't think they have opportunities there and they're worried about my future . . . Because of the economic downturn in the U.S. and everywhere else, people are looking for opportunities so obviously they're gonna go to an emerging economy. A lot of Viet Kieu have come back because at least they have a connection, whether culturally or . . . to possibly have a bigger advantage in Asia or somewhere else. I think the city will get more sophisticated, people here are nostalgic about the past.[16]

Doan believes the children of refugees are contributing to the city by bolstering its economy and improving Saigon's cultural sophistication. While building their resumes, Americanized Vietnamese subjects like Doan return to Saigon to try to reconnect with their Vietnamese roots, while bringing with them a less politicized memory of Saigon than their elders. Where many of Saigon's first-generation refugees are too old or rooted in the United States to undertake that journey back to the homeland (or opposed to the idea due to their hatred of communists), their well-heeled progeny can come back to occupy Saigon, making it wealthier and possibly democratic (as it was hoped during the war).

While the 1990s witnessed Vietnam's slow opening to the outside world, the economic developments of the 2000s bore fruit in the sprouting of Vietnam into a major exporting nation as well as destination site for transnational workers like Jenni Trang Le, one of many Vietnamese Americans bring technical expertise, investment funding, and cultural capital that Vietnam lacks (and they benefit from less economic pressures back home). Le was born in the United States but traveled to Saigon to find steady work and fell in love with it:

> I love Saigon. I feel super-Vietnamese whenever I'm here, but I know I'm not supposed to be here. I'm a foreigner, I guess, since I'm American but also my parents are refugees from the south. They have mixed feelings about me being here but they know I'm happy and I want to live here for as long as I can because there's so much going on and I want to be part of that.[17]

Following my interviewee around the city, I saw for example how Jenni moves easily around the city, meeting models, producers, directors, and actors, most of whom turned out to be Vietnamese Americans who came to Vietnam to realize their Hollywood-inspired dreams of fame. She says her fellow Việt Kiều community members hold a lot of power and wealth, but their status as the children of South Vietnam marks them as liminal subjects in Vietnam.

Per Fiona Ngô (2014), the global travels of formerly exiled subjects and their constant economic insecurities reflect the fact that "displacement is not universally available or desirable for many subjects, nor is it evenly experienced" (89). Following Ngô, I argue that Vietnamese Americans—1.5 and second generations— have returned with a sense of *owning* and *owing* Saigon, owning in the sense that this is their new home and owing in the sense that they have responsibility to make up for their parents' loss of home. Though she was not alive to personally witness the war, Tuyet says she holds some nostalgia about it, especially when she sees cafés tagged with the name "Saigon," quaint reminders of the fact that she is a child of refugees who fled that port city. Tuyet conjectures that in South Vietnam, perhaps owing to economic pressures to survive, or perhaps because of state censorship, there is less of an obsession about remembering the war. She believes the locals are not obsessed with what was because they have witnessed so many wars, revolutions, and changes in their country since 1975.[18] The Vietnamese, Tuyet says, are "looking only to the future," bearing future "expectations that it [Saigon] will change or develop much faster than it is so there's expectations [sic] that in 10 years, Saigon will be another Singapore."[19]

For a city historically marred by "underdevelopment" due to wartime and postwar problems, there is much anticipation that Saigon can leapfrog in time to become a global city like Singapore. Expectations of prosperity remain high, Tuyet admits, because Saigon is "cosmopolitan for those who can afford it. I can be if I choose it."[20] The neoliberal language of individual choice reflects the harried desire for change in a city where inequality and local identity are strong. At the same time, Tuyet views global cosmopolitanism from the vantage of her exiled parents who had, for many decades, wished for a cosmopolitan Saigon (meaning non-communist) that remains to be seen. Ultimately, her comments boil down to the realization that the city's wartime roots and refugee memory were never completely cancelled out by postwar globalization; at least for now, memory flows where cash flows. Liminality and change look different, however, from those who are not middle-class transplants but poor locals struggling to make ends meet.

Viewing Global Change from the Bottom

According to urban anthropologist Erik Harms (2011), the historical development of Ho Chi Minh City is sedimented: things build on top of one another and elements of the past blend into new mixed global-local realities. Harms's local interviewees believe that during the war South Vietnam had been economically ahead of many other Asian countries and could have become as modern as South Korea or Thailand had the Americans not left under the Vietnamization plan. Selective memories of Saigon as better off during the U.S. reign, according to Harms, function as a subtle criticism of U.S. Vietnamization policies as well as the socialist government's tanked policies to Vietnamize or nationalize once the Americans left. Development today, despite the government's efforts, has stalled through global economic shocks and local setbacks, and the silence of everyday people on Vietnam's stalled progress validates the dreams of a deferred pre-1975 capitalist future that is no less potent or essential today in the age of hyperindustrialization. Harms notes:

> Comparisons of present-day Ho Chi Minh City with American-backed wartime Saigon are themselves narrative constructions that silence certain elements of the past in order to make a commentary on the present state of affairs. People select elements to construct stories in ways that *become signifiers of a present that would have been, a future that remains to be achieved, a dream that is only now beginning to take shape.* These stories are no less constructed than the propagandistic counterparts offered by the state media and historical publications, but they offer an alternative interpretation of how social life might have been organized within history. (109; emphasis added)

Harms identifies two attitudes of everyday people toward history—one where the hopes of a better future point toward a time when the past is irrelevant; the other, a future colored by nostalgia for a simplified past.

Both wrongly give too much power to modernization schemes, he says, yet both are necessary as memory forms needed to survive in a harsh, ever-changing world without firm ground.

Why is it necessary to remember Saigon's past, and the war itself, when there is a need to push forward? During one of my visits to the American Center in downtown HCMC—a place of cultural exchange created by the U.S. Consulate to improve trust between the United States and Vietnam—I approached a male college student sitting alone after the end of a free educational session on American popular culture. He was clutching a small U.S. history textbook and I asked him why he thought learning about American history matters for Vietnamese today. He answered by saying the history matters so Vietnam and the United States can know more about one another to improve relations and become friends. When I reminded him about the contentious friendship of the United States with South Vietnam during the war, he replied, "That doesn't really matter as much now. Our countries are working together so that's all that matters really; we need to move on so we can become prosperous."[21] For this young man, the past seems irrelevant for the future, unless that history—a selective and heavily curated version of it—is a means to foster good binational relations. As the student went on to tell me, the "American War" means the U.S. Revolutionary War or Civil War, not the one where the United States fought the Vietnamese. Those U.S. wars offer great insights about Vietnam's own fight against colonization and desires for unification, he says, but the Second Indochinese War (and South Vietnam) is something they can skip over.

If there is a domestic population that cannot ignore the past, it is the aging soldiers of the south who never left Vietnam as refugees. For the soldiers of the fallen southern republic, many found their niche occupation after reeducation camps as cyclo drivers, unable to find other work because of their prior associations with the Americans. Meanwhile, the pro-communist fighters of the north were promised lofty positions in the government, which did not always materialize. Sixty-three-year-old Nguyễn Tuấn says he has been a peddler for 28 years, pulling Western tourists in his rented two-wheel rickshaw (see figure 5.2).[22] Though he was born in Saigon and grew up there, Tuấn joined the North Vietnam-

Figure 5.2. Driver Nguyễn Tuấn (photo by author).

ese Army because it was easier than finding a job with the communists than the U.S.-backed ARVN with its swelling number of applicants. He does not find it erroneous to fight for the north even though he hails from the south because he needed to earn a living, especially as Saigon was experiencing a tight labor market.[23] Be that as it may, Tuấn represents the crisis of Vietnamese identity during and after the war since these national heroes and defenders of the people did not fare that much better under communist rule. Poverty forced men like him to later take on an occupation associated with stigmatized southern soldiers. He has been pulling customers for a small fee ever since the days of the communist revolution but has yet to see the government reward him for his sacrifice. Indeed, that same government has made things more difficult as it seeks to develop under a capitalist system that favors Westerners and the nouveau rich (see figure 5.3).[24]

Figure 5.3. Sign barring cyclo drivers (photo by author).

When asked about the historical legacy of Saigon, he answers: "There is no South Vietnamese legacy. There's no American legacy. There's not even a communist legacy. From the top, everything looks global and modern, but it always looks terrible from the bottom. It's been this way since the war." He repeated the well-worn rhetoric that historical legacies are written by the victors, but rhetorically asked me who is winning when so many are struggling to attain a better life. His words highlight the necessity of looking at Vietnam's reality in the face of spreading class inequality and even hypocrisy. For day laborers like Tuấn, Saigon's glossy patina and rosy economy remain rather dire for many who netted few benefits from the U.S. Vietnamization of the Saigonese economy and the communist Vietnamization of globalization. If anything, communist and capitalist systems present a war against the common man.

Responding to my query if any recent changes implemented by the government are good for the people, the aging veteran says bluntly, "No, they don't care about everyday people like me. They want the Americans' money even though they speak of a Vietnam for Vietnamese. Saigon is a place for the rich like it's always been during the time of the Americans." Tuấn explained to me how the scores of ARVN veterans who once dominated the cyclo business to survive after the war have abandoned this hard vocation. In fact, most have been lucky enough to leave as sponsored refugees through the U.S. Orderly Departure Program for former southern political prisoners in the 1980s. It used to be difficult for the South Vietnamese, being on the "wrong side of history," he claims, but these days they are on the right side through their former connections to Americans and well-off overseas families, alongside their partial proficiency in English or trade skills learned under the Americans, which have allowed them to succeed where many veterans of the northern People's Army could not. While ARVN soldiers suffered tremendously after the communist takeover of Saigon, the tables of luck turned when the Communist Party began backpedaling on its position against foreigners and capitalism, thus giving kickbacks to Saigon's urbanized middle-class citizens. This fast turnaround splashes material success onto to those who can best exploit the new direction of the American-driven global market. Power, as my interviewee views it, has been put back in the hands of the United States, since "the Americans and Viet Kieu have come back." Personal stories like those from Tuấn should be read as allegories of power, illustrating the revolving door of winners and losers within contemporary Vietnamese history, a "glocal" history shaped by local events and global processes. Tuấn's rendition of truth suggests that what once worked, in retrospect, does not work now, and those who lost out during a prior moment gained something later, while the fates of others reversed (or stayed the same)—particularly when there is not one road but many roads to success.

Conclusion

Ho Chi Minh City/Saigon is a place that continues to change, but those changes do not displace the South Vietnamese experience of war, especially under the Americans, who rapidly changed the economy more than the more resource-extractive French. The scale of such major structural changes does not fall easily into the dustbins of history or the allure of the global present. Rather, this militarized experience gets another spin in an imperial moment when Vietnam finds rapprochement with the same foreign powers it had once furiously fought off. Beyond discussing how people remember the war back in the day, this chapter pays attention to the way memories of war operate in the life narratives for those living in Saigon. South Vietnamese-ness here serves as a *residual* formation of American empire and its Vietnamization of the war, even if it also being put to work in the economization and reconstruction of the city. This sense of the "Vietnamized" past as an economic force and symbolic marker for understanding the now is necessary to consider in the face of so many news articles with titles like "Capitalist Soul Rises as Ho Chi Minh City Sheds Its Past" (Fuller 2015). As Thu-Hương Nguyễn-Võ reminds us (2005), "empire builders are constructing a new universalism by historical amnesia," and it is our task to pay attention to local specificity and world history (165). If we want to draw back the curtains of memory to talk about current events, we can say that the ways the Americans Vietnamized (and Americanized) the war through fast-paced urbanization, then allowed the Communist Party, certain Saigonese elites, and former refugees to inherit certain residuals of empire.

Here, we can follow Michel Foucault's (1977) advice to write a "history of the present" (31). My framing of empire's residuals prevents wishful thinking for better times ahead or the wishing away of the past. It prohibits a selective attempt at historical revisionism to make the past digestible and fights against our celebratory instinct to brush aside what we no longer want to see under the banner of global progress. We must always ask how war still matters in places like Vietnam, despite its current industrial frenzy and capitalist takeoff. Sailing ahead toward a metropolitan vision of itself, Vietnam and the country's biggest city, Saigon, is an urban heterotopia, as Foucault might call it, not exclusively located in a past time or later time but a longer genealogy of "missed opportunities" for Vietnam, and especially South Vietnam, the spirit of which is only now being recaptured ironically under an anxious socialist regime trying to prove itself on the international market. The residuals of empire rattle our naïve faith that the march of time leads inexorably toward full democracy, freedom, and liberty. Here, we might recognize how prior hopes for a free South Vietnam are not dead in Saigon, but set in fast-changing times where the local and the global meet.

Epilogue

Returns of War identifies the distended legacy of South Vietnam as the "surplus" of history, obliging readers to remember that things do not wear away without leaving something behind or making their presence felt again. Where the figure of "Vietnam" is oft invoked as a metaphor of war that conjures up "a nightmare we cannot even imagine," South Vietnam flashes the image of a nebulous postcolonial dream we try to imagine (Jameson 1991: 43). Recognizing the defunct nation of South Vietnam as a "metaphor of sovereignty," a holdover from an older Cold War era that still holds salience today, I challenge the view of the Vietnam War as "over" (Lowe 2010). As important, the ghost of South Vietnam returns with a vengeance in this late stage of American empire, at a time when the United States is stretched thin by the morass of so many "Vietnamized" hot spots, similar to the simmering, and multiple, crises of the Cold War.

We have here turned and returned to the spoils of Vietnamization and have seen how a policy to salvage a war and the American reputation, and protect South Vietnam against communism, creates the perfect storm for the continued militarization of "Pax Americana," but also the militarization and politicization of Vietnamese refugee cultural memory and community-building. In short, the very term Vietnamization suggests that the making of free South Vietnam is a process with no terminable end. This raises unanswered questions about South Vietnam's demise and future, which are with us still, further amplified and confounded anew by the shake-up of our "post–Cold War" era.

In 1992, the United States normalized relations with Vietnam, and then President Bill Clinton called for more economic liberation in the socialist republic. Speaking after the end of his term, Clinton (2000) gestures toward a self-determined future placed entirely in Vietnamese hands. His call for interdependence between somewhat friendly nations (who do not quite fully trust one another) sounded very familiar, almost like a neoliberal version of Nixon's Vietnamization policy, asking Vietnamese to improve themselves with the assistance of the United States.[1] He called for a kind of Vietnamization of classic American ideals and said the Vietnamese needed a "declaration of interdependence, a clear, unequivocal statement that prosperity in the twenty-first century . . . your future should be in your hands, the hands of the Vietnamese people . . . We believe the Vietnamese people have the talent to succeed in this new global age as they have in the past . . . We have seen the talent and ingenuity of the Vietnamese who have come to settle in America" (ibid.).

This goodwill gesture seems to overlook the fact that the United States helped to block Vietnam from becoming economically independent in the postwar period by placing brutal sanctions and embargos in 1975 as revenge for the communists taking over South Vietnam. To add insult to injury to Vietnam's own botched socialist economic policies, Clinton cites the successes of former refugees of South Vietnam who have settled in the United States as examples for people in Vietnam to follow in order to succeed in the global modern world. This, of course, ignores the cultural/class differences among Vietnamese in Vietnam and Vietnamese Americans, but also the geopolitical difference between North and South Vietnam. As Clinton concludes: "In building that future, you, and only you now, can redeem the sacrifice of those who were lost on both sides in a terrible war" (ibid.).

In the midst of such proclamations, we know a more complicated reality. The Vietnam War is not a receding memory, best forgotten, of a grisly but increasingly distant past; rather, the memory of that war, and of South Vietnam as a whole, continues to percolate, as things that are still active today. Utilizing Vietnamization as a concept to analyze the returns on that war in the twenty-first century, I elucidated the need to recognize the "arrested development" of South Vietnam and its visibility within public discourse. That this term still holds enormous power hints at how the Fall of Saigon was not a fait accompli, just as Vietnamization was not a mission accomplished. Vietnamization, as we have seen throughout this book, discloses the terms through which South Vietnamese people have been brought unevenly into discourse as subjects of history and culture where "the lack of voice of America's South Vietnamese allies created a void for American discourse to dominate"

(Nguyen 2006: 111). Back then and now, Vietnamization presents a dilemma, as ethical as it is political, around what to do with those not deemed worthy of being rescued and remembered.

Scholars who are attuned to this cunning reason will bear witness to new global "relations between desire, power, and subjectivity . . . [within] advanced capitalist neocolonialism" (Spivak 1993: 68–69). According to Negri and Hardt (2000), the end of the Vietnam War ushered in a new imperial frontier, with the United States inheriting the mantle of leadership of an international market based on relations of neocolonial domination. In this order, the United States invades newer enemies like Iraq to tap into oil deposits, while posing as a friendly trade nation with former enemies like communist Vietnam. The cycles and crisis of capitalism and the falling rate of profit in global markets force a new "Vietnamized" paradigm shift that requires all of us to bear witness to specters of what Negri and Hardt called "two, three, many Vietnams" (261). Here, one must not remember that there is a South Vietnam and a North Vietnam, but the "'Nam" of the American popular imaginary, the Vietnamese communities scattered across the globe, and "future Vietnams" found in places like Iraq and Afghanistan. And though they are living reminders of one of the most famous wars in modern world history, the South Vietnamese constitute another kind of faceless Other in communist Vietnam as well as the United States as forsaken former allies during the war and later as refugees needing to be saved by Americans (Espiritu 2006). This image of the faceless Other is being renovated at a time when the U.S. government is waging preemptive wars and regional messes have sprung from a "new, economically pragmatic emergent ideology that needs the Other" (Polan 1996: 274). But rather than focus on governments, I chose to focus on how non-state cultural actors, organizations, and individuals put a face to these losers to say we must consider the returns of war and the price refugees (and others) pay for remembering (or being associated with) South Vietnam. Thousands of Vietnamese immigrants who were former supporters of the U.S.-backed regime are being sent back to Vietnam, even though they are protected by a bilateral treaty between Washington and Hanoi that prevents the deportation of those who came after 1975 and before 1995, the year diplomatic relations resumed. "These people don't really have a country to come back to," says former U.S. Ambassador to Vietnam, Ted Osius, and he claims the Hanoi government views these exiles as "destabilizing" elements and actors (Pearson 2018). Meanwhile, the Trump administration has labeled Vietnam as recalcitrant for not taking back these "nationals" (who are actually U.S. legal residents but not yet citizens).

All too often, the Vietnam War is studied in terms of the past, but I take stock of this calamitous neo-imperialist moment in time as the point of departure for studying Vietnamization of the future. If the contents and arguments of this book bear too much repetition, it is because there is no easy way of speaking about South Vietnam, the Vietnam War, empire, and refugees without returning to the same points again and again in a cycle of loss, memory, and trauma. While the United States seems to have moved on from its humiliating defeat in Vietnam, even if it is repeating the same wrongdoings in other places, it is because the Vietnamese paid and continue to pay for war's steep price.

So why does the Vietnam War or, for that matter, South Vietnam, still matter? As time wears on and the United States moves on to more wars, the memory of the way the American War in Vietnam was "Vietnamized" forwards a kind of refugee "structure of feeling" about reparations and redress (Williams 2006). The memory of the way the United States handled and Vietnamized the Vietnam War provides a kind of neocolonial discourse that enables us to think about forms of state formation and freedom-making that are always incomplete. What I foresee is a future where more and more American wars resemble the Vietnam War, and where collapsed client-states similar to South Vietnam must take on the onus of responsibility for winning wars on their own (and representing their needs as autonomous sovereign voices). Where past follies are never fully forgotten or even forgiven by survivors of war, the ghosts of history invariably insist upon some type of "returns" or indemnity for untimely mistakes. The chapters of this book provided a potential pathway to navigating those returns of war, where I started off first by looking for the Vietnamese presence in the archive and by accident returning to my own birthplace. I then sought to understand those economic and temporal returns in diasporic family bonds and anti-communist community politics, soldiers' transnational experiences with war, and Saigonese populations affected by globalization. Ultimately, these temporal returns of war hold out the precarious promise of liberation that remains open for all of us to ponder.

ACKNOWLEDGMENTS

Funding for this book came from numerous sources, including the University of California President's Postdoctoral Fellowship, University of Illinois Chancellor's Postdoctoral Fellowship, the UCSD Center for Global California Cultures, and the New Racial Studies Institute at the University of California, Santa Barbara. I thank everyone at NYU Press who worked on this book, most important, the forward-thinking Eric Zinner, who solicited me and shepherded this project early on, as well as David Lobenstine for outstanding editing. Much thanks to Lisha Nadkarni, Dolma Ombadykow, Alexia Traganas, and the two fantastic anonymous manuscript readers who were utterly patient with me and gave the most wonderful suggestions for finessing my words and thoughts into coherent form.

My deepest regards go to the faculty, staff, and students in the Department of Ethnic Studies at the University of California, San Diego, where this book began. All the love goes to my mentor, Yen Le Espiritu, and the rest of her family, especially Evyn, for proofreading an earlier draft of the book. Yen's guiding light and prescience encouraged me to face both the future (and past) with confidence. She reminds me that we must write about difficult things because we have lived them and people must know about us. The only way I can pay back this kind of loving support is to pay it forward, helping others to find their way. Ross Frank has been my guardian angel then and now. Denise Ferreira da Silva inspires me to imagine better worlds that includes spiritual ones. Lisa Lowe taught me how to listen to my own voice and own the words that I did not think I could grasp. Muchas gracias to Ricardo Dominguez for showing me how to do intellectual work and "artivism." He, along with Amy Sara Carroll, helped to sustain me. Lisa Park never gave up on me and I am forever grateful for her authenticity. Natalia Molina taught me the need for comparative work. Others who nurtured me included Roberto Alvarez, Ana Celia Zentella, Gabriel Mendes, Roshanak Kheshti, Wayne

Yang, Kirstie Dorr, and Mary Polytaridis. Yolanda Escamilla is my dearest friend forever.

Guides in the early academic path include undergraduate mentor Dorothy Fujita-Rony, who encouraged my graduate school aspirations. Linda Trinh Võ is my personal guru for everything; she is never wrong about anything. Further support at UC Irvine came from Claire Jean Kim, John M. Liu, Dan Tsang, Ivan Small, Quan Tran, and Glen Mimura. I felt so lucky when the inimitable Jodi Kim agreed to be my mentor at UC Riverside; she is the perfect model of innovative scholarship. She, alongside wonderful people like Mariam Lam, pushed me to be a more well-rounded scholar like her. Others include Emily Hue, Keith Miyake, Angelica Pepino, Tammy Ho, Daniel Olmos, Dylan Rodriguez, Grace Hong, Sarita See, David Lloyd, and Setsu Shigematsu. Other scholars in the field who have nurtured me include Felice Blake, Christina Schwenkel, Thu-Hương Nguyễn-Võ, Tu-Uyen Nguyen, Marguerite Nguyen, Michael Meere, Paula Park, Neda Atanasoski, and Julietta Hua. Kieu-Linh Valverde is a great teacher for community politics. Personal mentor Cathy Schlund-Vials got me through with her superpowers; there is no one like her and never will be. Lan Duong inspires me forever with her words and being; she is a model of scholar-activism at its best. Viet Thanh Nguyen is a model of critical scholarship for all of us. Viet Le is my hero, saving me too many times to count.

I have been very fortunate to have some admirable peers, among them Cathleen Kozen, Tomoko Tsuchiya, Angela Kong, Angela Kim, Arifa Raza, Thuy Vo-Dang, Quan Tran, Davorn Sisavath, Linh Nguyen, Mimi Khuc, Chrissy Lau, Traci Voyles, Maile Arvin, Traci Voyles, Jose Fuste, and Jade Powers-Sotomayor. Ma Vang and Kit Myers supported me in every stage of this professional life. Kudos to Ayako Sahara for a stimulating friendship. Sabrina Strings makes me laugh and think at the same time. Further nods go to Rashne Limki and Joseph Allen Ruanto-Ramirez, who are my co-conspirators for all things social justice. Vinh Nguyen is my Canadian brother. Thanks to Rebecca Kinney for camaraderie and cheer. Best friend Stevie Ruiz is an invested scholar, teacher, thinker, and friend who makes sense of everything in this life for me as a partner in crime. Martha Escobar makes me whole as a person, inspiring me to live my politics. Ofelia Cuevas molded me to become a better person by being my personal role model through her perseverance and fiery spirit. Buddy Tere Cesena formed a bond over a love of life and learning; she and Gina Opinaldo are my co-teachers. Much love to Wolfgang Shane for his humor and wit. Bestie Tram Le makes me wish I was born ten years earlier so we could share more amazing experiences. My amigo Carlos Dimas is special to me, because he speaks for me when I cannot. Carol Vu transformed my life as my best friend; she is the reason I even pursued this career. Patricia Nguyen helps me navigate the murky waters, while Ani Santorelli is my comrade in arms. A karmic bond ties me to Kim Anh Tran, who makes me not take anything for granted. I owe Ken Le much for being there from the beginning for the long journey and supporting me. Xuxa Rodriguez and Rehema Barber are sisters in the struggle. Ly Nguyen is my academic younger self who also taught me many things.

The wonderful folks at the University of Illinois, Urbana-Champaign welcomed me with open arms: Ariana Ruiz, Mike Atienza, Durell Callier, Soo Ah Kwon, Christina Chin, Karen Jaime, Augusto Espiritu, Martin Manalansan, Isabel Molina, and Jonathan X. Inda. Shantal Martinez, Genevieve Clutario, Christine Peralta, and Tessa Winkelmann are forever my intellectual coven. Thanks to big sister Sandra Ruiz for helping me tap into the other world for inspiration. Fiona Ngô has taught me many things in this life and past lifetimes; her honest advice never fails to inspire, heal, and transform. My twin Shantel Martinez grounds me with her healing magic, while Julie Dowling is indefatigable in her personal mentorship. Marisa Duarte is my model for doing community-based intellectual work. Arely Zimmerman is my greatest champion and confidante; I literally cannot imagine another academic sister. Lisa Cacho is the type of attentive public scholar I would like to emulate and become someday. Mimi Nguyen is that magical lodestar I follow to pursue the life of the mind without fear. I thank all artists, activists, and academics who I met in the field fighting for social justice. I entered academia wanting to make change and I am still inspired by this mission. I want to acknowledge the amazing people in the Department of Sociology and Program in Science and Technology Studies at Vassar College. At the University of California, Irvine, I also would like to thank Gloria Simpson in the Global and International Studies Department for all her incredible work, and Eve Darian-Smith and Philip McCarty for being such amazing scholars and even more amazing people along with Li

Zhang, Gustavo Oliveira, Vibhuti Ramachandran, Ruth Goldstein, and Yousef Al-Bolushi.

Finally, my refugee family is the reason why I am writing this book. My parents, siblings, cousins, and elders know what truly matters. Thuy, Thoa, Luan, Bac My, Co Ha, Chi Nhung, Hanh, and Lynh have suffered tremendously from the effects of war, but they have built the lives we want to live. I dedicate this book entirely to them.

NOTES

INTRODUCTION

1 The term is attributed first to Secretary of Defense Melvin Laird and later adopted by Richard Nixon in speeches. For more on the original development of this term, see Kimball (2006).
2 President Nixon's gave his address to the nation on the war in Vietnam on November 3, 1969 at the Midway Conference. The speech is also referred to as the "Silent Majority" speech, since it was directed to the many U.S. Americans who were against the more vocal liberal anti-war "minority." See Kimball (2006).
3 "Honorable withdrawal" is a phrased developed from the phrase "honorable peace" by former President Richard Nixon. Such rhetoric was tied to the reality that, should South Vietnam fall before a reelection, this would reflect badly upon Nixon.
4 Hughes suggests that this tactic would not get American POWs back even if the United States was adamant about not leaving South Vietnam until all American lives were recovered and accounted for.
5 While the French controlled Vietnam and the rest of Indochina from 1885 to 1954, forcibly subjugating all of Southeast Asia as a colonial territory, Hồ Chí Minh's Vietminh emerged as national revolutionary heroes in the first half of the twentieth century to eventually defeat the French during the first Indochina War (1946–1954). Hồ Chí Minh proclaimed the Democratic Republic of Vietnam in 1945 and sought U.S. assistance and support. Instead of supporting Minh's request for help from President Woodrow Wilson, the United States and other European powers legitimated French claims to Vietnam. The first Indo-China War was fought by the Việt Minh with the French from 1946 to 1954 and resulted in the division of the country into South and North Vietnam. By the mid-1960s, France, in the wake of another colonial war in Algeria, was too weak to be a colonial power there and the United States became the major supporter of South Vietnam.
6 This essay was originally published in 1954 in the same year as the Geneva Accords as an issue of the now defunct *Vietnam Generation Journal*, which devoted a whole issue to racism entitled "A White Man's War: Race Issues and Vietnam."
7 There are far too many sources to list here, but the following are some exemplary works: Hosmer, Kellen, and Jenkins (1978); Lâm (2001); Johnson (1970); Gartner (1998); Eggleston (2014); and Alexander (2008).

CHAPTER 1. ARCHIVAL OTHERS

1. Interview with Kelly Crager, September 23, 2010.
2. Every year the Texas state government has certain congressional line items in the state budget earmarked for special historical preservation projects, and the Vietnam Center and Archive is a beneficiary of this line item.
3. Interview with Kelly Crager, September 23, 2010. Three oral historians conduct the interviews and even the archive's current executive director was once the head oral historian, which shows the import of the oral history project.
4. I tried to get an interview with the only Vietnamese staff member in the VNCA, the associate director for Vietnamese Affairs, Dr. Khanh Cong Le, who works under the executive director, but he said he was not a staff member (even though he has official duties and a desk) and refused my request. He told me he was too busy to do interviews and did not want to do one so I respected his decision. His relationship with the Vietnamese American community as a representative of the archive is seemingly important but does not detract from my larger argument about the archive.
5. For more on how the Vietnam War connects to America's Indian Wars, see Slotkin (1992).
6. The vast majority of the archive's users as revealed to me by the reference archivist are American veterans. Interview with Amy Mondt, August 21, 2010.
7. This task is difficult given that Lubbock does not have a huge veteran population/association or military outfit/base and so the archive had begun out of the will and enterprising spirit of Dr. Reckner. The archive was funded with a shoestring budget from the university and the private funds of individuals like Dr. Reckner, which intuits the hesitance of Americans back then in commemorating, supporting, and institutionalizing the memory of the Vietnam War in public life. As the archive's founder, Reckner is the most significant individual in explaining the history and purpose of the archive, which is why most staff members referred me to him.
8. Reckner donated his personal documents and memoirs from his two tours of duty in Vietnam as the original materials to be included in the archive, including personal letters written to his parents and family. At the time of my interview with him, there was not yet an oral history featuring James Reckner.
9. Interview with James Reckner, September 25, 2010.
10. This need to call the war a "conflict" reveals the difficulty of assimilating the Vietnam War into American cultural history, since viewing the war *as* a war would immediately evoke loss and defeat for the United States. At the time of its founding, it was too controversial to call the Vietnam War an actual war since doing so conjures the idea of competing sides with winners and losers, whereas the term "conflict" provides a vague connotation. A formal proposal for establishment of the archive was approved later that year, calling for establishment of the Center for the Study of the Vietnam Conflict. For a more detailed time line and chronol-

ogy of the archive, see its website: "Highlights of the First Twenty Years," www.vietnam.ttu.edu.
11 The Vietnam Center is the logistical, publicity, and administrative service center for the Vietnam Archive, the latter concerned exclusively with archival preservation work.
12 Interview with James Reckner, September 25, 2010.
13 General Westmoreland infamously said in the award-winning 1974 documentary *Hearts and Minds* that the Oriental "does not put the same high price on life as does a Westerner," which some saw as justification of the military's cover-up of the My Lai massacre, the usage of Agent Orange and other defoliants, and other genocidal tactics that made Southeast Asia the primary site of violent state practices.
14 The archive contains material documents about the investigation of the My Lai atrocity, notes on the CIA's secret counterinsurgency efforts in Southeast Asia, legal briefs on the libel case against General William Westmoreland by CBS, and government reports of antiwar resistance from inside the military army.
15 When queries were sent by public citizens to the archive concerning the logo used on official newsletters which are sent out to the public and patrons, a statement was made about the logo in connection to the archive's philosophy. The logo used in informational literature is a reproduction of the special design of the medal-ribbon authorized by President Johnson in 1975, awarded to members of U.S. armed forces who served in Southeast Asia. As the archive staff responded to the questioners: "We selected this logo for our organization because it is the universally recognized symbol of American Vietnam Center and the Vietnam Archive at Texas Tech University are guided and very strongly supported by Vietnam veterans. Without their support, this organization would not exist. *Friends of the Vietnam Center Newsletter* 4 (2), July 1997 Vietnam Center Collection.
16 A comprehensive collection of South Vietnam records is the 1999 collection of 98 boxes that were donated from the Vietnamese embassy in Paris that contained South Vietnamese records and daily press releases.
17 The Families of Vietnamese Political Prisoners Association (FVPPA) helped over 10,000 former Vietnamese reeducation camp detainees and their families to immigrate to the United States and other countries through the United Nations High Commissioner for Refugee's Orderly Departure Program (ODP).
18 This also included the hiring of Vietnamese language specialists, translators, and archivists (mostly international exchange students who volunteer for the center).
19 A web page has been created where individuals can search a database of applicant file names, but the public cannot view the names and content of the files themselves unless they request it directly from the archive. The material on Vietnamese Americans is available only to individuals looking up their immigration records or those of their family members but is not open for public viewing to ensure anonymity and confidentiality.
20 The University of Texas at Austin is already starting its own Vietnamese American oral history project under the guidance of Khuc Minh Tho, a long-time commu-

nity activist and leader who has been a major supporter of the Vietnam Center and Archive.
21 Interview with James Reckner, September 25, 2010.
22 Because of the low pay scale of professors in Vietnam who are experts in both Vietnamese and English, Texas Tech staff members even go to Vietnam to have documents translated at low cost. On various trips to Vietnam, archival representatives present scholarships to students in Vietnam (as well as Cambodia) and provide archival seminars for Vietnamese universities.
23 Vietnamese families often had members who fought on both sides of the conflict with differing interpretations of what they were fighting for, yet the political divisions that split families were often not easily resolved.
24 Interview with Kelly Crager, September 23, 2010.
25 Kelly Crager says many of the veterans who volunteer their stories are proud of their service, but since the stories are on a voluntary basis, the sample pool might preclude the stories of those veterans who do not wish to speak, out of fear or political resistance to a historical project that seems to be associated with the state. By his own admission, the director says American veterans who resisted the government constitute a small minority of total stories, which shows that the more patriotic veterans are most represented in archive.
26 There is a small population of Vietnamese living in Lubbock. The director estimates that there are about 200 families in the area.
27 Last content analysis and update on May 14, 2011.
28 Interview with Kelly Crager, September 23, 2010.
29 Interview with Ann Mallott, September 24, 2010.
30 Informal conversation with Amy Mondt. In order to make sense of the term "gook," one must make sense of the racialized past, with the term gook serving as a signifier not only of war but the de-humanization of Vietnamese by the United States at not only an individual/group level but an institutional/national level as well. How would visitors ever look at and know about the term gook unless they ask the reference archivist; searching for the gook shows how racial meaning and terms live beyond their specific historical moment and have a longer shelf life than we think.
31 Informal conversation with James Reckner.
32 Vietnam Archive Oral History Project, Interview with Dr. Edward Feldman. Conducted by Stephen Maxner, November 27, December 11 and 14, 2000; January 8, 2001. Transcribed by Tammi Mikel.
33 The Vietnam Archive, Oral History Project, Interview with John Wear. Conducted by Steve Maxner, October 29, 2002. Transcribed by Jennifer McIntyre.
34 The Vietnam Archive, Oral History Project, Interview with David Crawley. Conducted by Stephen Maxner, February 27, 2001. Transcribed by Tammi Mikel Lyon.
35 As one African American veteran saw it: "I went to Boot Camp at Paris Island and we had a lot of brothers from Philly there and the common term used in discussing the brothers amongst the drill instructors, was they were "niggers." "Come

here nigger, do this nigger," I think this had a carry-over effect throughout the entire training." Veterans' Testimony on Vietnam—Need for Investigation. Written by Honorable Mark O. Hatfield (76 pages) (April 6, 1971).
36 In 1977, a group of wives of Vietnamese political prisoners formed a support group to advocate for their husbands and families. The group grew into a mutual assistance nonprofit organization incorporated in Virginia. This organization is named Families of Vietnamese Political Prisoners Association (FVPPA).
37 Pre-interview processing requires public documentation, which may include old personnel action notices, letters of recommendation, letters from former American colleagues, pay stubs, certificates, or verification notices or training.
38 While the archive focuses mostly on veterans of war, it also includes the widows and children of U.S. soldiers—something that promotes the family unit as the basis for national unity and storytelling.

CHAPTER 3. DISMEMBERED LIVES
1 Singers from Vietnam that come to the United States to perform are often seen as ambassadors of the socialist regime in Vietnam and are protested as such. Resettled Vietnamese American singers from the United States who try to hold concerts in Vietnam have been labeled as pro-communist supporters for going back. Vietnamese pop star Dam Vinh Hung, was pepper-sprayed by an anti-communist activist dressed as a woman, while performing at a July 2010 concert in the Santa Clara Convention Center. The person turned out to be U.S. citizen "freedom fighter" Ly Tong, who is also responsible for vandalizing the F.O.B. II exhibit artworks by Brian Doan and Steven Toly.
2 F.O.B. II is linked to a longer genealogy of art and activism in the Vietnamese community that reached a boiling point in the late 1990s, when a new generation of artists and youth began to articulate their own postwar subjectivities, facing anti-communist protests like the one at the San Jose Museum of Art (1993, 2000) over the displayed portrait of Hồ Chí Minh; the infamous Hi-Tek Video Store incident of 1999; as well as the closing of VAX (MTV-style program for Viet-American youth) in 2004 over the repeated display of that same photo of Minh on a documentary program.
3 Foot spas are part of the Asian service profession and industry of personal care, and the imposition of the flag's design on the foot spa points to the reliance of feminized labor in postwar ethnic enclave economies. The photos were published in Người Việt newspaper in the spring of 2008. Street protests erupted and the paper apologized to the public, eventually firing two top editors who sympathized with and understood the artist's intention of showing sacrifice not sacrilege for the Vietnamese people.
4 F.O.B. I was held in a building owned by Người Việt magazine, but political controversy since the foot spa incident has caused a stunning turnaround in the attitudes of Người Việt, which helped organize anti-VAALA protesters in the F.O.B. II protest.

5   With echoes of the Vietnamization policy which sent more troops to South Vietnam before disembarking, the United States was prepared to send thousands more troops to Iraq in a final surge before the Iraqi government took full control over security in Baghdad's fortified zones. This return to Iraqi sovereignty prompting newly elected President Barack Obama a month later to announce the end date for U.S. involvement.
6   Official press release statement from VAALA. F.O.B. II: Art Speaks: Multi-Art Show (December 2008).
7   The original quote is from www.thanhniencovang.com.
8   Like other female icons such as Wonder Woman, Rosie the Riveter, and the *Pho Hoa* girl, such poster art demonstrates the use of women to express the diasporic cultural desires of a community projecting itself into a powerful future, one eroticized and cathected through a dual form of hyperfeminine and hypermasculine energy.
9   Comment found on www.congdongnguoiviet.fr.
10 Quote from openly circulated letter, "Chống Triển Lãm F.O.B. Là Đúng," *Thtinfo*, accessed May 9, 2009, http://thtinfo.com.
11 The letter used the analogy of someone putting a picture of Hitler or a swastika flag in a community of Jews. He mentions Vietnam's autocratic regime, which restricts freedom of religion (and which many Americans take for granted) and here Tran says he does not support an outright ban on offensive art, given First Amendment rights, but that VAALA artists employ discretion toward displaying such art based on common wisdom about the needs and struggles of the many Vietnamese Americans who had tried to escape communist rule.
12 The curators created a slideshow of art that was banned in Vietnam featuring audio recordings and writings by dissidents from Vietnam. "I wanted to make the connections with Vietnamese artists that have been banned in Vietnam and this kind of repression that we face here in terms of voicing political opinions," Lan Duong said. "The forms of censorship are not equivalent, but they are similar." The exhibit also features a "Black Room," which has highly sensitive political materials including those most protested. See Tran (2009).
13 The groups were CCS and the VNCH.
14 Some of these organizations include the following groups: Đài phát thanh Diễn Đàn Chống Cộng (Great Anti-Communist Radio Forum), Hội Cựu Chiến Sĩ VNCH (Association of South Vietnamese Veterans), Ủy Ban Xây Dựng Sức Mạnh Cộng Đồng (Commission for Building Community Strength), Phong trào Tự Do Việt Nam (Freedom Movement of Vietnam), and Diễn Đàn Tiếng Nói Tự Do của Người Dân Việt Nam (Free Speech Forum of the People of Vietnam).
15 These anti-VAALA websites included the websites of *Vietbao* newspaper and *Thanh Nien Co Vang*, Youth for the Yellow Flag.
16 Letter written by the director of the Viet Art Center addressing VAALA organizers, January 21, 2009, http://vietamreview.blogharbor.com/.

17 When VAALA asked the Viet Art Center to join the political fight, Ms. Truong responded, "May I ask the battle is between 'who' and 'who'? Who is your 'enemy'? Are they [the protesters] 'terrorists'? Were they just 'exercising their rights of speech and assembly' and were they your family members? If 'yes' is your answer to these questions, I apologize that I cannot join you in this 'battle.' I can't fight against whom I love dearly."
18 Ibid.
19 Orange County Superior Court Judge Geoffrey T. Glass, who did not grant an injunction requested by the coalition, cited the 1995 Supreme Court ruling which made it constitutional for privately organized parades to exclude groups under the First Amendment of the U.S. Constitution.

CHAPTER 4. MILITARIZED FREEDOMS

1 Nixon hoped for reelection in 1972 against military hero George McGovern and worried about his chances against a decorated military veteran. Hoping not to appear soft on foreign policy or military affairs, he postponed not only formal peace negotiations but full-scale withdrawal of U.S. troops and personnel from Vietnam until after the election of 1972. See Berman (2001).
2 Military service is a path that can be motivated as much by economic reasons, as many poor people of color who, lacking many options for college, often see the military as an easy route to professionalization and employment as well as community-building. These groups historically enlist in the U.S. military in large numbers disproportionate to their actual numbers in U.S. society. It should be noted that Vietnamese Americans do not participate in large numbers compared with other ethnic groups, perhaps owing to their experiences with war or relatively better economic opportunities compared to other groups, but this cannot be assessed since the U.S. military does not track the final tally of Vietnamese in its ranks; it does note that Asians Pacific Islanders are underrepresented, since they only make up 1 percent of the military though they constitute 5 percent of the national population.
3 The United States along with the South Vietnamese invaded Cambodia in 1970 under the "Cambodian Campaign" and the consent of pro-U.S. General Lon Nol, who permitted these foreign allied forces to find a neutral base in the country's rural side to attack the Khmer Rouge as well Viet Cong. In 1972, Lon Nol staged a putsch that deposed the sovereign royal Pince Norodom Sihanouk. On April 1, 1975, the Lon Nol regime fell to the Khmer Rouge. See McMahon (1999) for a more comprehensive history of U.S. involvement in Southeast Asia during the Cold War.
4 CNN's *Newsroom*, broadcast on June 26, 2010.
5 I first contacted members of the Vietnamese American Armed Forces Association and asked them for references through a snowball method which led to a dozen interviews with members and non-members.
6 Email response interview, June 24, 2013.

7   Phone interview, July 14, 2002.
8   Face-to face-interview, July 12, 2012.
9   Email response to questionnaire, August 17, 2012.
10 Phone interview, July 7, 2012.
11 Quang tried to track down the CIA-sponsored group of Cuban pilots who flew with Americans in the failed Bay of Pigs mission and who made up part of the mass refugee movement from Cuba.
12 More than 320,000 soldiers were deployed from South Korea to fight in the Vietnam War. South Korean President Park Chung-hee and Lyndon Johnson believed it was the debt of South Koreans to pay the United States for aiding the country during the Korean War. See Hong-Koo (2006).

CHAPTER 5. EMPIRE'S RESIDUALS

1   Interview with Tuyet Nguyen in Saigon, May 2013.
2   HCMC contains various museums dedicated to history, such as the Ho Chi Minh City Museum, the Museum of Vietnamese History, the Revolutionary Museum, the Museum of Southeastern Armed Forces, the War Remnants Museum, the Museum of Southern Women, among others. There is a strong cultural industry creating, selling, and promoting Vietnam's military history across a range of social venues. Much criticism about the Vietnamese cultural memory of war has been directed at the tourism industry in Vietnam and the ways public notions of land, war, and people commingle in times of peace as a reminder of how major human catastrophe and events remain impervious to destruction by time.
3   Such pacification efforts included free-fire zones and the use of harsh hostage interrogation techniques that included torture in the CIA-backed Operation Phoenix program which ran from 1968 to 1972.
4   Military bases erected around Tân Sơn Nhất International Airport in Saigon, the country's largest airport, formerly the base of air landings for the French and drastically expanded during war, today serves as a depot for many public works, real estate, and media conglomerates (like American telecommunications service provider Motorola).
5   Some examples of this influence include the University of Michigan as the main education center for training or teaching South Vietnamese citizens and personnel, alongside the presence of the Peace Corps, the Pen Club, the USIS, the Rotary Club, the Asia Foundation, the Asia Cultural Association, and the U.S. Culture Centre. These institutions, along with films, comic strips, scholarships, and trips to the United States, the advisers, the GIs with their inevitable accompaniment of prostitution and brutalities, have done their work to Americanize Vietnamese local culture.
6   The name *Sài Gòn* comes from a Chinese loanword for an area originally part of the Khmer kingdom until the seventeenth century, when it was absorbed by Vietnam as the base for rule by the Nguyễn Lords. In modern times, it is recognized that the name Saigon referred to the educated class of Vietnamese but then

transformed into a sign of tribute to the Western colonialist. When Vietnam was forced to cede the Southern area to France in 1859, the area was renamed as a city. See Lang and Kolb (1980, nn. 1, 17).

7   On April 7, 1997, the United States and Vietnam signed an agreement in which Vietnam agreed to pay the roughly $145 million in debt, plus interest, South Vietnam incurred from 1960 to 1975 to support the development of economic infrastructure and to finance the importation of agricultural and other commodities. Committee on Foreign Relations, U.S. Senate, April 2010. "Report to the Chairman and Ranking Member." Vietnam Education Foundation, U.S. Government Accountability Office.

8   Part of the new urban culture is the emphasis on historical forgetfulness for trendy consumerism and leisure such as watching first-run movies in modern, air-conditioned cineplexes (featuring mostly American movies), where rich patrons pay for an hour of entertainment equal to a whole month's pay for government officials and day laborers. Meanwhile, Vietnam continues to adapt reality TV competition shows from the West into a local context. For more about the implications of this kind of Western cultural imperialism and the problems of translation in mass media entertainment programs, see Bui (2012).

9   Informal interview, June 6, 2013.

10 Saigon is constantly in dire straits with its quick integration into a staggering global economy, a lack of foreign capital investment, and a slowing of Vietnam's once enviable incipient "Dragon" economy. A speculative bubble in banking and real estate threatens to undo most of the country's progress, as does possible war with China.

11 Hence, the touristic logic of repackaging and making the war palatable for popular consumption sans political or historical context. Lots of makeshift stores sell Vietnamese war propaganda or relics like those found in the War Surplus Market, which offers American military gear and paraphernalia with an "authentic" collection of GIs' Zippo lighters from the war era.

12 Interview with Dinh Le at his home in Binh Chanh, June 1, 2013.

13 Face-to-face interview in HCMC, September 13, 2012.

14 Nguyễn Cao Kỳ, South Vietnam's former prime minister, even returned to the country in 2004, an action met with scorn by overseas Vietnamese anti-communist activists. Prominent exile artists such as the well-known composer Phạm Duy (whose music was verboten in Vietnam from 1975 to 2005) returned to Vietnam to perform or retire permanently.

15 Interview with Ky Nam Doan, January 18, 2016.

16 Interview with Ky Nam Doan, June 7, 2013.

17 Interview with Jenni in HCMC, August 18, 2012.

18 From the government's collectivization policies to later wars with countries like China and Cambodia to the Đổi Mới liberalization era and finally the era of global competition and economic trade wars, these many phases of Vietnam create a sense of ever-changing times in a country without a permanent historical sense of stability.

19 Interview with Tuyet Nguyen in Saigon, May 2013.
20 From the same interview with Tuyet Nguyen in Saigon, May 2013.
21 Informal interview at the American Center, June 26, 2012.
22 Informal interview in HCMC, September 20, 2012, Q. 1.
23 Fighting during the war disrupted food production, which had moved a large number of peasants from the southern countryside into the cities hoping to find employment in service jobs associated with the large American military or civil services related to it.
24 Police have been cracking down on cyclo drivers to make way for more efficient public transportation, so now most drivers turn to private motorbikes and customers hitch a ride for a small, negotiable fee with random individuals.

EPILOGUE

1 Bill Clinton was facing pressure from businesses wanting to do business in Vietnam but also faced demands to find the many missing American MIA/POWs still thought to be imprisoned or missing in Vietnam.

REFERENCES

Abbas, M. Ackbar. 1997. *Hong Kong: Culture and the Politics of Disappearance*. Minneapolis: University of Minnesota Press.
Adas, Michael. 2006. *Dominance by Design: Technological Imperatives and America's Civilizing Missions*. Cambridge, MA: Harvard University Press.
Agamben, Giorgio. 1998. *Homo Sacer*. Stanford, CA: Stanford University Press.
Aguilar-San Juan, K. 2009. *Little Saigons: Staying Vietnamese in America*. Minneapolis: University of Minnesota Press.
Alexander, Nathan. 2008. *Abandoning Vietnam: How America Left and South Vietnam Lost Its War*. Lawrence: University Press of Kansas.
Allen-Kim, Erica. 2016. "Saigon in the Suburbs: Protest, Exclusion, and Visibility." In *Conflict, Identity, and Protest in American Art*, eds. Makeda Best and Miguel de Baca. Newcastle: Cambridge Scholars Publishing, 155–171.
Altenbaumer, Kara. 1999a. "Conflict of Emotions: Vietnam Symposium, Memorial Stir Contrasting Reactions." *Avalanche Journal* (April 16).
———. 1999b. "Montford, James Reckner Embark on Vietnam Trip." *Avalanche Journal* (July 29).
Anderson, Benedict. 1991. *Imagined Communities: Reflections on the Origin and Spread of Nationalism*. New York: Verso.
Anderson, David L. and John Ernst, eds. 2007. *The War that Never Ends: New Perspectives on the Vietnam War*. Lexington: University Press of Kentucky.
Angry Asian Man blog. 2014. "LGBT Organizations Will March in Orange County Tet Parade." (January 6); www.angryasianman.com.
Appadurai, Arjun. 1996. *Modernity at Large*. Minneapolis: University of Minnesota Press.
Archive of Modern American Warfare. "Vision." www.amaw.ttu.edu.
Asselin, Pierre. 2002. *A Bitter Peace: Washington, Hanoi, and the Making of the Paris Agreement*. Chapel Hill: University of North Carolina Press.
———. 2009. "Memorializing the Anti-American Resistance: The 'Vietnam War' in Vietnamese Film." In *Thirty Years After: New Essays on Vietnam War Literature, Film, and Art*, ed. Mark Heberle. Cambridge, UK: Cambridge Scholars Publishing.
Atanasoski, Neda. 2006. "'Race' Toward Freedom: Post–Cold War US Multiculturalism and the Reconstruction of Eastern Europe." *Journal of American Culture* 29: 213–226.
———. 2013. *Humanitarian Violence: The U.S. Deployment of Diversity*. Minneapolis: Minnesota University Press.

Babbin, Jed. 2005. "The Vietnamization of Iraq." *American Spectator* (November 28); http://spectator.org.
Bài Việt. 2009. "Hey Brian Đoàn." *Bài Việt* (February 8); http://huongvebinhthuan.org.
Barath, Deepa. 2009. "Vietnamese Artists' Exhibit Shut Down by Threat of Protests." *Orange County Register* (January 16); www.ocregister.com.
Beck, Ulrich. 2000. *The Brave New World of Work*. Cambridge, UK: Polity Press.
Benjamin, Walter. 1968. *Illuminations*. New York: Harcourt Brace Jovanovich.
Berman, Larry. 2001. *No Peace, No Honor: Nixon, Kissinger, and Betrayal in Vietnam*. New York: Simon & Schuster.
Berndtson, Erkki. 2000. "Globalization as Americanization." In *Power in Contemporary Politics: Theories, Practices, Globalizations*, ed. Henri Goverde and Howard H. Lentner. London: Sage, 155–169.
Bhabha, Homi. 1994. *The Location of Culture*. New York: Routledge.
Bhaduri, Madhu. 1977. "From Saigon to Ho Chi Minh City." *Economic and Political Weekly* 12, no. 40: 1696–1699.
Bharath, Deepa. 2009. "'F.O.B II: Art Speaks' Closed Today after Little Saigon Community Members Protested a Photo with Image of Hồ Chí Minh." *Orange County Register* (January 16); www.ocregister.com.
Blackburn, Elliott. 2006. "Conference to Address Contributions of South Vietnamese forces in War." *Avalanche-Journal* (March 17).
Blight, David. 2002. *Beyond the Battlefield: Race, Memory and the American Civil War*. Amherst: University of Massachusetts Press.
Bourdieu, Pierre and Jean-Claude Passero. 1998. "Foundations of a Theory of Symbolic Violence." In *Reproduction in Education, Society and Culture*. Trans. Richard Nice. 2nd edition. London: Sage, viii–68.
Bradley, Mark Philip. 2000. *Imagining Vietnam and America: The Making of Postcolonial Vietnam, 1919–1950*. Chapel Hill: University of North Carolina Press.
———. 2001. "Contests of Memory: Remembering and Forgetting War in the Contemporary Vietnamese Cinema." In *The Country of Memory: Remaking the Past in Late Socialist Vietnam*, ed. Hue-Tam Ho Tai. Berkeley: University of California Press, 196–226.
Bradsher, Keith. 2006. "Vietnam's Roaring Economy Set for World Stage." *New York Times* (October 25); A1.
Brady, Mary Pat. 2002. *Extinct Lands, Temporal Geographies: Chicana Literature and the Urgency of Space*. Durham, NC: Duke University Press.
Brigham, Robert Kendall. 2006. *ARVN: Life and Death in the South Vietnamese Army*. Lawrence: University Press of Kansas.
Bui, Long T. 2015. "The Debts of Memory: Historical Amnesia and Refugee Knowledge." *Journal of Asian American Studies* 18, no. 1: 73–97.
———. 2016. "The Global War City: Traces of the Militarized Past in Saigon's Urbanized Future." *Verge: Studies in Global Asias* 2, no. 1: 141–169.
Butler, Judith. 1997. *The Psychic Life of Power: Theories in Subjection*. Stanford, CA: Stanford University Press.

Byrd, Jodi. 2011. *The Transit of Empire: Indigenous Critiques of Colonialism*. Minneapolis: University of Minnesota Press.

Calvino, Manuel. 1998. "Reflections on Community Studies." *Journal of Community Psychology* 26, no. 3: 253–259.

Cam, Tran Do and Nguyen Manh Tr. 2011. "Two Generations, One Aspiration." www.saigonecho.com (August).

Canaday, Margot. 2003. "Building a Straight State: Sexuality and Social Citizenship under the 1944 GI Bill." *Journal of American History* 90, no. 3: 935–957.

Cao, Lan. 1998. *Monkey Bridge*. New York: Penguin.

———. 2014. *The Lotus and the Storm*. New York: Penguin.

Caplan, Nathan, John K. Whitmore, and Marcella H. Choy. 1989. *The Boat People and Achievement in America: A Study of Family Life, Hard Work, and Cultural Values*. Ann Arbor: University of Michigan Press.

Carruthers, Ashley. 2008. "Saigon from the Diaspora." *Singapore Journal of Tropical Geography* 29: 68–86.

Carter, James. 2008. *Inventing Vietnam: The United States and State Building, 1954–1968*. New York: Cambridge University Press.

CBS News2014, February 1. "Gay Community Allowed in Vietnamese Lunar New Year." www.losangeles.cbslocal.com/.

Chakravartty, Paula and Denise Ferreira da Silva. 2012. "Accumulation, Dispossession, and Debt: The Racial Logic of Global Capitalism—An Introduction." *American Quarterly* 64, no. 3: 361–385.

Chan, Kwok B. and David Loveridge. 1987. "'Refugees in Transit': Vietnamese in a Refugee Camp in Hong Kong." *International Migration Review* 21, no. 3: 745–759.

Chang, Richard. 2009a. "Photographer Set Off Little Saigon." *Orange County Register* (January 30); www.ocregister.com.

———. 2009b. "Vietnamese American Artworks Vandalized." *Orange County Register* (January 20); www.ocregister.com.

———. 2009c. "Protesters Shut down 'F.O.B. II' Exhibition." *Orange County Register* (January 16); www.ocregister.com.

———. 2009d. "Assemblyman Van Tran Responds." *Orange County Register* (February 13); www.ocregister.com.

———. 2012. "O.C. Native Aimee Phan Writes Novel about Reeducation Camps," *Orange County Register* (March 23); www.ocregister.com.

Cheng, Anne. 2000. *The Melancholy of Race: Psychoanalysis, Assimilation, and Hidden Grief*. New York: Oxford University Press.

Chesneaux, Jean. 1955. "Stages in the Development of the Vietnam National Movement 1862–1940." *Past and Present* 7: 63–75.

Chomsky, Noam. 1991. "Visions of Righteousness." In *The Vietnam War and American Culture*, ed. Rick Berg and John Carlos Rowe. New York: Columbia University Press.

Chong, Sylvia Shin Huey. 2005. "Restaging the War: The Deer Hunter and the Primal Scene of Violence." *Cinema Journal* 44, no. 2 (Winter): 89–106.

"Chống Triển Lãm F.O.B. Là Đúng." n.p. *Thtinfo*; http://thtinfo.com/.

Chow, Rey. 1993. *Writing Diaspora: Tactics of Intervention in Contemporary Cultural Studies*. Bloomington: Indiana University Press.

Chuh, Kandice. 2003. *Imagine Otherwise: On Asian Americanist Critique*. Durham, NC: Duke University Press.

Clinton, Bill. 2000. Speech at Hanoi National University. Le Viêt Nam (November 17); http://patrick.guenin2.free.fr.

"Cờ máu, hình Hồ và VAALA tại Nam California." 2009. *Nhóm Nhà Văn Quân Đội* (December 1); http://thtinfo.com/.

Cohen, Cathy J. 1999. *The Boundaries of Blackness: AIDS and the Breakdown of Black Politics*. Chicago: University of Chicago Press.

Collet, Christian and Nadine Selden. 2003. "Separate Ways . . . Worlds Apart?: 'Generation Gap' in Vietnamese America as Seen Through *The San Jose Mercury News* Poll." *Amerasia Journal* 29, no. 1: 199–217.

Committee on Foreign Relations, U.S. Senate. 2010. "Report to the Chairman and Ranking Member." Vietnam Education Foundation. U.S. Government Accountability Office (April).

Coutin, Susan Bibler. 2010. "Originary Destinations: Re/membered Communities and Salvadoran Diasporas." *Urban Anthropology and Studies of Cultural Systems and World Economic Development* 39: 47–72.

Cuevas, Ofelia. 2012. "Welcome to My Cell: Housing and Race in the Mirror of American Democracy." *American Quarterly* 64, no. 3: 605–624.

Cvetkovich, Ann. 2003. *An Archive of Feelings: Trauma, Sexuality, and Lesbian Public Cultures*. Durham, NC: Duke University Press.

Dacy, Douglas C. 1986. *Foreign Aid, War, and Economic Development: South Vietnam, 1955–1975*. Cambridge, UK: Cambridge University Press.

Daddis, Gregory A. 2011. *No Sure Victory: Measuring U.S. Army Effectiveness and Progress in the Vietnam War*. New York: Oxford University Press.

Dao, Anh Thang Dao. 2012. "Exile of Freedom: The Nation-State and Exile in Linda Lê's Slander." *positions* 20, no. 3: 713–736.

Davis, Peter, dir. 1974. *Hearts and Minds*. BBS Productions.

Diehl, Jackson. 2009. "It's Vietnam, Again." *Washington Post* (October 25); www.washingtonpost.com.

"Dinh Q. Lê in Conversation with Zoe Butt." 2013. *Guggenheim UBS MAP Global Art Initiative* (January 22); http://blogs.guggenheim.org/.

Do, Anh. 2013. "Tired of Being Marginalized, Viet Gay Rights Group Stops Playing Nice." (December 8); www.latimes.com.

Do, Hien Duc. 1999. *The Vietnamese Americans*. Westport, CT: Greenwood Press.

Doan, Brian. 2009. "Photographer Delivers Lecture at Cypress College." (February 4); http://artsblog.freedomblogging.com/.

Dorais, Louis-Jacques. 2001. "Defining the Overseas Vietnamese." *Diaspora: A Journal of Transnational Studies* 10, no. 1: 3–27.

Douglass, Mike and Liling Huang. 2007. "Globalizing the City in Southeast Asia: Utopia on the Urban Edge—The Case of Phu My Hung, Saigon." *International Journal of Asian Pacific Studies* 3, no. 2: 1–42.

Drummond, Lisa. 2000. "Streetscapes: Practices of Public and Private Spaces in Vietnamese Cities." *Urban Studies* 37, no. 12: 2377–2391.

Duiker, William J. 1977. "Ideology and Nation-Building in the Democratic Republic of Vietnam." *Asian Survey* 17, no. 5 (May): 413–431.

Dulles, John Foster and Richard M. Nixon. 1995. "Taking Up the White Man's Burden: Two American Views." In *Vietnam and America: A Documented History*, ed. Marvin E. Gettleman, Jane M. Franklin, Marilyn Young, and H. Bruce Franklin. New York: Grove/Atlantic Press.

Duong, Lan. 2005. "Manufacturing Authenticity: The Feminine Ideal in Tony Bui's *Three Seasons*." *Amerasia Journal* 31, no. 2: 1–19.

———. 2009. "Vietnamese Americans and the United States of War." *Official F.O.B. II Art Speaks Catalogue*.

———. 2012. *Treacherous Subjects: Gender, Culture, and Trans-Vietnamese Feminism*. Philadelphia: Temple University Press.

Duong, Lan and Isabelle Thuy Pelaud. 2012. "Vietnamese American Art and Community Politics: An Engaged Feminist Perspective." *Journal of Asian American Studies* 15, no. 3: 241–269.

Earl, Catherine. 2004. "Leisure and Social Mobility in Ho Chi Minh City." In *Social Inequality in Vietnam and the Challenges to Reform*, ed. Phillip Taylor. Singapore: Seng Lee Press, 2377–2392.

Edkins, Jenny. 2003. *Trauma and the Memory of Politics*. New York: Cambridge University Press.

Eggleston, Michael. 2014. *Exiting Vietnam: The Era of Vietnamization and American Withdrawal Revealed in First-Person Accounts*. Jefferson, NC: McFarland and Co.

Ehrenhaus, Peter. 1989. "Commemorating the Unwon War: On Not Remembering Vietnam." *Journal of Communication* 39, no. 1: 96–107.

Eng, David L. and David Kazanjian, eds. 2002. *Loss: The Politics of Mourning*. Berkeley: University of California Press.

Enloe, Cynthia. 1993. *The Morning After: Sexual Politics at the End of the Cold War*. Berkeley: University of California Press.

Espiritu, Yen Le. 2003. *Home Bound: Filipino Lives Across Cultures, Communities, and Countries*. Berkeley: University of California Press.

———. 2005a. "Thirty Years AfterWARd: The Endings That Are Not Over." *Amerasia Journal* 31, no. 2: xiii–xxvi.

———. 2005b. "Vietnamese Women in the United States: A Critical Transnational Perspective." In *Le Vietnam au Feminin/Vietnam: Women's Realities*, ed. Gisele Bousquet and Nora Taylor. Paris: Les Indes Savantes, 307–321.

———. 2006a. "The 'We-Win-Even-When-We-Lose' Syndrome: U.S. Press Coverage of the Twenty-Fifth Anniversary of the 'Fall of Saigon.'" *American Quarterly* 58, no. 2: 329–352.

———. 2006b. "Toward a Critical Refugee Study: The Vietnamese Refugee Subject in US Scholarship." *Journal of Vietnamese Studies* 1, nos. 1–2: 410–433.

———. 2014. *Body Counts: The Vietnam War and Militarized Refugees*. Berkeley: University of California Press.

Forbes, Dean. 1996. "Urbanization, Migration, and Vietnam's Spatial Structure." *Sojourn: Journal of Social Issues in Southeast Asia* 11, no. 2: 24–51.

Foucault, Michel. 1977. *Discipline and Punish: The Birth of the Prison*. New York: Random House.

———. 2003. *Society Must Be Defended: Lectures at the College de France 1975–1976*. Trans. David Macey. New York: Picador.

Fuller, Thomas. 2015. "Capitalist Soul Rises as Ho Chi Minh City Sheds Its Past." *New York Times* (July 20): A1.

Furuya, Hiroyo and Christian Collet. 2009. "Contested Nation: Vietnam and the Emergence of Saigon Nationalism in the United States." In *The Transnational Politics of Asian Americans*, ed. Christian Collet and Pei-te Lien. Philadelphia: Temple University Press, 56–73.

Gainsborough, Martin. 2003. *Changing Political Economy of Vietnam: The Case of Ho Chi Minh City*. London: Routledge.

Gallagher, John and Ronald Robinson. 1953. "The Imperialism of Free Trade." *Economic History Review* 6, no. 1: 1–15.

Gartner, Scott Sigmund. 1998. "Differing Evaluations of Vietnamization." *Journal of Interdisciplinary History* 29, no. 2: 243–262.

Gibbs, Jessica and Alex Goodall. 2009. "Conflict and Cooperation: Cuban Exile Anti-Communism and the United States, 1960–2000." In *Anti-Communist Minorities in the U.S.*, ed. Ieva Zake. New York: Palgrave Macmillan, 233–253.

Giddens, Anthony. 1991. *Modernity and Self-Identity: Self and Society in the Late Modern Age*. Cambridge, UK: Polity.

Gilmore, Ruth Wilson. 2002. "Fatal Couplings of Power and Difference: Notes on Racism and Geography." *Professional Geographer* 54, no. 1: 15–24.

Glissant, Édouard. 1997. *Poetics of Relation*. Trans. Betsy Wing. Ann Arbor: University of Michigan Press.

Goldstein, Alyosha. 2014. "Introduction: Toward a Genealogy of the U.S. Colonial Present." In *Formations of United States Colonialism*, ed. Alyosha Goldstein. Durham, NC: Duke University Press.

Gopinath, Gayatri. 2005. *Impossible Desires: Queer Diasporas and South Asian Public Cultures*. Durham, NC: Duke University Press.

Gordon, Avery. 1997. *Ghostly Matters: Haunting and the Sociological Imagination*. Minneapolis: University of Minnesota Press.

Gough, Kathleen. 1984. "The War against Women." *Manushi* 21: 29–32.

Gravel, Mike, ed. 1971. *Pentagon Papers*. Gravel edition, volume 3. Boston: Beacon Press.

Grewal, Inderpal. 2014. "American Humanitarian Citizenship." In *Gender, Globalization, and Violence: Postcolonial Conflict Zones*, ed. Sandra Ponzanesi. London: Routledge Press, 64–81.

Griswold, Charles and Stephen S. Griswold. 1986. "The Vietnam Veterans Memorial and the Washington Mall: Philosophical Thoughts on Political Iconography." *Critical Inquiry* 12, no. 4 (Summer): 688–719.

Guevarra, Anna Romina. 2009. *Marketing Dreams, Manufacturing Heroes: The Transnational Labor Brokering of Filipino Workers*. New Brunswick, NJ: Rutgers University Press.

Gustafsson, Mai Lan. 2007. "The Living and the Lost: War and Possession in Vietnam." *Anthropology of Consciousness* 18, no. 2: 56–73.

Hagedorn, Jessica Tarahata. 1990. *Dogeaters*. New York: Penguin.

Hagopian, Patrick. 2003. "Virtual Vietnam Archive." *Journal of American History* 90, no. 1 (June).

———. 2009. *The Vietnam War in American Memory: Veterans, Memorials, and the Politics of Healing*. Amherst: University of Massachusetts Press.

Halloran, Richard. 2005. "Vietnamese Americans Repay the U.S. with Military Service." *Taipei Times* (October 17); www.taipeitimes.com.

Hamilton, Annette. 2009. "Renovated: Gender and Cinema in Contemporary Vietnam." *Visual Anthropology* 22, nos. 2–3: 141–154.

Hanhimaki, Jussi M. 2004. *The Flawed Architect: Henry Kissinger and American Foreign Policy*. New York: Oxford University Press.

Hardt, Michael and Antonio Negri. 2000. *Empire*. Cambridge, MA: Harvard University Press.

Harms, Erik. 2011. *Saigon's Edge: On the Margins of Ho Chi Minh City*. Minneapolis: University of Minnesota Press.

Harvey, David. 1990. *The Condition of Postmodernity: An Enquiry into the Origins of Cultural Change*. Cambridge: Blackwell.

Hass, Kristin Ann. 1986. *Carried to the Wall: American Memory and the Vietnam Veterans Memorial*. Berkeley: University of California Press.

Herrera, Andrea O'Reilly. 1998. "'The Consciousness of Exile': Memory and the Vicarious Imagination in Cuban-American Literature and Art." *Journal of West Indian Literature* 8, no. 1: 82–98.

Herring, George C. 2007. "'Peoples Quite Apart': Americans, South Vietnamese, and the War in Vietnam." *Diplomatic History* 14, no. 1: 1–26.

Herring, George W. 1991/92. "America and Vietnam: The Unending War." *Foreign Affairs* 70, no. 5 (Winter): 104–119.

Hien, Phong and Van Hao Le. 1975. "Aspects of Neo-Colonialist Culture." *Vietnamese Studies* 41, no. 1: 110–150.

Hirsch, Marianne. 2008. "The Generation of Postmemory." *Poetics Today* 29, no. 1: 103–128.

Hirsh, Michael. 2004. "Endgame; How Will We Know When We Can Finally Leave?" *Washington Post* (September 26): B01.

Hoang, Kimberly Kay. 2010. "Economies of Emotion, Familiarity, Fantasy, and Desire: Emotional Labor in Ho Chi Minh City's Sex Industry." *Sexualities* 13, no. 2: 255–272.

Hoang, Tuan. 2016. "From Reeducation Camps to Little Saigons: Historicizing Vietnamese Diasporic Anti-communism." *Journal of Vietnamese Studies* 11, no. 2: 43–95.
Hoelscher, Steven and Derek H. Alderman. 2004. "Memory and Place: Geographies of a Critical Relationship." *Social and Cultural Geography* 5, no. 3: 347–355.
Hong Koo, Han. 2006. "South Korea and the Vietnam War." In *Developmental Dictatorship and the Park Chung-Hee Era: The Shaping of Modernity in the Republic of Korea,* ed. Lee Byeong-Cheon. Paramus, NJ: Homa and Sekey Books, 248–270.
Horowitz, Irving L. 1999. "The Vietnamization of Yugoslavia Society." *Society* 36, no. 5: 3–10.
Hosmer, Stephen T., Konrad Kellen, and Brian M. Jenkins. 1978. *The Fall of South Vietnam: Statements by Vietnamese Military and Civilian Leaders.* No. RAND/R-2208-OSD (HIST). Santa Monica: Rand Corporation.
Hughes, Ken. 2010. "Fatal Politics: Nixon's Political Timetable for Withdrawing from Vietnam." *Diplomatic History* 34, no. 3 (June): 497–506.
Huynh, Luu, Doan Huynh. 1993. "The American War in Vietnamese Memory." In *The Vietnam War: Vietnamese and American Perspectives,* ed. Mark Bradley, Jayne S. Werner, and Luu Doan Huynh. Armonk, NY: M.E. Sharpe.
Ikul, Eikoh. 2001. "Reprogramming Memories: The Historicization of the Vietnam War from the 1970s through the 1990s." *Japanese Journal of American Studies* 12: 41–63.
Isaacs, Arnold R. 1997. *Vietnam Shadows: The War, Its Ghosts, and Its Legacy.* Baltimore, MD: Johns Hopkins University Press.
Jackson, Lynette. 2010. "Where Are the Girls? War, Displacement and the Notion of Home among Sudanese Refugee Children." In *Gender, Migration and the Public Sphere,* ed. Marlou Schrover and Eileen Yeo. New York: Routledge Press, 160–177.
Jameson, Fredric. 1991. *Postmodernism, or, the Cultural Logic of Late Capitalism.* Durham, NC: Duke University Press.
———. 1992. *The Geopolitical Aesthetic: Cinema and Space in the World System.* Bloomington: Indiana University Press.
———. 2013. *The Political Unconscious: Narrative as a Socially Symbolic Act.* London: Routledge.
Jervis, Robert. 2010. "The Politics of Troop Withdrawal: Salted Peanuts, the Commitment Trap, and Buying Time." *Diplomatic History* 34, no. 3: 507–516.
Johnson, Chalmers. 2004. *The Sorrows of Empire: Militarism, Secrecy, and the End of the Republic.* New York: Metropolitan Books.
Johnson, Robert H. 1970. "Vietnamization: Can It Work?" *Foreign Affairs* (July): 629–647.
Jolly, Margaret. 2008. "Moving Masculinities: Memories and Bodies across Oceania." *Contemporary Pacific* 20, no. 1: 1–24.
Kang, Laura Hyun Yi. 2002. *Compositional Subjects: Enfiguring Asian/American Women.* Durham, NC: Duke University Press Books.
Kang, Namsoon. 2014. *Diasporic Feminist Theology: Asia and Theopolitical Imagination.* Minneapolis, MN: Augsburg Fortress Publishers.

Kaplan, Lawrence. 2011. "Vietnamization: Enemy Body Counts Make a Grim Return." *New Republic* (March 3): 9.

Ken, Danny Wong Tze. 2014. "Vietnam-Champa Relations and the Malay-Islam Regional Network in the 17th–19th Centuries." *Kyoto Review of Southeast Asia*. Issue 5 (March).

Kessler, Glenn and Thomas E. Ricks. 2006. "The Realists' Repudiation of Policies for a War, Region." *Washington Post* (December 7).

Kibria, Nazli. 1993. *Family Tightrope: The Changing Lives of Vietnamese Americans*. Princeton, NJ: Princeton University Press.

Kiernan, V. G. 1974. "American Hegemony under Revision." *Socialist Register* 11, no. 11: 302–330.

Kim, Annette M. 2012. "The Mixed-Use Sidewalk." *Journal of the American Planning Association* 78, no. 3: 225–238.

Kim, Jodi. 2010. *Ends of Empire: Asian American Critique and the Cold War*. Minneapolis: University of Minnesota Press.

Kimball, Jeffrey. 2006. "The Nixon Doctrine: A Saga of Misunderstanding." *Presidential Studies Quarterly* 36, no. 1: 59–74.

———. 2011. "Richard M. Nixon and the Vietnam War: The Paradox of Disengagement with Escalation." In *Columbia History of the Vietnam War*, ed. David L. Anderson. New York: Columbia University Press.

King, Victor T. 2008. "The Middle Class in Southeast Asia: Diversities, Identities, Comparisons and the Vietnamese Case." *IJAPS* 4, no. 2: 73–109.

King, Victor, Phương An Nguyên, and Nguyên Hữu Minh. 2008. "Professional Middle Class Youth in Post-Reform Vietnam: Identity, Continuity and Change." *Modern Asian Studies* 42, no. 4: 783–813.

Kirkus Reviews. 2012. "The Reeducation of Cherry Truong." (March 15); www.kirkus-reviews.com/.

Klein, Kerwin Lee. 2000. "On the Emergence of Memory in Historical Discourse." *Representations* 69: 127–150.

Knight, Kathleen Abowitz and Jason Harnish. 2006. "Contemporary Discourses of Citizenship." *Review of Educational Research* 76, no. 4: 653–690.

Kochiyama, Yuri. 1994. "The Impact of Malcolm X on Asian-American Politics and Activism." In *Blacks, Latinos, and Asians in Urban Americas: Status and Prospects for Politics and Activism*, ed. James Jennings. London: Praeger.

Komarow, Steven. 2005. "30 Years Later: Are We Still Warring over Vietnam? *USA Today* (April 29): 8A.

Kopetman, Roxana. 2013. "Vietnamese Americans to LGBT: Don't Join the Parade." *Orange Counter Register* (November 15).

Krapp, Peter. 2004. *Déjà Vu: Aberrations of Cultural Memory*. Minneapolis: University of Minnesota Press.

Kwan, Yvonne. 2015. "Intergenerational Refugee Resilience." In *Navigating the Great Recession: Immigrant Families' Stories of Resilience*, ed. Ana Sanchez-Munoz, Gina

Masequesmay, Eunai Shrake, and Tracy Buenavista. Dubuque, IA: Kendall Hunt Publishing, pp. 21–25.

Labaeye, Adrien et al. 2012. "Reality Check: Ho Chi Minh City, Vietnam." *Resilient Cities* 2: 367–376.

Laderman, Scott. 2009. *Tours of Vietnam: War, Travel Guides, and Memory*. Durham, NC: Duke University Press.

Laird, Melvin R. 2005. "Iraq: Learning the Lessons of Vietnam." *Foreign Affairs* 84, no. 6: 22–43.

Lam, Andrew. 2005. *Perfume Dreams: Reflections on the Vietnamese Diaspora*. Berkeley, CA: Heyday Books.

———. 2007. "An American Tragedy." *The Nation* 12 (March); www.thenation.com.

Lâm, Quang Thi. 2001. *The Twenty-Five-Year Century: A South Vietnamese General Remembers the Indochina War to the Fall of Saigon*. Denton: University of North Texas Press.

Lang, Michael and Barry Kolb. 1980. "Locational Components of Urban and Regional Public Policy in Postwar Vietnam: The Case of Ho Chi Minh City (Saigon)." *GeoJournal* 4, no. 1: 13–18.

Le, Huong. 2008. "Economic Reforms, Cultural Policy: Opportunities and Challenges to the Arts and Culture in Vietnam in the Age of Globalization." *Journal of Arts Management, Law, and Society* 38, no. 1 (Spring): 5–18.

Le, Long. 2011. "Exploring the Function of the Anti-communist Ideology in the Vietnamese American Diasporic Community." *Journal of Southeast Asian American Education and Advancement* 6: 1–26.

Le, T. D. 2007. "Vietnamese Americans in the Military." *Vietbaomagazine* (July 13); www.vietbao.com.

Lê, Thi Diem Thúy. 2011. *The Gangster We Are All Looking For*. New York: Anchor.

Lê, Việt. 2005. "The Art of War: Vietnamese American Visual Artists Đình Q. Lê, Ann Phông and Nguyễn Tân Hoàng." *Amerasia Journal* 31, no. 2: 23–35.

Lemarchand, René. 2012. *The Dynamics of Violence in Central Africa*. Philadelphia: University of Pennsylvania Press.

Leshkowich, Ann Marie. 2008. "Wandering Ghosts of Late Socialism: Conflict, Metaphor, and Memory in a Southern Vietnamese Marketplace." *Journal of Asian Studies* 67: 5–41.

———. 2012. "Finances, Family, Fashion, Fitness, and . . . Freedom? The Changing Lives of Urban Middle-Class Vietnamese Women." In *The Reinvention of Distinction: Modernity and the Middle-Class in Vietnam*, ed. Van Nguyen-Marshall, Lisa B. Welch, and Danièle Bélanger. Dordrecht: Springer Netherlands, 95–113.

Leventman, Seymour and Paul Camacho. 1980. "The 'Gook' Syndrome: The Vietnam War as a Racial Encounter." In *Strangers at Home*, ed. C. R. Figley. New York: Praeger, 55–70.

Lieberman, Kim-An. 2003. "Virtually Vietnamese: Nationalism on the Internet." In *AsianAmerica.Net: Ethnicity, Nationalism, and Cyberspace*, ed. Rachel C. Lee and Sau-ling Cynthia Wong. New York: Routledge, 71–97.

Lieu, Nhi T. 2011. *The American Dream in Vietnamese*. Minneapolis: University of Minnesota Press.
Linh, Tiểu. 2010. "Đạo diễn Bùi Thạc Chuyên: Những tâm sự trong nghề." *TinMoi*. www.tinmoi.vn.
Lowe, Lisa. 1996. *Immigrant Acts: On Asian American Cultural Politics*. Durham, NC: Duke University Press.
———. 2010. "Metaphors of Sovereignty." In *America and the Misshaping of a New World Order*, ed. Giles Gunn and Carl Gutierrez-Jones. Berkeley: University of California Press, 191–214.
Lutz, Catherine. 2006. "Empire Is in the Details." *American Ethnologist* 33, no. 4: 593–611.
Ly, Phuong. 2003. "Former Refugees Now Able to Return and Enjoy Vietnam." *Washington Post* (October 12); www.washingtonpost.com.
Maier, Charles S. 2000. "Consigning the Twentieth Century to History: Alternative Narratives for the Modern Era." *American Historical Review* 105, no. 3 (June): 807–831.
Man, Simeon. 2014. "Radicalizing Currents: The GI Movement in the Third World." In *The Rising Tide of Color: Race, State Violence, and Radical Movements across the Pacific*, ed. Jung Moon-Ho. Seattle: University of Washington Press, 266–298.
Mariscal, Jorge. 2005."Homeland Security, Militarism, and the Future of Latinos and Latinas in the United States." *Radical History Review* 93 (Fall): 39–52.
Markell, Patchen. 2003. *Bound by Recognition*. Princeton, NJ: Princeton University Press.
Martin, Randy. 2007. *An Empire of Indifference: American War and the Financial Logic of Risk Management*. Durham, NC: Duke University Press.
Martini, Edwin. 2007. *Invisible Enemies: The American War on Vietnam, 1975–2000*. Amherst: University of Massachusetts Press.
Marx, Karl. 1973. *Grundrisse*. Harmondsworth, UK: Penguin Books.
Masequesmay, Gina. 2012. "Queering Tet." In *Asian Pacific American Experiences: Past, Present, and Future*, ed. Eunai Shrake and Edith Chen. Dubuque, IA: Kendall Hunt Publishing, 323–334.
Maxner, Stephen. 2011. "Celebrating 20 Years of Preserving the Past for a Better Future." Vietnam Center and Archive (May 20). www.vietnam.ttu.edu.
Mbembé, Achille. 2003. "Necropolitics." *Public Culture* 15, no. 1: 11–40.
McCollum, James K. 1983. "The CORDS Pacification Organization in Vietnam: A Civilian-Military Effort." *Armed Forces and Society* 10, no. 1: 105–122.
McGee, Terry G. 2009. "Interrogating the Production of Urban Space in China and Vietnam under Market Socialism." *Asia Pacific Viewpoint* 50, no. 2: 228–246.
McKelvey, Robert S. 2002. *A Gift of Barbed Wire: America's Allies Abandoned in South Vietnam*. Seattle: University of Washington Press.
McMahon, Robert J. 1999. *The Limits of Empire: The United States and Southeast Asia Since World War II*. New York: Columbia University Press.
Mcnichols, Mary. 2010. "A Conversation with Susan Aaron-Taylor, August 2009." *Jung Journal* 4, no. 2: 110–122.

McQuaid, Cate. 2010. "Symbolic Power: Brian Doan's Meditations on Vietnamese History Say More Than They Show." *Boston.com* (December 22); http://articles.boston.com.

Miller, Edward and Tuong Vu. 2009. "The Vietnam War as a Vietnamese War: Agency and Society in the Study of the Second Indochina War." *Journal of Vietnamese Studies* 4, no. 3: 1–16.

Minh, Dang Nhat and Pham Thu Thuy. 2003. "Representations of Đổi Mới Society in Contemporary Vietnamese Cinema." In *Consuming Urban Culture in Contemporary Vietnam*, ed. Lisa Drummond and Mandy Thomas. London: Routledge Curzon, 191–201.

Minh-Ha, Trinh. 2011. *Elsewhere, Within Here: Immigration, Refugeeism and the Boundary Event*. New York: Taylor and Francis.

Morrison, Toni. 1991. *Beloved*. New York: Signet.

Mulvey, Laura. 1975. "Visual Pleasure and Narrative Cinema." *Screen* 16, no. 3: 6–18.

Muppidi, Himadeep. 2006. "Shame and Rage: International Relations and the World School of Colonialism." In *Interrogating Imperialism: Conversations on Gender, Race, and War*, ed. Naeem Inayatullah and Robin Riley. New York: Palgrave Macmillan, 51–61.

Naber, Nadine Suleiman. 2014. "Imperial Whiteness and the Diasporas of Empire." *American Quarterly* 66, no. 4: 1107–1115.

Nelson, Vern. 2014. "Viet Bigotry Melts to Manageable Size, LGBT to March in Tet Parade!" *Orange Juice Blog* (January 4); www.orangejuiceblog.com.

Ng, Celeste. 2015. *Everything I Never Told You*. New York: Penguin.

Ng, Fae Myenne. 1993. *Bone*. New York: HarperPerennial.

Ngô, Fiona. 2014. *Imperial Blues: Geographies of Race and Sex in Jazz Age New York*. Durham, NC: Duke University Press.

Nguyen, Huy. 2009. "Bài và Hình." *Người Việt*. (January 16); www.nguoi-viet.com.

———. 2009. "Hai Tổ Chức Cựu Chiến Sĩ VNCH Họp Để Tìm Cách Phản Đối Cuộc Triển Lãm 'Nghệ Thuật Lên Tiếng.'" *Người Việt* (January 13); www.nguoi-viet.com.

Nguyen, Jimmy. 2014. "Return of LGBT Groups to Little Saigon's 'Tet' Parade Is a Community Win." *Huffington Post* (January 6); www.huffingtonpost.com.

Nguyen, Kim. 2010. "'Without the Luxury of Historical Amnesia': The Model Postwar Immigrant Remembering the Vietnam War through Anti-communist Protests." *Journal of Communication Inquiry* 34, no. 2: 134–150.

Nguyen, Linh. 2013. "Recalling the Refugee: Cultural Clash and Melancholic Racial Formation in Daughter from Danang." *Amerasia Journal* 39, no. 3: 101–121.

Nguyen, Mimi Thi. 2012. *The Gift of Freedom: War, Debt, and Other Refugee Passages*. Durham, NC: Duke University Press.

Nguyen, Nathalie Huynh. 2009. *Memory Is Another Country: Women of the Vietnamese Diaspora*. Westport, CT: Praeger.

Nguyen, Phuong. 2017. *Becoming Refugee American: The Politics of Rescue in Little Saigon*. Champaign: University of Illinois Press.

Nguyen, Qui Duoc. 2009. "The VAALA Exhibit—A View from Inside." *Damau* (April 2), http://damau.org/.

Nguyen, Viet Thanh. 2002. *Race and Resistance: Literature and Politics in Asian America*. Cary: Oxford University Press.

———. 2005. "What Is the Political? American Culture and the Example of Viet Nam." In *Asian American Studies after Critical Mass*, ed. Kent Ono. Malden, MA: Blackwell, 19–39.

———. 2006. "Speak of the Dead, Speak of Vietnam: The Ethics and Aesthetics of Minority Discourse." *CR: The New Centennial Review* 6, no. 2: 7–37.

———. 2016. *Nothing Ever Dies*. Cambridge, MA: Harvard University Press.

Nguyen, Xuan Lai. 1975. "Vietnamization in the Economic Sphere (1969–1972)." *Vietnamese Studies* 42, no. 1: 188–250.

Nguyen-Akbar, Mytoan. 2016. "Finding the American Dream Abroad? Narratives of Return Among 1.5 and Second Generation Vietnamese American Skilled Migrants in Vietnam." *Journal of Vietnamese Studies* 11, no. 2: 96–121.

Nguyễn-Võ, Thu-Hương. 2005. "Forking Paths: How Shall We Mourn the Dead?" *Amerasia* 31, no. 2: 157–175.

———. 2010. "The Feminine Coordinate: Staging Asian Modernity and Neoliberal Globality in Vietnam." Keynote speech, Gendering Asia Network Conference. Copenhagen University Asian Dynamics Initiative.

Ninh, Erin Khuê. 2005. *Ingratitude: The Debt-Bound Daughter in Asian American Literature*. New York: New York University Press.

Nixon, Richard. 1969. "Address to the Nation on the War in Vietnam." www.nixonlibrary.gov.

———. 1972. "Address on the State of the Union Delivered Before a Joint Session of the Congress." University of California Santa Barbara American Presidency Project.

Nora, Pierre. 1989. "Between Memory and History: Les Lieux de Mémoire." *Representations* 26 (Spring): 7–24.

———. 2001. "Aestheticizing Urban Space: Modernity in Postcolonial Saigon and Hanoi." *L'Esprit Créateur* 41, no. 3: 73–87.

Ong, Aihwa. 2003. *Buddha Is Hiding: Refugees, Citizenship, the New America*. Berkeley: University of California Press.

Ong, Nhu-Ngoc T. and David S. Meyer. 2004. "Protest and Political Incorporation: Vietnamese American Protests, 1975–2001." Center for the Study of Democracy, UC Irvine. http://repositories.cdlib.org.

Orange Juice Blog. 2009. "Van Tran Is No Hero, But Brian Doan Is!" *Orange Juice Blog* (February 1); http://www.orangejuiceblog.com/.

Orderly Departure Program (ODP) Application File for Dang Minh Tam, March 28, 1989. Item Number: 1849006072000, Families of Vietnamese Political Prisoners Association (FVPPA) Collection, Vietnamese American Heritage Foundation.

Oropeza, Lorena. 2005. *Raza Sí!, Guerra No!: Chicano Protest and Patriotism During the Viet Nam War Era*. Berkeley: University of California Press.

Parsons, Dana. 2009. "Vietnamese Americans' Hatred of Communism Shouldn't Inhibit Free Speech." *Los Angeles Times* (January 16); www.latimes.com.

Paterson, Thomas G. 1988. "Historical Memory and Illusive Victories: Vietnam and Central America." *Diplomatic History* 12, no. 1: 1–18.

Pearson, James. 2018. "U.S. Seeks to Deport Thousands of Vietnamese Protected by Treaty: Former Ambassador." *Reuters* (April 12); www.reuters.com.

Pedroza, Art. 2010. "Gay Protesters Targeting Saturday's Tet Festival Parade, in Westminster." *Orange Juice Blog* (February 12); www.orangejuiceblog.com.

Pelaud, Isabelle Thuy. 2010. *This Is All I Choose to Tell: History and Hybridity in Vietnamese American Literature.* Philadelphia: Temple University Press.

Pettus, Ashley. 2003. *Between Sacrifice and Desire: National Identity and the Governing of Femininity in Vietnam.* New York: Routledge.

Pham, Andrew T. 2010. "The Returning Diaspora: Analyzing Overseas Vietnamese (Viet Kieu): Contributions Toward Vietnam's Economic Growth." M.Sc. thesis, London School of Economics.

Pham, Quang X. 2005a. *A Sense of Duty: My Father, My American Journey.* New York: Ballantine Books.

———. 2005b. "Duty and Deceit." *Boston Globe* (June 27); www.bostonglobe.com.

Phan, Aimee. 2012. *The Reeducation of Cherry Truong.* New York: St. Martin's.

Polan, Dana. 1996. "Globalism's Localisms." In *Global/Local: Cultural Production and the Transnational Imaginary*, ed. Rob Wilson and Wimal Dissanayake. Durham, NC: Duke University Press.

Potts, Andrew. 2013. "Judge Rules LGBT Vietnamese Groups Can Be Legally Excluded from Orange County Tet Parade." *Gay Star News* (February 9).

Pratt, Mary Louise. 1991. "Arts of the Contact Zone." *Profession 91*: 33–40.

Ray, Richard. 1970. "War and Language-the Vietnamization of the Human Spirit." *Journal of Social Philosophy* 1, no. 1 (September): 10–13.

Reckner, James. 1994. "Why Are America's Top Vietnam Veterans Supporting Texas Tech University's Center for the Study of the Vietnam Conflict?" *Friends of the Vietnam Center Newsletter* 1, no. 1 (May): 3. Vietnam Center Collection. The Vietnam Archive, Texas Tech University.

———. 1998. "Approaching Vietnam." *Friends of the Vietnam Center Newsletter* 5, no. 3 (October): 3. Vietnam Center Collection. The Vietnam Archive, Texas Tech University.

———. 2002. "From the Director." *Friends of the Vietnam Center Newsletter* 9, no. 2 (June): 2. Vietnam Center Collection. The Vietnam Archive, Texas Tech University.

———. 2004. "From the Director." *Friends of the Vietnam Center Newsletter* 11, no. 3 (Fall): 2. Vietnam Center Collection. The Vietnam Archive, Texas Tech University.

Renan, Ernest. 1990. "What Is a Nation?" In *Nation and Narration*, ed. Homi K. Bhabha. London: Routledge, 8–22.

Rodriguez, Dylan. 2010. *Suspended Apocalypse: White Supremacy, Genocide, and the Filipino Condition.* Minneapolis: University of Minnesota Press.

Rose, Nikolas. 1996. "Governing 'Advanced' Liberal Democracies." In *The Anthropology of the State: A Reader*, ed. Aradhana Sharma and Akhil Gupta. Malden, MA: Blackwell, 144–162.

Rowe, John Carlos. 2002. "'Bringing It All Back Home': American Recycling of the Vietnam. War." In *The Violence of Representation. Literature and the History of Violence*, ed. Nancy Armstrong and Leonard Tennenhouse. London: Routledge, 197–204.

Sahagun, Louis and My-Thuan Tran. 2009. "Vietnamese Americans Protest Art Exhibit in Santa Ana." *Los Angeles Times* (January 18); www.latimes.com.

Sahara, Ayako. 2012. "Theater of Rescue: Cultural Representations of U.S. Evacuation from Vietnam." *Journal of American and Canadian Studies* 30: 55–84.

Said, Edward. 1994. *Orientalism*. New York: Vintage Books.

Saito, Leland T. 1998. *Race and Politics: Asian Americans, Latinos, and Whites in a Los Angeles Suburb*. Urbana: University of Illinois Press.

Sanger, David. 1997. "Hanoi Agrees to Pay Saigon's Debts to U.S." *New York Times* (March 1): www.nytimes.com.

SarDesai, D. R. 2005. *Vietnam, Past and Present*. Boulder, CO: Westview Press.

Sassen, Saskia. 1996. *Losing Control?: Sovereignty in an Age of Globalization*. New York: Columbia University Press.

Schlund-Vials, Cathy. 2012. *War, Genocide, and Justice: Cambodian American Memory Work*. Minneapolis: University of Minnesota Press.

———. 2014. "Vietnamization, Soldier Remorse, and Marvel Comics." In *Drawing New Color Lines: Transnational Asian American Graphic Narratives*, ed. Monica Chiu. Hong Kong: Hong Kong University Press, 189–208.

Schram, Martin. 2010. "Vietnamization of Afghanistan." *War Korea Times* (June 16); www.koreatimes.com.

Schwenkel, Christina. 2006. "Recombinant History: Transnational Practices of Memory and Knowledge Production in Contemporary Vietnam." *Cultural Anthropology* 21, no. 1 (February): 3–30.

Scott, Joan. 1991. "The Evidence of Experience." In *Questions of Evidence, Proof, Practice, and Persuasion across the Disciplines*, ed. James Chandler, Arnold I. Davidson, and Harry Harootunia. Chicago: University of Chicago Press, 363–387.

Sekula, Allan. 1986. "The Body and the Archive." *October* 39: 3–64.

Silva, Denise Ferreira da. 2005. "A Tale of Two Cities: Saigon, Fallujah, and the Ethical Boundaries of Empire." *Amerasia* 31, no. 2: 121–134.

———. 2007. *Toward a Global Idea of Race*. Minneapolis: University of Minnesota Press.

Silverman, Kaja. 2000. *World Spectators*. Stanford, CA: Stanford University Press.

Slotkin, Richard. 1992. *Gunfighter Nation: The Myth of the Frontier in Twentieth Century America*. New York: HarperCollins.

Small, Ivan V. 2012. "'Over There' Imaginative Displacements in Vietnamese Remittance Gift Economies." *Journal of Vietnamese Studies* 7, no. 3: 157–183.

Smith, Linda Tuhiwai. 2013. *Decolonizing Methodologies: Research and Indigenous Peoples*. London: Zed Books Ltd.

Soddu, Marco. 2012. "Truman Administration's Containment Policy in Light of the French Return to Indochina." *Foreign Policy Journal* (December 13): 1–7.

"South Vietnamese Colors Fly in Baghdad, Iraq." 2005. *Navy Mobile Riverine Force Mekong Delta, Vietnam War History (April 9)*; www.riverinesailor.com.

Spanos, William V. 2008. *American Exceptionalism in the Age of Globalization: The Specter of Vietnam*. New York: SUNY Press.

Speece, Mark. 2002. "Consumer Value Orientation in Vietnam's Urban Middle Class." *der markt* 41, no. 4: 157–168.

Spivak, Gayatri Chakravorthy. 1993. "Can the Subaltern Speak?" In *Colonial Discourse and Post-Colonial Theory: A Reader*, ed. Patrick Williams and Laura Chrisman. London: Harvester Wheatsheaf, 66–111.

Stoler, Ann Laura. 2006. "Intimidations of Empire: Predicaments of the Tactile and Unseen." *Haunted by Empire: Geographies of Intimacy in North American History*. Durham, NC: Duke University Press, 1–22.

———. 2008. "Imperial Debris: Reflections on Ruins and Ruination." *Cultural Anthropology* 23, no. 2: 191–219.

Sturken, Marita. 1991. "The Wall, the Screen, and the Image: The Vietnam Veterans Memorial." *Representations* 35 (Summer): 118–142.

———. 1997. *Tangled Memories: The Vietnam War, the AIDS Epidemic, and the Politics of Remembering*. Berkeley: University of California Press.

Tadiar, Neferti Xina M. 2009. *Things Fall Away: Philippine Historical Experience and the Makings of Globalization*. Durham, NC: Duke University Press.

Tang, Eric. 2015. *Unsettled: Cambodian Refugees in the New York City Hyperghetto*. Philadelphia: Temple University Press.

Tartarski, Michael. 2017. "Vietnam's Tale of Two Metros, One Built by the Japanese and the Other by the Chinese." *This Week in Asia* (July 30); www.scmp.com.

Tatum, James. 1996. "Memorials of the America War in Vietnam." *Critical Inquiry* 22, no. 4 (Summer): 634–678.

Taylor, Diana. 2003. *The Archive and the Repertoire: Performing Cultural Memory in the Americas*. Durham, NC: Duke University Press.

Taylor, Nora. 2009. "The Art of Many Vietnams." *Official F.O.B. II: Art Speaks Catalogue*.

———. 2012. "Exhibiting Middle Classness: The Social Status of Artists in Hanoi." In *The Reinvention of Distinction*. Dordrecht: Springer Netherlands, 115–127.

Taylor, Philip. 2001. *Fragments of the Present: Searching for Modernity in Vietnam's South*. Honolulu: University of Hawai'i Press.

Thach, James Van. 2009. "Another Generation's War: Vietnamese American Voices from IRAQ." http://iraq.pigstye.net/article.php.

Thanh Nien Co Vang (TNCV). (January 16, 2009); https://www.tncvonline.com/cms.

Thomassen, Lasse. 2011. "(Not) Just a Piece of Cloth: Begum, Recognition and the Politics of Representation." *Political Theory* 39, no. 3: 1–27.

Thrift, Nigel. 1987. "'Difficult Years: Ideology and Urbanization in South Vietnam, 1975–1986,'" *Urban Geography* 8, no. 5: 420–439.

Thrift, Nigel and Dean Forbes. 2006. *The Price of War: Urbanization in Vietnam, 1954–1985*. London: Routledge.

Thuyên, Nhã. *The Marginal Position: Open-Mouth Group's Poetic Experiments from a Cultural Perspective*. MA thesis, Hanoi National University of Education.

Tran, Do Cam and Nguyen Manh Tri. 2011. "Two Generations, One Aspiration." (August 11); www.saigonecho.com.

Tran, My-Thuan. 2009. "Vietnamese Art Exhibit Puts Politics on Display." *Los Angeles Times* (January 10).

Tran, Nu-Anh. 2006. "South Vietnamese Identity, American Intervention, and the Newspaper Chính Luan, 1965–1969." *Journal of Vietnamese Studies* 1, no. 1–2: 169–209.

Tran, Qui-Phiet. 1993. "Contemporary Vietnamese American Feminine Writing: Exile and Home." *Amerasia Journal* 19, no. 3: 71–83.

Trần, Tôn Nữ Quỳnh and Nguyễn Trọng Hoà. 2007. *Văn Hoá Hẻm Phố Sài Gòn*. HCM: NXB Tong Hop.

Tran, Tri Vu. 1988. *Lost Years: My 1,632 Days in Vietnamese Reeducation Camps*. Trans. Nguyen Phuc. Berkeley: University of California Press.

Truitt, Allison. 2008. "On the Back of a Motorbike: Middle-Class Mobility in Ho Chi Minh City, Vietnam." *American Ethnologist* 35, no. 1: 3–19.

———. 2012. "Banking on the Middle Class in Ho Chi Minh City." In *The Reinvention of Distinction*. Dordrecht: Springer Netherlands, 129–141.

———. 2013. *Dreaming of Money in Ho Chi Minh City*. Seattle: University of Washington Press.

TuoiTreNews. 2013. "VN Ranks 7th in Overseas Remittance." (June 8); http://tuoitrenews.vn.

Twining, Daniel. 2007. "America's Grand Design in Asia." *Washington Quarterly* 30, no. 3: 79–94.

Tyner, James. 2009. *War, Violence, and Population: Making the Body Count*. New York: Guilford Press.

Ullman, Harlan. 2005. "The 'Vietnamization' of Iraq; With U.S. Support and Deliberate Speed." *Washington Times* (November 23): A17.

Um, Khatharya. 2005. "The 'Vietnam War': What's in a Name?" *Amerasia Journal* 31, no. 2: 134–139.

Underhill, Julie Thi. 2014. "You Didn't Kill US All, You Know—Part Two." (April 24); www.diacritics.com.

VAALA. "F.O.B. II Exhibition Opens This Weekend at New VAALA Center in Santa Ana." www.vaala.org.

———. "VAALA ngưng triển lãm tranh vì thiếu giấy phép." 2009. *Người Việt Daily News* (January 16); http://www.nguoi-viet.com/.

Valverde, Kieu Linh. 2009. "If Art Speaks, It Can Also Be Silenced." (January 9); http://loungemonkey.blogspot.com.

———. 2012. *Transnationalizing Viet Nam: Community, Culture, and Politics in the Diaspora*. Philadelphia: Temple University Press.

Vang, Ma. 2012. "The Refugee Soldier: A Critique of Recognition and Citizenship in the Hmong Veterans' Naturalization Act of 1997." *positions* 20, no. 3: 685–712.

Vietnam Center and Archive. 1996. *Friends of the Vietnam Center Newsletter* 6, no. 1, February.
———. 1997. *Friends of the Vietnam Center Newsletter* 4, no. 2, July.
———. 1998. *Friends of the Vietnam Center Newsletter* 5, no. 2, May.
———. 1999. *Friends of the Vietnam Center Newsletter* 6, no. 1, February.
———. 2001. *Friends of the Vietnam Center Newsletter* 8, no. 3, August.
———. 2002. *Friends of the Vietnam Center Newsletter* 9, no. 2, June.
———. 2004. *Friends of the Vietnam Center Newsletter* 11, no. 3, Fall.
———. "About the Vietnam Center and Archive." www.vietnam.ttu.edu.
"Vietnam Unique Tours or Rubicon." 2007. http://www.vietnamuniquetours.com/.
Vietnamese American Arts and Letters Association. "History & Mission." http://www.vaala.org/.
VietNamNet Bridge. 2011. "Viet Kieu Bring Money, but also Knowledge and Technology." http://english.vietnamnet.vn.
Vigdor, Jacob L. 2008. "Measuring Immigrant Assimilation in the United States. Civic Report No. 53." New York: Manhattan Institute for Policy Research.
Vinh, Cam. 2005. "*Sống Trong Sợ Hãi* Chiếu Trong . . . Sợ Hãi!." http://tuoitre.vn.
Vlastos, Stephen. 1991. "America's 'Enemy': The Absent Present in Revisionist Vietnam War History." In *The Vietnam War and American Culture*, ed. John Carlos Rowe and Rick Berg. New York: Columbia University Press, 52–74.
"VNCA Special Projects." The Vietnam Center and Archive; www.vietnam.ttu.edu.
Võ, Linda. 2009. "Transforming an Ethnic Community: Little Saigon, Orange County." In *Asian America: Forming New Communities, Expanding Boundaries*, ed. Huping Ling. New Brunswick, NJ: Rutgers University Press, 87–103.
Vo, Nghia M. 2011. *Saigon: A History*. Jefferson, NC: McFarland Publishing.
Vo-Dang, Thuy. 2005. "The Cultural Work of Anticommunism in the San Diego Vietnamese American Community." *Amerasia Journal* 31, no. 2: 64–86.
———. 2008. *Anti-communism as Cultural Praxis: South Vietnam, War, and Refugee Memories in the Vietnamese American Community*. PhD Dissertation, University of California, San Diego.
Vu, Roy. 2013. "Natives of a Ghost Country." In *Asian Americans in Dixie: Race and Migration in the South*, ed. Jigna Desai and Khyati Y. Joshi. Urbana: University of Illinois Press, 165–189.
Wagner-Pacific, Robin Barry Schwartz. 1991. "The Vietnam Veterans Memorial: Commemorating a Difficult Past." *American Journal of Sociology* 97, no. 2: 376–420.
———. 2005. "The Cultural Work of Anti-communism in the San Diego Vietnamese American Community." *Amerasia Journal* 31, no. 2: 65–85.
Ward, Clarissa and Sadie Bass. 2009. "Left Vietnam as a Refugee, Returns as a U.S. Navy Captain." *ABC News*, November 13.
Warrior, Robert. 2009. *Tribal Secrets: Recovering American Indian Intellectual Traditions*. Minneapolis: University of Minnesota Press.
Werner, Jayne S. 2006. "Between Memory and Desire: Gender and the Remembrance of War in Doi Moi Vietnam." *Gender, Place and Culture* 13, no. 3: 303–315.

Westbrook, Ray. 2005. "South Vietnam's Takeover by North Left Turmoil." *Avalanche-Journal* (April 30); www.lubbockonline.com.

Westheider, James E. 1997. *Fighting on Two Fronts: African Americans and the Vietnam War.* New York: New York University Press.

White, Hayden. 1987. *The Content of Form: Narrative Discourse and Historical Representation.* Baltimore, MD: Johns Hopkins University Press.

Wiest, Andrew A. 2008. *Vietnam's Forgotten Army: Heroism and Betrayal in the ARVN.* New York: New York University Press.

Willbanks, James H. 2004. *Abandoning Vietnam: How America Left and South Vietnam Lost Its War.* Lawrence: University Press of Kansas.

Williams, Raymond. 1977. *Marxism and Literature.* New York: Oxford University Press.

———. 2006. "The Analysis of Culture." In *Cultural Theory and Popular Culture*, ed. John Storey. Athens: University of Georgia Press, 32–40.

Wilson, Richard. 2001. *The Politics of Truth and Reconciliation in South Africa: Legitimizing the Post-Apartheid State.* Cambridge: Cambridge University Press.

Winichakul, Thongchai. 1994. *Siam Mapped: A History of the Geo-Body.* Honolulu: University of Hawaii Press.

Yoneyama, Lisa. 1999. *Hiroshima Traces: Time, Space, and the Dialectics of Memory.* Berkeley: University of California Press.

Youngsuk, Chae. 2007. *Politicizing Asian American Literature: Towards a Critical Multiculturalism.* London: Routledge.

Zelizer, Craig. 2010. "Laughing Our Way to Peace or War: Humour and Peacebuilding." *Journal of Conflictology* 1, no. 2: 1–8.

Zinn, Howard. 2003. *A People's History of the United States.* New York: New Press.

INDEX

Aaron-Taylor, Susan, 89
Afghanistan, 13, 140–42, 147, 155–56
African Americans, 212n35
Agamben, Giorgio, 69
Air Force, U.S., 137
allies, 8, 88, 148
Al Qaeda, 136
American Dream, 71, 73
Americanization Syndrome, 131
American Syndrome, 164, 166
American War. *See* Vietnam War
amnesia, historical, 70–71
"Another Generation's War: Vietnamese American Voices from IRAQ" (article), 136
anticolonial resistance, 14
anti-communism, 107–8, 110, 118–20; protesters to, 55; South Vietnam and, 12, 105; South Vietnamese nationalism with, 101–2; U.S.-South Vietnamese relations and, 105; Vietnamese Americans influenced by, 37–39; of Vietnamese refugees, 97, 112–13
anti-democratic forces, 4
antiwar protesters, 27
Arab Muslims, 48
archival others, 40, 49, 54–56; Vietnamese as, 28, 33, 47, 51
archives, 26, 33, 49, 54; My Lai atrocity in, 211n14; organization logo in, 211n15; Vietnam translations for, 212n22. *See also* Vietnam War Center and Archive
Army of the Republic of Vietnam (ARVN), 9, 11–12, 41, 59–60

Army Reserves, U.S., 125
art displays, 189, 213n2, 214
articles, 136
artworks, 91, 99–101
ARVN. *See* Army of the Republic of Vietnam
Asian Americans, 58, 62, 79, 81–82, 90–91
Asian femininity, 98–99
Association of South Vietnamese Veterans, 103
asylum status, 53
Atanasoski, Neda, 139
authoritarian violence, 65

Bảo Đại imperial regime, 15
Battle of Điện Biên Phủ, 15
Beck, Ulrich, 182
benevolent paternalism, 76
benign assimilation, 176
Benjamin, Walter, 109, 186
Brazilinization, 182
Bui, Thao Thanh, 135–36, *136*
burden of proof, 53
Bush, George W., 128, 163
By Land, By Air, Or By Sea (Toly), 97, *97*

calamity of errors, 144
Calvino, Manuel, 89
Cambodia, 132, 215n3
Cao, Lan, 62
capitalism, 180, 184–85, 195, 203; communist regime with, 179, 197; global, 173, 186; socialist control and, 170, 181–82
Castro, Fidel, 117

censorship, 93–99, 135, 214n12
Chae, Youngsuk, 63
chemical warfare, 16
Cheng, Anne, 152
children, 73, 109–10
China, 172–73
Chuh, Kandice, 71
Chung-hee, Park, 216n12
civilian life, of Pham, Q., 159–60
civil rights, gay, 116–18
civil war, 5
class inequality, 197
Clinton, Bill, 201–2, 218n1
Cochinchina, 174
Cold War, 156, 165, 170; Vietnamization policy of, 29; Vietnam War enabling victory in, 35, 128–29
collective pain, 58
Collet, Christian, 113
colonial empires, 170–71
colonial history, 177–78
commercialism, urban, 187
commodity supply chains, 184
communications, 92
Communist Party, 22, 181, 185, 197
communist regime, 59–60, 95–96, 103–4; capitalism in, 179, 197; farming collectives of, 174, 180; middle-class status in, 190; nationalism and, 121; Pham, Q., dinner with officer of, 160; popular culture attack against, 177; reeducation camps of, 50, 79–80; South Vietnam and, 12, 44, 66; South Vietnamese reaction to, 91; U.S. military fighting, 138–39; Vietnamese Americans opposed to, 41; Vietnamese hating, 107; Vietnamization extending territory of, 7, 175–76; Vietnam War containment of, 16. See also anti-communism
communities, 87–89, 93, 102, 112, 119–20
community-as-family, 109
community-based archives, 33

community-based phenomenon, 22
complex personhood, 84
condos, high-rise, 173
Confucian Asian culture, 118
công nghiệp hóa (industrialization), 183
consciousness, double, 61
contact zone, 177
contemporary art scene, 189
corporal violence, 89–90
cosmopolitan colonial roots, 178
Crager, Kelly, 44, 212n25
critical illiteracy, 68
culture, 20, 63, 101, 214n8, 216n5; Americanization effort and, 177; Confucian Asian, 118; hybrid subjects of, 124; integrity of, 108; racist, 153; urban, 217n8; wars over, 120
Cvetkovich, Ann, 40
cyclo drivers, 194, 196

Daddis, Gregory, 9
Dao, Anh Thang, 84
debt, 21, 81–82
debt of blood, 60
decolonization, 12–13
dehumanizing, of Vietnamese, 48–49
demilitarized zone, 15
democracy, 88, 125–27, 140–42
Democratic Republic of Vietnam (DRV), 5, 209n5
diasporic culture, 214n8
diasporic identity, 67–68, 108
Diệm, Ngô Đình, 116
Điện Biên Phủ, battle of, 15
differential inclusion, 55
digital electronic processes, 54
Dinh, Tino, 136–37
diplomacy, 32, 40–41, 72, 203–4
disengagement with escalation, 5
dismemberment, 89–90, 99, 119–20; fear and, 102; protesters and community, 112; of South Vietnam, 92, 113
Doan, Brian, 93–94, 96, 99, 104, 191

documentary, 211n13
đô thị hóa. *See* urbanization
double consciousness, 61
Dragon economy, 217n10
DRV. *See* Democratic Republic of Vietnam
dual nationality, 92, 135–36
Dulles, John, 16
Duoc, Nguyen Qui, 108
Duong, Lan, 93, 100, 104, 214n12
Duy, Phạm, 217n14

economics, 169–70, 182–84, 191, 217n10
Edkins, Jenny, 39, 123
educated class, 216n6
education, 76, 85. *See also* reeducation
Ellis Island, 51
embargo, 187, 202
empires, 128, 162–64, 170–71, 198–99
Enloe, Cynthia, 162
Espiritu, Yen Le, 35, 55, 106, 126
Eurocentric white societies, 69
European immigrants, 51

faceless other, 203
Fall of Saigon, 56, 65, 160, 165–66, 174
Families of Vietnamese Political Prisoners Association (FVPPA), 31, 211n17, 213n36
family, 53, 62, 65–66, 71–78, 212n23
farming collectives, 174, 180
fear, dismemberment and, 102
Federation of Former Republic of Vietnam Veterans, 100
Feldman, Edward, 47
Ferreira da Silva, Denise, 9–10
field training, 153
Filipinization, 10–11
financial independence, 183–84
financial losses, 181
First Indochina War, 14–15, 209n5
flags, 101, 104, 136, *136*
F.O.B. *See* Fresh off the Boat

F.O.B. II Show, 91–100, 107; art and activism of, 213n2; artists views of protesters of, 110; community dismemberment and, 119–20; politics on display at, 102–3
food production, 218n23
foot spa controversy, 91–93, 213n3
forced urbanization, 182
foreign investment, 172, 180–81
foreign policy, U.S., 4–5, 127–30, 148
Foucault, Michel, 198
fractionalized nation, 90
France, 65, 71, 77–78, 84
freedom, 4, 7–9, 104–6, 116; defenders of, 88; democracy and, 125; gift of, 66–67, 76; joint ventures for militarized, 148; militarized, 123, 130–31, 139, 142–43, 147–48, 156–57, 166, 168; multiple definitions of, 167; paradise of, 176; power relationships of, 67; Vietnam War and, 156–57, 166, 168; wars protecting, 140
free-market socialist Vietnam, 72
free trade, 181
Fresh off the Boat (F.O.B.), 90
Friends of the Vietnam Center (newsletter), 32
Furuya, Hiroyo, 113
FVPPA. *See* Families of Vietnamese Political Prisoners Association

gay civil rights, 116–18
gendered discourse, 99, 106–7
gendered practices, 58–59, 82
Geneva Peace Accords (1954), 15, 209n6
geopolitical failures, 164–65
geopolitical relationships, 140
gift of freedom, 66–67, 76
Glass, Geoffrey T., 215n19
Glissant, Édouard, 60
global capitalism, 173, 186
global development, 172
global imperialism, 186

global investments, 179
globalization, 73, 172–73, 181–86
global/local realities, 193
global South, 171
good life, 85
gooks, 46–49, 47, 153, 212n30
Gordon, Avery, 84
government intelligence, 56
Green Berets, 16
Grewal, Inderpal, 148
Gulf of Tonkin, 16

Hagopian, Patrick, 12
Hardt, Michael, 171–72, 203
Harms, Erik, 193
HCMC. *See* Ho Chi Minh City
Hearts and Minds (documentary), 211n13
hegemonic power, 140
hiện đại hóa (modernization), 183
historical amnesia, 70–71, 123
historical memory, 31
historical oblivion, 49–50
Hoa (fictitious character), 75–78
Hoa, Alex, 189–90
Hồ Chí Minh, 14–15, 93, 103, 209n5
Ho Chi Minh City (HCMC), 72, 147; colonial history of, 177–78; economic development in, 169–70; global capitalism in, 173; global/local realities in, 193; metro-system projects of, 185–86; museums in, 216n2; Saigon as, 174; structural changes of, 198; Vietnamese American living in, 188
homeland, 70–72, 88, 107
honorable withdrawal, 209n3
humanitarianism, 69
humanitarian violence, 139
human rights, 38, 115–18
Hung (fictitious character), 75, 80
Hung, Dam Vinh, 213n1
Hussein, Saddam, 126
Huynh, Chau, 91
hyperindustrialization, 193

identity, 59, 67–68, 108–9; crisis, 111, 195; sexual, 119
illiteracy, 68
immigrant bubble, 187
immigrants, European, 51
Immigration and Naturalization Act (1965), 52
imperialism, 9, 11–12, 148, 171, 186
independent nation f, 10–11
industrialization (công nghiệp hóa), 183
intellectual sovereignty, 28
international trading markets, 184
Internet campaign, 100
interrogation techniques, 216n3
intraethnic conflict, 112
investments, 172, 179, 180–81
Iraq, 13, 135–37, 140–42, 147, 155–56; U.S. troops to, 214n5
Iraqification, 126–27

Johnson, Lyndon B., 5, 149, 216n12

Kang, Laura, 32
Kang, Namsoon, 19
Kennedy, John F, 15, 142
key economic zones (KEZs), 185
key word search, 46
KEZs. *See* key economic zones
Kibria, Nazli, 74
Kim, Jodi, 128, 156
Kim-Vo, 71, 80
Kissinger, Henry, 6, 8
Kolb, Barry, 177
Korean War, 46
Kuwait, 155
Kwan, Yvonne, 83
Kỳ, Nguyễn Cao, 217n14
Kynam (property developer), 190–91

labor, masculine, 148
Laderman, Scott, 186
Laird, Melvin, 4
Lam, Andrew, 28, 47

Lam, Long, 146
Lan, Vu Hoang, 104
Lang, Michael, 177
Laos, 132
Laotian Civil War, 157
LA Times, 111
Le, Dinh Q., 188–89
Le, Hung Ba, 134
Le, Jenni Trang, 191–92
Le, Khanh Cong, 210n4
Le, Tram, 92
Le, Ysa, 104
LGBT, 114–19
liberal exceptionalism, 112
liberalism, 66
liberation, ARVN dreams of, 11–12
Lieu, Nhi, 73
Little Saigon enclave (the O.C.), 1, 64, 72, 113–15, 120
living memorial, 30
Long, Keira, 147
The Lotus and the Storm (Cao), 62
Lowe, Lisa, 20
Lu, Lan, 41
Lum (fictitious character), 73–74
Luong, Viet, 134–35

Mahayana Buddhism, 116
Malaysian refugee camp, 58
Mallett, Ann, 45, 51
management of life, 69
Marines, U.S., 154
Mariscal, Jorge, 129
masculine labor, 148
Maxner, Stephen, 41
Mbembé, Achille, 69
memoirs, 28, 42, 124, 150–51, 162
memory, 31, 64, 68, 146–47; culture as repository for, 20; of the future, 49–50; refugees, 19–23, 86, 110, 145; of South Vietnam, 61–62; South Vietnam's discredited, 18
metro-system projects, 185–86

middle-class ideals, 73
middle-class status, 190
militarized freedoms, 123, 130–31, 139, 142–43, 147–48; Vietnam War and, 156–57, 166, 168
militarized masculinity, 162
military, U.S., 124; ARVN relations breakdown with, 9; backing out of commitments by, 137, 164–65; communism fought by, 138–39; enlistment in, 215n2; interventions by, 88, 130–31; national growth stimulated by, 175; racist culture of, 153; Vietnamese Americans and, 131–32; Vietnamese refugees in, 129–30; Vietnam War and, 13–14, 122
Miller, Edward, 32
Minh-Ha, Trinh, 82–83
model minority, 73–74, 79, 90–91
modernization (hiện đại hóa), 183
Mondt, Amy, 46, 212n30
Monkey Bridge (Cao), 62
multicultural humanitarianism, 69
multiple voices, 102
museums, in HCMC, 216n2
Muslim Arabs, 48
My Lai atrocity, 211n14

national flag, 101
national healing, 26–27
National Historical Research and Publications Commission, 36
nationalism, 14, 101, 115–16, 121, 177
National Liberation Front (Việt Cộng), 17, 153
national security, 56
native informants, 28–29, 122
NATO. *See* North Atlantic Treaty Organization
Navy Seal Training, 142
Negri, Antonio, 171–72, 203
neocolonial discourse, 13, 204
neocolonial domination, 203
neoliberal economies, 3

newsletters, 32
newspapers, 134
Newton, Natalie, 118
Ngô, Fiona, 192
Người Việt (Vietnamese people), 94, 213n3
Nguyen, Chuong, 141–42
Nguyen, Dina, 116
Nguyen, Hieu, 118
Nguyen, Hung P., 115
Nguyen, Jimmy, 116
Nguyen, Kim, 70
Nguyen, Mimi, 66–67, 76
Nguyen, Nathalie Huynh, 66
Nguyen, Phuc, 96
Nguyen, Phuong, 18
Nguyen, Tina, 110
Nguyen, Tuyet, 169, 192
Nguyen, Viet, 48, 55, 88
Nguyen, Viet Thanh, 62
Nguyễn-Võ, Thu-Hương, 174, 198
Ninh, Erin, 60, 81
Niu, Phan Tan, 100
Nixon, Richard, 4–5, 8–10, 16, 140; China visit of, 172–73; forced urbanization by, 182; honorable withdrawal from, 209n3; Vietnamization program from, 3, 53, 166–67, 175; Vietnamization speech of, 6–7, 122, 209n2; Vietnam War troop withdrawal by, 215n1
Nol, Lon, 215n3
Nora, Pierre, 107
North Atlantic Treaty Organization (NATO), 9
North Ireland, 14
North Vietnamese soldiers, 40–41, 194–95
nước Mỹ (Vietnamese for the United States), 149

Obama, Barack, 106, 214n5
O.C. *See* Little Saigon enclave
"O.C. Native Writes About Reeducation Camps" (article), 64
ODP. *See* Orderly Departure Program
offensive materials, 100–101
Operation Desert Storm, 56, 155, 156
Operation Enduring Freedom, 163
Operation Iraqi Freedom, 126, 163
oral histories, 42–47, 52–54, 210n4
Orange County, 43, 64, 72, 90, 133
Orange County Register, 106, 112, 118
Orderly Departure Program (ODP), 50, 52–53, 197, 211n17
Osius, Ted, 203
Our Sense of Duty: Our Journey from Vietnam to America (Pham, Q.), 124
overseas Vietnamese (Việt Kiều), 42, 70, 169, 186–87, 190

painting, 97–99, *98*
parade, in Little Saigon enclave, 114–15, *117*, 119
paradise of freedom, 176
paternalism, benevolent, 76
Paterson, Thomas, 131
patriotic language, 32
Pelaud, Isabelle Thuy, 67, 104–5
People's Army of Vietnam, 160
Persian Gulf War, 163
personal life story, 60
personhood, 129
Pham, Quang X., 124, 138, 149, 159–65; father's death of, 157–58; father sent to reeducation camp, 150–52, 158; *A Sense of Duty: Our Journey from Vietnam to America* by, 149, 151; as South Vietnam son, 151; U.S. fought for by, 155–56; U.S. home for mother of, 152; U.S. never welcoming father of, 154; veteran's reunion attended by, 157
Pham, Van Hoa, 154
Phan, Aimee, 69, 75; *The Reeducation of Cherry Truong* by, 57–64, 67, 71, 73, 77–86; raised in U.S., 64; *We Shall Never Meet* by, 71

Phan, Chris, 142–43, 145
Philippines, 132
Philippines War, 46
Phong, Nguyen Xuan, 41–42
political prisoners, 31, 36, 59–62, 79, 86
politics, 53–54, 60–61, 78–79, 93; anticommunist, 37–39, 55; autonomy, 42; conservatism, 118; cultural, 20, 101; F.O.B. II show displaying, 102–3; opinions, 135; projects, 39; reeducation, 2; refugees, 3, 50; unconscious, 19; Vietnamese American's anti-communism, 119–20
Pol Pot, 132
popular culture, 177
postcolonial freedom, 4
postwar households, 77
postwar refugee families, 65–66, 74–75, 77
postwar trauma, 68, 70, 85–86, 113
poverty, 195
power relationships, 67
preservation discourse, 108
PRG. *See* Viet Cong
prisoner of consciousness, 85
protesters, 27, 93–99, 112–13; to anticommunist politics, 55; communist symbols disturbing, 103–4; F.O.B. II show and, 107, 110; at parade, *117*
protracted afterlife, 156
pro-war propaganda, 12
psychological delusions, 82
public reproach, 94
public schools, 84

Al Qaeda, 136
queer people ban, 114

race, 45–46, 48, 126, 152–53
rail system, 185
rape, 82–83
Reckner, James, 30, 34–41, 45–46, 210n7, 210n8
red capitalism, 180
reeducation, 59–61, 84–85; communist camps of, 50, 79–80; debt concepts in, 81–82; Pham, Q., father sent to, 150–52, 158; of South Vietnamese soldiers, 2–3, 57, 65, 68–69, 79–80
The Reeducation of Cherry Truong (Phan, A.), 57–64, 67, 71–73, 77–86
refugee body politics, 87–88, 90, 106–7, 114–20
refugees, 18, 28, 49, 58, 71–72; communist regime resentment of, 96; communities, 93; displacement, 150; double consciousness of, 61; Little Saigon enclave of, 1, 64; losing everything, 51–52; memory, 19–23, 86, 110, 145; political economy of, 78–79; political obstacles to, 50; politics, 3, 50; postwar, 65–66, 74–75, 77; reeducation as asset to, 61; reeducation camp for, 61, 68, 84–85; retelling stories of, 64; subjection process of, 67; transportation, 97; U.S. debt of gratitude from, 134–35, 145–46; U.S. receiving economic, 77–78; U.S. rescuing helpless, 61; veteran sacrifices of, 125; will to survive of, 81. *See also* South Vietnamese refugees; Vietnamese refugees
regional hegemony, 16
remembering, 58–61, 99
rememberment, 88–90
Republic of Vietnam (RVN), 1
residuals, 170–71, 198–99
returns of war, 21
reunification government, 174, 179
revolutionary government, 177
rice paddies, *47*
rickshaws, 194, *195*
Rodriguez, Dylan, 130
Rosen, Mark, 116
Rowe, John Carlos, 26
RVN. *See* Republic of Vietnam

Sahara, Ayako, 149
Saigon, 71, 150, 179–84; with capitalism, 185; Dragon economy of, 217n10; educated class of, 216n6; fall of, 56, 65, 160, 165–66, 174; legacy of, 196–97; nationalism of, 115–16; revolutionary government banning name of, 177; south, 169, *173*; as urban heterotopia, 198–99; U.S. influence on, 188–89. *See also* Ho Chi Minh City; Little Saigon enclave
Sài Gòn, 216n6
Saigon South, 169, *173*
sanctions, 202
Sanh (fictitious character), 79–80
Schlund-Vials, Cathy, 167
Schmidtt, Carl, 9
search engines, 54
second-generation, 57, 63, 92, 123–24, 192; youth, 37, 96
Second Indochinese War, 194
secret wars, 165
A Sense of Duty: My Father, My American Journey (Pham, Q.), 151
A Sense of Duty: Our Journey from Vietnam to America (Pham, Q.), 149, 151, 162–63
service-oriented manufacturing, 180
sexual identity, 119
sexual symbolism, 105–7
sexual violence, 83–84
Sihanouk, Norodom, 215n3
silence, quiet wisdom of, 83
Silverman, Kaja, 84
Smith, Linda Tuhiwai, 33
socialism, 72, 96, 170, 177, 181–82
Socialist Republic of Vietnam, 38, 40, 54–55, 213n1
social life, 95
social waste, 171
soldiers, U.S., 3, 32–35, 46–49, 135
South Vietnam: anti-communism and, 12, 105; arrested development of, 202; Asian femininity in, 98–99; capitalist roots of, 180; as childlike, 12; protected against communist regime, 12, 44, 66; communist threat to, 44; cosmopolitan colonial roots of, 178; discredited memory of, 18; dismemberment of, 92, 113; Fall of Saigon and forgotten, 165–66; financial independence for, 183–84; financial losses of, 181; flag poster exhibit of, 104; freedom for, 8–9, 116; gift of freedom to, 66–67; as independent nation, 10–11; memory of, 61–62; military-induced capitalism in, 184–85; national flag of, 101; neocolonial history of, 14–17; Nixon and liability of, 8; only memory left of, 146–47; Pham, Q., son of, 151; as political unconscious, 19; postcolonial freedom hopes of, 4; preserving story of, 42; racial order inequalities and, 126; refugees political views about, 3; short existence of, 18–19; Thiệu president of, 7; U.S. abandonment of, 32, 35, 43, 66, 113–14; U.S. and protected territory of, 15; U.S. born children beholden to, 109–10; U.S. culture influencing, 216n5; U.S. economic relations with, 59; U.S. failing to save, 161; U.S. friend/ally to, 8, 88, 148; U.S. ignorance about, 11; U.S. military relations breakdown with, 9; U.S. relations with, 80; U.S. reliance of, 145; U.S. withdrawal from, 19; U.S. with history of, 104–5; Vietnamese Americans and, 3, 110–11; Vietnamization as failure to, 10, 19, 139–42, 176–77, 201; VNCA preserving story of, 42
South Vietnamese, 101–2, 120–21, 144; burden of proof on, 53; communist regime reaction of, 91; community-as-family of, 109; dual nationality of, 92, 135–36; veterans groups of, 108, 157; Vietnam War price paid by, 158–59

South Vietnamese refugees, 1–3, 53–54; cultural deficit objects and, 63; failure and triumph of, 73–74; homeland loss of, 17–19, 51; as transparent subjects of representation, 68; transportation used by, 97; U.S. entered as, 51; U.S. institutions not memorializing, 37–38; as U.S. resident aliens, 52; U.S. with nationalism of, 22; Vietnamese American identity and, 108–9; Vietnam return of, 186–93, 203–4; VNCA and, 27–28, 33–34, 36–52, 56
South Vietnamese soldiers, 29, 41–42; protest movement led by, 95–96; reeducation camps for, 2–3, 57, 65, 68–69, 79–80; VNCA honoring, 32–33
sponsor countries settlement, 69–70
State Records and Archive Department, 54
subjection process, 67
subjects of war, 70
Super F.O.B. Beauty Queen (painting), 97–99, *98*
supply chains, 184
The Sympathizer (Nguyen, V. T.), 62

Tang, Eric, 145
Tatum, James, 33
Taylor, Phillip, 178–79
territory occupation, 148
terrorism, 113, 140
Texas Tech University, 30, 54, 212n22
Thanh Niên Cờ Vàng (TNCV), 96
Thiệu, Nguyễn Văn, 7
Third World outsiders, 111
Tho, Khuc Minh, 211n20
TNCV. *See* Thanh Niên Cờ Vàng
To, Michael, 139
Toly, Steven, 96–98, *97*
Tong, Ly, 105–6, 213n1
Tonkin Gulf Resolution (1964), 161
trade balance, 11
Tran, Ha Son, 115
Tran, Hung, 140
Tran, Van, 100
transnational elites, 187
transparent subjects of representation, 68
transportation, refugee, 97
trauma, 2, 23, 83; archival project including, 49; dismemberment and, 120; historical amnesia and, 123; memory pitfalls and, 64; moral injury and, 36; postwar, 68, 70, 85–86, 113; Vietnamese refugees, 74, 109; Vietnam War causing, 150–51, 158
Truman, Harry, 15
Trung, Ly Chanh, 177
Tuấn, Nguyễn, 194–97, *195*
Tuyet (fictitious character), 58, 71, 75, 80–81

Ulsterisation, 14
UN High Commission for Refugees (1979), 50
United States (U.S.): Afghanistan and Iraq conflicts of, 13; Air Force, 137; anti-communism and, 105; Army Reserves, 125; democracy building by, 126–27; Filipinization strategy of, 10–11; F.O.B. II show protesters and, 107; foreign policy, 4–5, 127–30, 148; future Vietnams of, 166; geopolitical failures of, 164–65; global development and, 172; hegemonic power of, 140; helpless refugees rescued and, 61; imperialism of, 148; Iraq and Afghanistan and, 155–56; Iraq and troops of, 214n5; Iraqification by, 126–27; Le, J., born in, 191–92; Lum refuses return to, 73; Marines of, 154; military interventions by, 88, 130–31; neocolonial domination of, 203; Nixon's foreign policy for, 4–5; ODP initiated by, 52; Pham, Q., and, 160–64; Pham, Q., father never welcomed by, 154; Pham, Q., fighting for, 155–56; Pham, Q., mother finding home in, 152; Phan, A., raised in, 64;

United States (*cont.*)
Philippines annexation by, 132; political autonomy given by, 42; political refugee obstacles in, 50; poor economic refugees to, 77–78; public shunning Vietnam veterans of, 34; racial prejudices held in, 45–46, 48; refugees debt of gratitude to, 134–35, 145–46; regional hegemony of, 16; resident aliens in, 52; responsibility abnegation of, 7; Saigon influenced by, 188–89; secret wars of, 165; Socialist Republic of Vietnam diplomatic relations with, 40; soldiers, 3, 32–35, 46–49, 135; South Vietnam and children born in, 109–10; South Vietnam culture influenced by, 216n5; South Vietnam economic relations with, 59; South Vietnamese nationalism in, 22; South Vietnamese pawned by, 144; South Vietnamese refugee not memorialized in, 37–38; South Vietnamese refugees entering, 51; South Vietnam failure of, 161; South Vietnam friend/ally to, 8, 88, 148; South Vietnam history alive in, 104–5; South Vietnam ignorance of, 11; South Vietnam protected territory and, 15; South Vietnam relations with, 80; South Vietnam's reliance on, 145; South Vietnam withdrawal of, 19; Vietnam bridging space between, 151; Vietnamese American in military of, 124; Vietnamese Americans with homes in, 18, 31–32; Vietnamese refugees coming to, 129–30, 152; Vietnam history of, 131; Vietnamization abandoning South Vietnam, 32, 35, 43, 66, 113–14; Vietnamization imperial contract with, 9; Vietnamization policy of, 7–8, 97, 127–30; Vietnam signing agreement with, 217n7; Vietnam's relations with, 183, 201–2; Vietnam's trade embargo from, 187, 202; Vietnam's trust with, 194; Vietnam wanting money from, 197; Vietnam War and war-mongering of, 133; Vietnam War entered by, 16–17; Vietnam War opposition in, 5. *See also* Vietnamese Americans

University of Texas, 211n20
unwon war, 34
urban commercialism, 187
urban culture, 217n8
Urban heterotopia, 198–99
urbanization, 175–76, 182
U.S. *See* United States
"U.S. Neo-colonialism in South Vietnam: The 'Vietnamization' of the War," 176

VAAFA. *See* Vietnamese American Armed Forces Association
VAALA. *See* Vietnamese American Arts and Letters Association
Valverde, Caroline Kieu Linh, 102
vandalism, 106
Vang, Ma, 157
Verne, Richard, 35
veteran sacrifices, 125
Việt Cộng (National Liberation Front), 17, 153
Viet Cong (PRG), 5
Việt Kiều (overseas Vietnamese), 42, 70, 169, 186–87, 190
Việt Minh nationalist party, 14–15
Vietnam: archive translations in, 212n22; billionaires living in, 189; children born outside of, 73; class inequality in, 197; emerging economy of, 191; foreign investment in, 172; free-market socialist, 72; global investments of, 179; identity crisis of, 195; looking to future, 192; Pham, Q., love of, 149, 160; socialist regime of, 38, 213n1; social life in contemporary, 95; South Vietnamese refugees returning to, 186–93, 203–4; State Records and Archive Department of, 54; U.S. bridging space

between, 151; U.S. history in, 131; U.S. money wanted in, 197; U.S. relations with, 183, 201–2; U.S. signing agreement with, 217n7; U.S. trade embargo on, 187, 202; U.S. trust with, 194
Vietnamese: benevolent paternalism toward, 76; censorship of, 96–97; communist regime hated by, 107; dehumanizing of, 48–49; diasporic identity of, 67–68; divergent lives portrayed of, 94; gook term used for, 46–49, 47; heritage reclaimed of, 188; sponsor countries settlement of, 69–70; as Third World outsiders, 111; VNCA with documents related to, 50; women, 106
Vietnamese American Armed Forces Association (VAAFA), 138, 143
Vietnamese American Arts and Letters Association (VAALA), 87, 90–92, 95–96, 109; freedom protected by, 105; offensive materials and, 100; veterans opposing exhibit of, 103; women organizers of, 107
Vietnamese American Federation, 115
Vietnamese American Heritage Foundation, 31, 36
Vietnamese American Heritage Project, 36, 45, 51
Vietnamese Americans: anti-communism politics of, 119–20; anti-communist politics influencing, 37–39; communist regime opposed by, 41; double loss of, 137–38; experience of, 63–64; HCMC life of, 188; identity crisis of, 111; LGBT and, 117, 119; middle-class ideals of, 73; militarized freedoms concept and, 123; model minority and, 73–74; privileged generation of, 169; refugee body politics of, 87–88; refugee story of, 28; South Vietnam and, 3, 110–11; South Vietnamese refugees and identity of, 108–9; stories of, 52; as subjects of war, 70; U.S. home for, 18, 31–32; U.S. military and, 131–32; VNCA participation of, 38–39, 41, 44–45
Vietnamese American soldiers, 2–3, 122, 124, 133
Vietnamese Army, 146
Vietnamese communist party, 22
Vietnamese for the United States (nước Mỹ), 149
Vietnamese people (Người Việt), 94
Vietnamese refugees, 74–78, 109, 129–30, 152; anti-communism of, 97, 112–13; communities of, 87–88; Eurocentric white societies and, 69; homeland remembrance of, 70; liberal exceptionalism and, 112; management of life and, 69; queer people as, 114; war memories passed on by, 86
Vietnamization, 110; as benign assimilation, 176; of capitalism, 180; Cold War policy of, 29; communists extending territory after, 7, 175–76; as community-based phenomenon, 22; decolonization deferred by, 12–13; disengagement with escalation through, 5; of globalization, 181–86; historical oblivion from, 49–50; imperial contract formed by, 11; of Iraq, 135; nature of war changed by, 6; as neocolonial discourse, 13; Nixon's program of, 3, 53, 166–67, 175; Nixon's speech on, 6–7, 122, 209n2; of other countries, 125–26; South Vietnam and failure of, 10, 19, 139–42, 176–77, 201; South Vietnamese soldiers armed in, 29; U.S. abandoning South Vietnam in, 32, 35, 43, 66, 113–14; U.S. foreign policy of, 7–8, 97, 127–30; U.S. imperial contract through, 9; of Vietnam War, 3–10
"The Vietnamization of Iraq" (article), 127
Vietnamization Syndrome, 130
Vietnam memorial, 37
Vietnam Symposium, 40

Vietnam Syndrome, 13, 130, 133, 163–64
Vietnam veterans, U.S., 34
Vietnam Veterans Memorial, 26
Vietnam War, 46; archive dedicated to, 26; as calamity of errors, 144; Cold War victory from, 35, 128–29; communism containment of, 16; as conflict, 210n10; cultural politics remembering, 20; historical amnesia and, 123; militarized freedoms and, 156–57, 166, 168; national healing from, 26–27; neocolonial discourse about, 204; Nixon withdrawing troops in, 215n1; Pham, Q., attitude toward, 159; phases of, 217n18; postwar trauma and, 68; propaganda of, 217n11; reeducation following, 84–85; South Vietnamese paying price of, 158–59; students lack of knowledge about, 30; trauma caused by, 150–51; traumatic experience of, 150–51, 158; U.S. and future, 166; U.S. entering, 16–17; U.S. military losses in, 13–14, 122; U.S. opposition to, 5; U.S. soldier sacrifice in, 34–35; U.S. war-mongering and, 133; Vietnamization of, 3–10. *See also* First Indochina War; Second Indochinese War; war

Vietnam War Center and Archive (VNCA), 2, 25–26; art displays and, 214; ARVN contributions theme of, 41; differential inclusion in, 55; digital electronic processes used by, 54; experiences material records in, 27; gook term in, 46–49; of historical memory, 31; as living memorial, 30; memory of future in, 49–50; native informants for, 28–29; oral histories collected by, 42–47, 52–54; political projects of, 39; refugees losing everything and, 51–52; Socialist Republic of Vietnam signing agreement with, 54–55; soldiers honored in, 32–33; South Vietnamese refugee and, 27–28, 33–34, 36–50, 56; South Vietnam story preserved in, 42; unwon war honored in, 34; Vietnamese American Heritage Foundation donation to, 36; Vietnamese Americans participation in, 38–39, 41, 44–45; Vietnamese-related documents in, 50; Vietnam Symposium of, 40; Westmoreland visit to, 35

Vietnam War Memorial, 88
Viet Rainbow of Orange County (VROC), 87, 115
Vinda, Linda, 111
violence, 65, 83–84, 89–90, 139
Virtual Vietnam, 54
visions of righteousness, 8
VNCA. *See* Vietnam War Center and Archive
Võ, Linda T., 101
Vo-Dang, Thuy, 108
VROC. *See* Viet Rainbow of Orange County
Vu, Truong, 32

war, 34, 60, 86, 107–8, 171
warfare, chemical, 16
War on Terror, 13, 21, 124, 136, 147–48
We Shall Never Meet (Phan, A.), 71
Westmoreland, William, 12, 30, 35, 211n3
white societies, 69
will to survive, 81
Wilson, Woodrow, 15, 209n5
women, 66, 74–75, 81–82, 99, 106–7; diasporic culture projected by, 214n8
World Bank, 181
World Trade Organization, 181
World War II, 14

Xuan (fictitious character), 83–84

Yoneyama, Lisa, 186
youth, 73, 80, 85, 109; second-generation, 37, 96
Yugoslavia, 126

ABOUT THE AUTHOR

Long T. Bui is Assistant Professor in the Global and International Studies Department at the University of California, Irvine.